회화를 제대로 살리는

주제별 영단어

정희영 · 봉영아 공저

머리말

    학원에서 회화를 가르치면서 가장 많이 받는 질문들 중 하나는, 어떻게 하면 빠른 시일 내에 효과적으로 외국인과 무리 없이 영어로 의사 소통이 가능하게 되는가 하는 것입니다. 일단 기본적으로 의사소통을 하기 위한 어휘를 갖고 있어야 하는 것은 당연한 일입니다.
    그렇다면 기본 단어들을 내 것으로 만들어서 제대로 활용하기 위해서는 어떻게 해야 할까요? 기본 단어라고 해도 영어를 배우는 초기 단계에서는 상당한 분량인데 이를 효과적으로 소화할 수 있는 방법은 무엇일까요? 기억법의 한 방법이기도 하지만 바로 우리가 이미 알고 있는 상황들과 익혀야 할 단어를 연관시키는 것입니다. 즉, 단어를 익힐 때 알파벳 순으로 하나하나 개별적으로 취급하는 것이 아니라 같은 상황에서 사용될 법한 단어들을 하나의 주제로 엮어서 같이 기억하는 것입니다.
    이 책의 구성내용을 보면 13가지 커다란 주제가 있고 다시 여기에 속하는 101가지 작은 주제가 있어, 각각의 소 주제에 대해 28개 정도의 중요 단어들을 선별하였습니다. 26내지 28개의 단어묶음 중에서도 관련 정도에 따라 A · B · C · D로 다시 나누어서 눈에 쉽게 들어오게 편집한 덕분에 암기가 간편합니다. 또한, 28가지에 속하지 못한 기타 관련 단어들 및 중학 수준의 기본 단어들이 활용 예문과 함께 실렸고, 영문 색인을 넣어서 사전적 검색이 가능하게 하여 최대한 여러분의 학습에 도움이 되고자 하였습니다.
    영어의 의사소통 능력의 중요성이 강조되면서 공식 영어 시험에 speaking 부분이 추가 되고 있는 상황을 볼 때, 단지 단어를 알기만 해서는 부족합니다. 막상 주제를 정하고 프리 톡킹을 하려 하면 적합한 단어 및 표현을 떠올리기가 쉽지 않습니다. 따라서 이 책을 이용하여 주제별로 익힌 단어들을 적극 활용하기 위해서는 이를 회화 공부와 연결시켜야 합니다. 가능하다면 두 명 혹은 네 명 정도의 그룹을 이루어서 주제별 단어를 이용한 문장을 만들어보거나 만들어진 문장을 가지고 영어로만 대화를 해보는 식으로 스터디를 해보면 의외로 많은 도움이 될 것입니다.

금방 몇 달 안에라도 영어가 가능할 것 같은 비법서들이 매일매일 쏟아지고 있지만 외국어를 공부하면서 단 시일에 가능한 것은 없습니다. 언제나 즐거운 마음을 갖고 꾸준히 노력하는 게 가장 좋은 방법입니다.

마지막으로 흔쾌히 교정을 도와준 친구 Skye, Cheryl, 그리고 글로벌 어학원 영어 선생님들께 감사의 마음을 전합니다.

chapter 1 — Basic Ideas

1. 기수 · 8
2. 서수 · 11
3. 시간 · 14
4. 하루 / 낮 / 요일 · 17
5. 달 / 계절 · 20
6. 날씨 · 23
7. 국가 · 26
8. 국적 · 29
9. 색 · 32
10. 공휴일 / 파티 · 35
11. 위치 · 38

chapter 2 — Daily life

12. 가족 · 42
13. 생활용품 · 45
14. 일상생활 · 48
15. 대중교통 · 51
16. 탈것 · 54
17. 전화 · 57
18. 주거 · 60
19. 집 · 63
20. 부엌 · 66
21. 가전제품 · 69
22. 가구 · 72
23. 의복 및 신발 · 75
24. 악세서리 · 78
25. 잡화 · 81
26. 문구용품 · 84
27. 가게 · 87

chapter 3 — Human Body & Feeling

28. 감정(명사) · 92
29. 감정(동사/형용사) · 95
30. 성격 · 98
31. 신체 1 · 101
32. 신체 2 · 104
33. 얼굴 · 107
34. 성장 · 110

chapter 4 — Plants & Animals

35. 곡물 · 114
36. 식물 / 나무 · 117
37. 꽃 · 120
38. 과일 · 123
39. 야채 · 126
40. 동물 · 129
41. 곤충 · 132
42. 물고기 및 바다생물 · 135
43. 새 · 138

chapter 5 — Food

44. 요리 · 142
45. 조미료 · 145
46. 식사 · 148
47. 후식 및 술 · 151
48. 식당 및 양식 · 154

chapter 6 — Health & Disease

49. 건강 · 158
50. 질병 · 161
51. 병원 1 · 164
52. 병원 2 · 167

chapter 7 — Education

53. 교육 · 172
54. 학교 · 175
55. 교과목/학문 · 178
56. 역사 · 181
57. 수업 · 184
58. 수학 · 187

chapter 8 — Economics, Business, Media & Government Institutions

59. 경제 · 192
60. 비즈니스 · 195
61. 회사 1 · 198
62. 회사 2 · 201
63. 산업 · 204
64. 무역 / 거래 · 207
65. 정치 · 210
66. 직업 1 · 213
67. 직업 2 · 216
68. 우체국 · 219
69. 은행 · 222
70. 전쟁 · 225
71. 매스미디어 · 228
72. 범죄 · 231
73. 사건 및 재난 · 234
74. 법률 · 237

chapter 9 — Hobbies & Leisure

75. 취미 · 242
76. 여행 · 245
77. 관광 · 248
78. 호텔 · 251
79. 공항 · 254
80. 쇼핑 1 · 257
81. 쇼핑 2 · 260
82. 스포츠 1 · 263
83. 스포츠 2 · 266
84. 놀이 · 269

chapter 10 — Culture & Art

85. 음악 · 274
86. 문학 · 277
87. 패션 및 화장품 · 280

chapter 11 — Culture & Society

88. 사교 · 284
89. 사랑 및 교제 · 287
90. 신앙 1 · 290
91. 신앙 2 · 293
92. 의사소통 · 296

chapter 12 — Science & Technology

93. 우주 · 300
94. 지구 1 · 303
95. 지구 2 · 306
96. 인터넷 · 309
97. 화학 · 312

chapter 13 — Miscellaneous

98. 물질 1 · 316
99. 물질 2 · 319
100. 추상명사 1 · 322
101. 추상명사 2 · 325

1 Basic Ideas

Part 001 Numbers 기수

A
- cardinal number
- one
- two
- three
- four
- five
- six

B
- seven
- eight
- nine
- ten
- eleven
- twelve
- thirteen

C
- fourteen
- fifteen
- sixteen
- seventeen
- eighteen
- nineteen
- twenty

D
- thirty
- forty
- hundred
- thousand
- ten thousand
- million
- billion

Part 1

#	Word	Pronunciation	Meaning
1	**cardinal number**	[káːrdənl nʌ́mbər] n.	기수
2	**one**	[wʌn] n. a.	하나
3	**two**	[tuː] n. a.	둘
4	**three**	[θriː] n. a.	셋
5	**four**	[fɔːr] n. a.	넷
6	**five**	[faiv] n. a.	다섯
7	**six**	[siks] n. a.	여섯
8	**seven**	[sévən] n. a.	일곱
9	**eight**	[eit] n. a.	여덟
10	**nine**	[nain] n. a.	아홉
11	**ten**	[ten] n. a.	열
12	**eleven**	[ilévən] n.	열하나
13	**twelve**	[twelv] n. a.	열둘
14	**thirteen**	[θəːrtíːn] n. a.	열셋
15	**fourteen**	[fɔːrtíːn] n. a.	열넷
16	**fifteen**	[fiftíːn] n. a.	열다섯
17	**sixteen**	[sikstíːn] n. a.	열여섯
18	**seventeen**	[sevəntíːn] n. a.	열일곱
19	**eighteen**	[eitíːn] n. a.	열여덟
20	**nineteen**	[naintíːn] n. a.	열아홉
21	**twenty**	[twénti] n. a.	스물
22	**thirty**	[θə́ːrti] n. a.	서른
23	**forty**	[fɔ́ːrti] n. a.	마흔
24	**hundred**	[hʌ́ndrəd] n. a.	백
25	**thousand**	[θáuzənd] n. a.	천
26	**ten thousand**	[ten θauzənd] n. a.	만
27	**million**	[míljən] n. a.	백만
28	**billion**	[bíljən] n. a.	십억

Basic Ideas

⋯⋯▸ Two plus three equals five.
2에 3을 더하면 5가 됩니다.

⋯⋯▸ Seven minus five equals two.
7에서 5를 빼면 2가 됩니다.

⋯⋯▸ Nine divided by three equals three.
9 나누기 3은 3입니다.

⋯⋯▸ Millions of people gathered.
백만 명 정도의 사람들이 모였습니다.

⋯⋯▸ He turns thirty-five years old this year.
올해 그는 서른다섯 살이 됩니다.

＊ **fifty**	[fífti] n. a.	쉰
＊ **sixty**	[síksti] n. a.	예순
＊ **seventy**	[sévənti] n. a.	일흔
＊ **eighty**	[éiti] n. a.	여든
＊ **ninety**	[náinti] n. a.	아흔
＊ **ten million**	[ten míljən] n. a.	천만
＊ **hundred million**	[hándrəd míljən] n. a.	1억
＊ **trillion**	[tríljən] n. a.	조
＊ **zero**	[zíərou] n.	영
＊ **odd number**	[ɑd nÁmbər] n.	홀수
＊ **even number**	[í:vən nÁmbər] n.	짝수

Part 002 Numbers 서수

A
- ordinal number
- first
- second
- third
- fourth
- fifth
- sixth

B
- seventh
- eighth
- ninth
- tenth
- eleventh
- twelfth
- thirteenth

C
- fourteenth
- fifteenth
- sixteenth
- seventeenth
- eighteenth
- nineteenth
- twentieth

D
- thirtieth
- fortieth
- hundredth
- thousandth
- ten thousandth
- millionth
- billionth

Basic Ideas

#	Word	Pronunciation	Meaning
1	**ordinal number**	[ɔ́:rdənəl nʌ́mbər] n.	서수
2	**first**	[fə:rst] n. a.	첫번째
3	**second**	[sékənd] n. a.	두번째
4	**third**	[θə:rd] n. a.	세번째
5	**fourth**	[fɔ:rθ] n. a.	네번째
6	**fifth**	[fifθ] n. a.	다섯번째
7	**sixth**	[siksθ] n. a.	여섯번째
8	**seventh**	[sévənθ] n. a.	일곱번째
9	**eighth**	[eitθ] n. a.	여덟번째
10	**ninth**	[nainθ] n. a.	아홉번째
11	**tenth**	[tenθ] n. a.	열번째
12	**eleventh**	[ilévənθ] n. a.	열한번째
13	**twelfth**	[twelfθ] n. a.	열두번째
14	**thirteenth**	[θə:rtí:nθ] n. a.	열세번째
15	**fourteenth**	[fɔ:rtí:nθ] n. a.	열네번째
16	**fifteenth**	[fiftí:nθ] n. a.	열다섯번째
17	**sixteenth**	[síkstí:nθ] n. a.	열여섯번째
18	**seventeenth**	[sevəntí:nθ] n. a.	열일곱번째
19	**eighteenth**	[eití:nθ] n. a.	열여덟번째
20	**nineteenth**	[naintí:nθ] n. a.	열아홉번째
21	**twentieth**	[twéntiiθ] n. a.	스무번째
22	**thirtieth**	[θə́:rtiiθ] n. a.	서른번째
23	**fortieth**	[fɔ́:rtiiθ] n. a.	마흔번째
24	**hundredth**	[hʌ́ndrədθ] n. a.	백번째
25	**thousandth**	[θauzəndθ] n. a.	천번째
26	**ten thousandth**	[ten θauzəndθ] n. a.	만번째
27	**millionth**	[míljənθ] n. a.	백만번째
28	**billionth**	[bíljənθ] n. a.	십억번째

⋯ He divorced his second wife.
그는 두번째 부인과 이혼했습니다.

⋯ We have only one millionth of possibility to solve the problem now.
지금 그 문제를 해결하는 데에 단지 백만분의 일의 가능성이 있을 뿐입니다.

⋯ All of the family gathered to celebrate her fifteenth birthday.
온 가족이 그녀의 15번째 생일을 축하하기 위해 모였습니다.

⋯ Finally she succeeded in discovering it in the hundredth times try.
마침내 백 번째 시도에서 그녀는 그것을 발견하는데 성공했습니다.

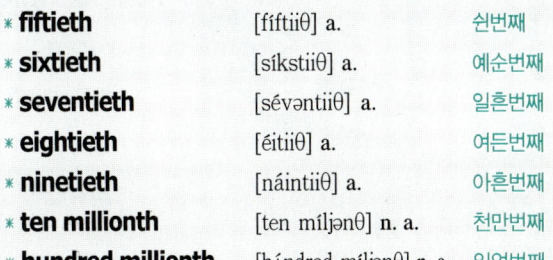

* fiftieth	[fíftiiθ] a.	쉰번째
* sixtieth	[síkstiiθ] a.	예순번째
* seventieth	[sévəntiiθ] a.	일흔번째
* eightieth	[éitiiθ] a.	여든번째
* ninetieth	[náintiiθ] a.	아흔번째
* ten millionth	[ten míljənθ] n. a.	천만번째
* hundred millionth	[hʌ́ndrəd míljənθ] n. a.	일억번째

003 Time 시간

A
- first
- end
- recently / lately
- for the first time
- the last
- once upon a time
- these days / nowadays

B
- past
- present
- future
- once
- at noon
- at midnight

C
- quarter
- half
- half past three
- late
- previous
- forever
- forward

D
- ever
- later
- next
- at the moment
- someday
- sometimes

Part 1

#	Word	Pronunciation	Meaning
1	**first**	[fəːrst] a.	처음
2	**end**	[end] n.	끝
3	**recently / lately**	[ríːsəntli] / [léitli] ad.	최근
4	**for the first time**	[fɔːr ðə fəːrst taim]	최초
5	**the last**	[ðə læst] ad.	마지막
6	**once upon a time**	[wʌns əpán ə taim] ad.	옛날
7	**these days/nowadays**	[ðiːz deiz] / [náuədéiz] ad.	오늘날
8	**past**	[pæst] n.	과거
9	**present**	[prézənt] n.	현재
10	**future**	[fjúːtʃər] n.	미래 / 장래
11	**once**	[wʌns] ad.	한때
12	**at noon**	[æt nuːn]	정오에
13	**at midnight**	[æt mídnàit]	자정에
14	**quarter**	[kwɔ́ːrtər] n.	15분
15	**half**	[hæf] n.	30분
16	**half past three**	[hæf pæst θriː]	3시 반
17	**late**	[léit] a. ad.	늦은, 늦게
18	**previous**	[príːviəs] a.	이전의
19	**forever**	[fərévər] ad.	영원히
20	**forward**	[fɔ́ːrwəːrd] ad.	앞으로
21	**ever**	[évər] ad.	이전에 / 언제나
22	**later**	[léitər] ad.	나중에
23	**next**	[nekst] a.	다음에
24	**at the moment**	[æt ðə móumənt] n.	지금은
25	**someday**	[sʌ́mdèi] ad.	언젠가(미래)
26	**sometimes**	[sʌ́mtàimz] ad.	때때로

Basic Ideas

⋯▸ It was a long time ago.
그것은 옛날 일입니다.

⋯▸ It's a quarter past ten.
10시 15분입니다.

⋯▸ Let's meet this coming Friday.
이번 주 금요일에 만납시다.

⋯▸ He got married last year.
그는 작년에 결혼했습니다.

⋯▸ Come over to my house if you have some time.
시간이 나면 우리 집에 놀러오세요.

∗ **this year**	[ðis jiə:r]	올해
∗ **last year**	[læst jiə:r]	작년
∗ **next year**	[nekst jiə:r]	내년
∗ **the year before last**	[ðə jiə:r bifɔ́: læst]	재작년
∗ **the year after next**	[ðə jiə:r ǽftər nekst]	내후년
∗ **every year**	[évri jiə:r]	매년
∗ **half year**	[hæf jiə:r]	반년
∗ **the end of the year**	[ði endɔv ðə jiə:r]	연말
∗ **the end of the month**	[ði endɔv ðə mʌnθ]	월말
∗ **during the week**	[djúəriŋ ðə wi:k]	주중에
∗ **on weekends**	[ɔn wí:kèndz]	주말에

Part 004 Days
하루 / 낮 / 요일

A
- in the morning
- in the afternoon
- in the evening
- at night
- last night
- tonight
- yesterday

B
- today
- tomorrow
- the day before yesterday
- the day after tomorrow
- at dawn
- at sunset
- at sunrise

C
- eve
- stay up all night
- all day long
- calender
- at the beginning of
- in the middle of
- at the end of

하루

D
- Monday
- Tuesday
- Wednesday
- Thursday
- Friday
- Saturday
- Sunday

#	영어	발음	뜻
1	in the morning	[inː ðə mɔ́ːrniŋ]	아침에
2	in the afternoon	[inː ði ǽftərnúːn]	오후에
3	in the evening	[inː ði íːvniŋ]	저녁에
4	at night	[æt nait]	밤에
5	last night	[læst nait]	어젯밤
6	tonight	[tənáit] n. ad.	오늘밤
7	yesterday	[jéstərdèi] n. ad.	어제
8	today	[tədéi] n. ad.	오늘
9	tomorrow	[təmɔ́ːrou] n. ad.	내일
10	the day before yesterday	[ðə dei bifɔ́ːr jéstərdèi]	그저께
11	the day after tomorrow	[ðə dei ǽftər təmɔ́ːrou]	모레
12	at dawn	[æt dɔːn]	새벽에
13	at sunset	[æt sʌ́nsèt]	해질녘에
14	at sunrise	[æt sʌ́nràiz]	해뜰 무렵에
15	eve	[iːv] n.	전날 / 전날 밤
16	stay up all night	[stei ʌp ɔːl nait]	밤샘하다
17	all day long	[ɔːl dei lɔːŋ]	하루 종일
18	calender	[kǽləndər] n.	달력
19	at the beginning of	[æt ðə bigíniŋ ʌv]	초순
20	in the middle of	[inː ðə mídl ʌv]	중순
21	at the end of	[æt ði end ʌv]	하순
22	Monday	[mʌ́ndei] n.	월요일
23	Tuesday	[tjúːzdei] n.	화요일
24	Wednesday	[wénzdèi] n.	수요일
25	Thursday	[θə́ːrzdei] n.	목요일
26	Friday	[fráidei] n.	금요일
27	Saturday	[sǽtərdèi] n.	토요일
28	Sunday	[sʌ́ndei] n.	일요일

⋯▶ I go jogging with the dog every morning.
저는 매일 아침 개와 조깅을 합니다.

⋯▶ He was called to work in the middle of night.
그는 한밤중에 일 때문에 불려 나갔습니다.

⋯▶ I am going to have a blind date the day after tomorrow.
내일 모레 소개팅을 합니다.

⋯▶ I stayed at home all day long.
하루 종일 집에 있었습니다.

⋯▶ Monday follows Tuesday.
월요일 다음날은 화요일입니다.

∗ able	~할 수 있는
∗ abroad	외국으로 / 해외로
∗ absorb	흡수하다
∗ according to	~에 따라 / ~에 따르면
∗ actually	사실상 / 실제로
∗ admit	허락하다 / 인정하다
∗ advance	전진
∗ affect	영향을 미치다
∗ agree	동의하다
∗ ahead	앞으로
∗ alarm	놀람 / 경보
∗ almost	거의

Part 005 Months & Seasons
달 / 계절

A
- January
- February
- March
- April
- May
- June
- July

B
- August
- September
- October
- November
- December
- at the beginning of the month
- at the end of the month

C
- season
- spring
- summer
- autumn
- winter
- in the middle of summer
- in the middle of winter

D
- all year long
- the summer solstice
- the winter solstice
- lunar calendar
- solar calendar
- leap year

Part 1

Basic Ideas

1	January	[dʒǽnjuèri] n.	일월
2	February	[fébruèri] n.	이월
3	March	[mɑːrtʃ] n.	삼월
4	April	[éiprəl] n.	사월
5	May	[mei] n.	오월
6	June	[dʒuːn] n.	유월
7	July	[dʒuːlái] n.	칠월
8	August	[ɔ́ːgəst] n.	팔월
9	September	[səptémbər] n.	구월
10	October	[ɑktóubər] n.	시월
11	November	[nouvémbər] n.	십일월
12	December	[disémbər] n.	십이월
13	at the beginning of the month		월초에
14	at the end of the month		월말에
15	season	[síːzən] n.	계절 / 철
16	spring	[spriŋ] n.	봄
17	summer	[sʌ́mər] n.	여름
18	autumn	[ɔ́ːtəm] n.	가을
19	winter	[wíntər] n.	겨울
20	in the middle of summer		한여름
21	in the middle of winter		한겨울
22	all year long		일년 내내
23	the summer solstice	[sʌ́mər sɑ́lstis]	하지
24	the winter solstice	[wíntər sɑ́lstis]	동지
25	lunar calendar	[lúːnər kǽləndər]	음력
26	solar calendar	[sóulər kǽləndər]	양력
27	leap year	[liːp jiəːr]	윤년

21

⋯▸ **Spring passes and summer comes.**
　　봄이 지나면, 여름이 옵니다.

⋯▸ **The four seasons are distinct in Korea.**
　　한국은 사계절이 확실합니다.

⋯▸ **It's hot like in the middle of summer.**
　　마치 한여름과 같은 더위입니다.

⋯▸ **My birthday is March 20th.**
　　저의 생일은 3월 20일입니다.

⋯▸ **Africa is hot throughout the year.**
　　아프리카는 일년 내내 덥습니다.

∗ always	늘 / 언제나
∗ amazing	놀라운 / 굉장한
∗ another	또 하나의
∗ anyway	어쨌든 / 아무튼
∗ appeal	호소하다
∗ appear	나타나다 / ~인 듯하다
∗ appetite	식욕
∗ apply	적용하다 / 지원하다
∗ appoint	지명하다 / 정하다
∗ assemble	모으다 / 소집하다
∗ assign	할당하다 / 지정하다
∗ assist	돕다

Part 006 Weather 날씨

A
- rain
- snow
- wind
- cloud
- fog
- frost
- shower

B
- downpour
- hail
- climate
- typhoon
- thunder
- snowstorm
- lightning

C
- weather forecast
- temperature
- Fahrenheit
- Celsius
- below zero
- above zero
- monsoon season

D
- rainbow
- blow
- freeze
- drizzle
- warm
- wet
- humid

Part 1

Basic Ideas

#	Word	Pronunciation	Meaning
1	rain	[rein] n.	비
2	snow	[snou] n.	눈
3	wind	[wind] n.	바람
4	cloud	[klaud] n.	구름
5	fog	[fɔ(:)g] n.	안개
6	frost	[frɔːst] n.	서리
7	shower	[ʃóuər] n.	소나기
8	downpour	[dáunpɔ́ːr] n.	폭우
9	hail	[heil] n.	싸락눈, 우박
10	climate	[kláimit] n.	기후
11	typhoon	[taifúːn] n.	태풍
12	thunder	[θʌ́ndər] n.	천둥
13	snowstorm	[snóustɔ́ːrm] n.	눈보라
14	lightning	[láitniŋ] n.	번개
15	weather forecast	[wéðər fɔ́ːrkæ̀st] n.	일기예보
16	temperature	[témpərətʃuər] n.	기온
17	Fahrenheit	[fǽrənhàit] n.	화씨
18	Celsius	[sélsiəs]	섭씨
19	below zero	[bilóu zíərou] n.	영하
20	above zero	[əbʌ́v zíərou] n.	영상
21	monsoon season	[mɑnsúːn síːzən] n.	장마
22	rainbow	[réinbòu] n.	무지개
23	blow	[blou] v.	(바람이)불다
24	freeze	[friːz] vi.	얼다
25	drizzle	[drízl] n.	이슬비가 내리다
26	warm	[wɔːrm] a.	따뜻한
27	wet	[wet] a.	젖은
28	humid	[hjúːmid] a.	습기 찬

- I got caught in a shower.
  갑자기 소나기를 맞았습니다.
- It's getting chilly these days.
  요새 점점 추워지고 있습니다.
- According to the weather forecast, we will have a typhoon tomorrow.
  일기예보에 의하면, 내일은 태풍이 온다고 합니다.
- Monsoon season usually starts at the end of June.
  장마기 6월 하순에 시작됩니다.

* **mist**	[mist] n.	안개
* **dew**	[djuː] n.	이슬
* **sunny**	[sʌ́ni] a.	맑은
* **heavy**	[hévi] a.	(비, 바람이)심한
* **hot**	[hɑt] a.	더운
* **windy**	[windi] a.	바람이 부는
* **cloudy**	[kláudi] a.	흐린 / 구름이 많은
* **rainy**	[réini] a.	비가 오는
* **clear**	[kliər] a.	맑은
* **foggy**	[fɔ́(ː)gi] a.	안개 낀
* **drizzling**	[drízliŋ] n.	이슬비가 내리는
* **freezing**	[fríːziŋ] a.	얼음처럼 찬
* **thermometer**	[θəːrmɑ́mitər] n.	온도계
* **degree**	[digríː] n.	도
* **hurricane**	[hə́rəkèin] n.	허리케인
* **tornado**	[tɔːrnéidou] n.	회오리폭풍
* **ice**	[ais] n.	얼음
* **storm**	[stɔːrm] n.	폭풍(우)

Part 007 Country 국가

A
- foreign country
- mother country
- President
- Prime Minister
- Vice Prime Minister
- diplomat
- mayor

B
- citizen
- capital city
- government
- cabinet
- political party
- diplomacy
- embassy

C
- patriotism
- capitalism
- socialism
- communism
- communist
- democracy
- democrat

D
- legislation
- judicature
- administration
- developed country
- developing country
- underdeveloped country
- govern / rule

Part 1

Basic Ideas

#	Word	Pronunciation	Meaning
1	**foreign country**	[fɔ́(:)rin kʌ́ntri]	외국
2	**mother country**	[mʌ́ðər kʌ́ntri]	모국
3	**President**	[prézidənt] n.	대통령
4	**Prime Minister**	[praim mínistər] n.	총리
5	**Vice Prime Minister**	[vais praim mínistər] n.	부총리
6	**diplomat**	[dípləmæt] n.	외교관
7	**mayor**	[méiər] n.	시장
8	**citizen**	[sítəzən] n.	시민
9	**capital city**	[kǽpitl síti] n.	수도
10	**government**	[gʌ́vərnmənt] n.	정부
11	**cabinet**	[kǽbənit] n.	내각
12	**political party**	[pəlítikəl pá:rti] n.	정당
13	**diplomacy**	[diplóuməsi] n.	외교
14	**embassy**	[émbəsi] n.	대사관
15	**patriotism**	[péitriətizəm]	애국심
16	**capitalism**	[kǽpitəlìzəm] n.	자본주의
17	**socialism**	[sóuʃəlìzəm] n.	사회주의
18	**communism**	[kámjənìzəm] n.	공산주의
19	**communist**	[kámjənist] n.	공산주의자
20	**democracy**	[dimákrəsi] n.	민주주의
21	**democrat**	[déməkræt] n.	민주주의자
22	**legislation**	[lèdʒisléiʃən] n.	입법
23	**judicature**	[dʒú:dikətʃər] n.	사법
24	**administration**	[ædmìnəstréiʃən] n.	행정
25	**developed country**	[divéləpt kʌ́ntri]	선진국
26	**developing country**	[divéləpiŋ kʌ́ntri]	개발도상국
27	**underdeveloped country**	[ʌ̀ndərdivéləpt kʌ́ntri]	후진국
28	**govern / rule**	[gʌ́vərn]/[ru:l] v.	통치하다

⋯▶ Seoul is the capital city of Korea.
서울은 한국의 수도입니다.

⋯▶ He was elected President.
그는 대통령으로 선출되었습니다.

⋯▶ Is Korea a democratic country?
한국은 민주주의 국가입니까?

⋯▶ She went to the American Embassy for a visa interview.
그녀는 비자 인터뷰를 하기 위해 미국 대사관에 갔습니다.

⋯▶ He used to work in a government office.
그는 이전에 공무원이었습니다.

*king	[kiŋ] n.	왕
*kingdom	[kíŋdəm] n.	왕국
*queen	[kwiːn] n.	여왕 / 왕비
*prince	[prins] n.	왕자
*princess	[prínses] n.	공주 / 왕자비
*civil	[sívəl] a.	시민의
*royal	[rɔ́iəl] a.	왕의

Part 008
Countries & Nationalities 국적

A
Asia
Europe
Africa
continent
The United States
American
Japan / Japanese

B
Korea / Korean
China / Chinese
North Korea
Hawaii
The United Kingdom
Briton
Germany / German

C
Italy / Italian
Switzerland / Swiss
Canada / Canadian
Russia / Russian
Greece / Greek
Netherlands / Dutch
Mexico / Mexican

D
Thailand / Thai
France / French
Philippines / Filipino
Turkey / Turkish
Australia / Australian
New Zealand / New Zealander
Spain / Spaniard

Basic Ideas

#	Word	Pronunciation	Korean
1	**Asia**	[éiʒə] n.	아시아
2	**Europe**	[júərəp] n.	유럽
3	**Africa**	[ǽfrikə] n.	아프리카
4	**continent**	[kántənənt] n.	대륙
5	**The United States**	[ði juːnáitid steitz] n.	미국
6	**American**	[əmérikən] n. a.	미국인
7	**Japan / Japanese**	[dʒəpǽn] / [dʒæ̀pəníːz]	일본 / 일본인
8	**Korea / Korean**	[kəríːə] / [kəríːən]	대한민국 / 한국인
9	**China / Chinese**	[tʃáinə] / [tʃainíːz]	중국 / 중국인
10	**North Korea**	[nɔːrθ kəríːə] n.	북한
11	**Hawaii**	[həwáiiː] n.	하와이
12	**The United Kingdom**	[ði juːnáitid kíŋdəm] n.	영국
13	**Briton**	[brítn] n.	영국인
14	**Germany / German**	[dʒə́ːrməni] / [dʒə́ːrmən]	독일 / 독일인
15	**Italy / Italian**	[ítəli] / [itǽljən]	이탈리아 / 이태리인
16	**Switzerland / Swiss**	[swítsərlənd] / [swis]	스위스 / 스위스인
17	**Canada / Canadian**	[kǽnədə] / [kənéidiən]	캐나다 / 캐나다인
18	**Russia / Russian**	[rʌ́ʃə] / [rʌ́ʃən]	러시아 / 러시아인
19	**Greece / Greek**	[griːs] / [griːk]	그리스 / 그리스인
20	**Netherlands / Dutch**	[néðərləndz] / [dʌtʃ]	네덜란드 / 네덜란드인
21	**Mexico / Mexican**	[méksikòu] / [méksikən]	멕시코 / 멕시코인
22	**Thailand / Thai**	[táilænd] / [tai]	태국 / 태국인
23	**France / French**	[fræns] / [frentʃ]	프랑스 / 프랑스인
24	**Philippines / Filipino**	[fíləpìːnz] / [filəpíːnou]	필리핀 / 필리핀인
25	**Turkey / Turkish**	[tə́ːrki] / [tə́ːrkiʃ]	터키 / 터키인
26	**Australia / Australian**	[ɔːstréiljə] / [ɔːstréiljən]	호주 / 호주인
27	**New Zealand / New Zealander**	[njuːzíːlənd] / [njuːzíːləndə]	뉴질랜드 / 뉴질랜드인
28	**Spain / Spaniard**	[spein] / [spǽnjərd]	스페인 / 스페인사람

- Korea and Japan are geographically close but culturally distant countries.
  한국과 일본은 지리적으로 가깝지만 문화적으로 먼 나라입니다.

- I am going to the America to study English.
  미국으로 어학 연수하러 갈 작정입니다.

- I want to visit Rome, the capital city of Italy someday.
  저는 언젠가는 이탈리아의 수도, 로마를 방문하고 싶습니다.

- Korea, China, and Russia belong to Northeast Asia.
  한국과 중국과 러시아는 동북아시아에 속합니다.

- The Olympic Games were held in Greece for the first time.
  올림픽 경기는 그리스에서 처음 시작됐습니다.

*international	[ìntərnǽʃənəl] a.	국제의
*Southeast Asian countries	[sàuθíːst éiʒən kʌ́ntriz]	동남아시아
*Central Asia	[séntrəl éiʒə]	중앙아시아
*Central and South America	[séntrəl sauθ əmérikə]	중남미
*Mongolia	[maŋgóuliə] n.	몽골
*Mongol	[máŋgəl] n.	몽골사람

Part 009 color 색

A
- red
- blue
- white
- black
- yellow
- green

B
- brown
- light blue
- peach
- gold
- silver
- gray

C
- pink
- navy blue
- purple
- orange
- light green
- beige

D
- cream
- bright
- dark
- golden
- brownish gold
- bluish

Part 1

Basic Ideas

#	Word	Pronunciation	Meaning
1	**red**	[red] a.	빨간색
2	**blue**	[bluː] a.	파란색
3	**white**	[hwait] n.	흰색
4	**black**	[blæk] a.	검정색
5	**yellow**	[jélou] n.	노랑색
6	**green**	[griːn] a.	녹색
7	**brown**	[braun] n.	갈색
8	**light blue**	[lait bluː] n.	하늘색
9	**peach**	[piːtʃ] n.	복숭아 색
10	**gold**	[gould] n.	금색
11	**silver**	[sílvər] n.	은색
12	**gray**	[grei] n.	회색
13	**pink**	[piŋk] n.	핑크색
14	**navy blue**	[néivi bluː] n.	짙은 청색
15	**purple**	[pə́ːrpl] a.	보라색
16	**orange**	[ɔ́(ː)rindʒ]	오렌지 색
17	**light green**	[lait griːn]	연두색
18	**beige**	[beiʒ] n.	베이지색
19	**cream**	[kriːm] a.	크림색
20	**bright**	[brait] a.	밝은 / 똑똑한
21	**dark**	[dɑːrk] a.	어두운 / 캄캄한
22	**golden**	[góuldən] a.	금빛의 / 귀중한
23	**brownish gold**	[bráuniʃ gould] a.	갈색 빛이 도는 금색
24	**bluish**	[blúːiʃ] a.	푸르스름한

33

- He wears a blue dot-printed shirt.
  그는 파란색 물방울무늬 셔츠를 입고 있습니다.
- I'll have this light green apron.
  이 연두색 앞치마를 살게요.
- My favorite color is navy blue.
  내가 좋아하는 색은 짙은 청색입니다.
- The kid painted the Sun yellow.
  아이는 해를 노란색으로 칠했습니다.
- We couldn't see anything in the dark basement.
  우리는 어두운 지하실에서 아무것도 볼 수 없었습니다.

* attach	붙이다
* available	이용할 수 있는 / 사용가능한
* avoid	피하다 / 회피하다
* awfully	아주 / 몹시
* ax	도끼
* bake	굽다
* balance	균형
* ball	공 / 구
* balloon	풍선
* basic	기초적인
* basket	바구니
* bat	박쥐

Part 010 Public Holiday / Party
공휴일 / 파티

A
- New Year's Day
- Lunar New Year's Day
- Valentine's Day
- Independence Movement Day
- Easter
- Arbor Day
- Children's Day

B
- Parents' Day
- Teacher's Day
- Memorial Day
- Constitution Day
- Independence Day
- Korean Thanksgiving Day
- Foundation Day

C
- Hangul Proclamation Day
- Halloween
- Christmas Day
- New Year's Eve
- 100th day after birth
- the first birthday
- the 60th birthday

D
- wedding anniversary
- housewarming party
- potluck party
- surprise party
- farewell party
- welcome party
- year-end party

1	**New Year's Day**	[njuːjiəːrz dei]	설날(1.1)
2	**Lunar New Year's Day**	[lúːnər njuːjiəːrz dei]	음력 설날(음1.1)
3	**Valentine's Day**	[væləntàinz dei]	발렌타인 데이(2.14)
4	**Independence Movement Day**	[ìndipéndəns múːvmənt dei]	삼일절(3.1)
5	**Easter**	[íːstər] n.	부활절
6	**Arbor Day**	[áːrbər dei]	식목일(4.5)
7	**Children's Day**	[tʃíldrənz dei]	어린이날(5.5)
8	**Parents' Day**	[péərənts dei]	어버이날(5.8)
9	**Teacher's Day**	[tíːtʃəːrz dei]	스승의 날(5.15)
10	**Memorial Day**	[mimɔ́ːriəl dei]	현충일(6.6)
11	**Constitution Day**	[kánstətjúːʃən dei]	제헌절(7.17)
12	**Independence Day**	[ìndipéndəns dei]	광복절(8.15)
13	**Korean Thanksgiving Day**	[kəríːən θæ̀ŋksgíviŋ dei]	추석
14	**Foundation Day**	[faundéiʃən dei]	개천절
15	**Hangul Proclamation Day**	[háːŋgul prákləméiʃən dei]	한글날
16	**Halloween**	[hæləwíːn]	할로윈
17	**Christmas Day**	[krísməs dei]	크리스마스(12.25)
18	**New Year's Eve**	[njuːjiəːrz iːv]	섣달 그믐(12.31)
19	**100th day after birth**	[hʌ́ndrədθ dei ǽftə bəːrθ]	백일
20	**the first birthday**	[ðə fəːrst bə́ːrθdèi]	돌
21	**the 60th birthday**	[ðə síkstiiθ bə́ːrθdèi]	회갑
22	**wedding anniversary**	[wédiŋ æ̀nəvə́ːrsəri]	결혼기념일
23	**housewarming party**	[háuswɔ̀ərmiŋ páːrti]	집들이
24	**potluck party**	[pátlʌ́k páːrti]	각자의 음식을 가져오는 파티
25	**surprise party**	[sərpráiz páːrti]	깜짝 파티
26	**farewell party**	[fɛ̀ərwél páːrti]	송별회
27	**welcome party**	[wélkəm páːrti]	환영회
28	**year-end party**	[jiər end páːrti]	송년 파티

···▶ We went to a Halloween party at Universal Studio.
우리는 유니버설 스튜디오의 할로윈 파티에 갔습니다.

···▶ Most Koreans celebrate Lunar New Year's Day.
대부분의 한국인들은 음력설을 지냅니다.

···▶ I went to a department store to buy a gift for Parents' Day.
어버이날 선물을 사러 백화점에 갔습니다.

···▶ Easter is a very important holiday on the Christian calendar.
부활절은 기독교에서 매우 중요한 축제일입니다.

···▶ We're preparing a surprise party for him.
우리는 그를 위한 깜짝 파티를 준비하고 있습니다.

✻ beast	짐승
✻ beg	구걸하다 / 간청하다
✻ behave	행동하다
✻ behind	~뒤에 / 늦어
✻ belong	속하다 / 소속이다
✻ besides	게다가 / 그밖에
✻ betray	배반하다 / 누설하다
✻ beyond	~의 너머로 / ~의 지나서
✻ big	큰
✻ bind	묶다
✻ birth	탄생
✻ bite	물다

Part 011 Location 위치

A
- east
- west
- south
- north
- above
- below
- opposite

B
- top
- bottom
- front
- back
- side
- inside
- outside

C
- surface
- between
- range
- direction
- area
- space
- district

D
- both sides
- middle
- near
- far
- center
- outer
- inner

Part 1

#	Word	Pronunciation	Meaning
1	east	[iːst] n.	동(쪽)
2	west	[west] n.	서(쪽)
3	south	[sauθ] n.	남(쪽)
4	north	[nɔːrθ] n.	북(쪽)
5	above	[əbˊʌv] ad.	위쪽에
6	below	[bilóu] prep.	아래쪽에
7	opposite	[άpəzit] a.	맞은편
8	top	[tɑp] n.	위
9	bottom	[bάtəm] n.	밑바닥
10	front	[frʌnt] n.	앞/정면
11	back	[bæk] n.	뒤
12	side	[said] n.	옆
13	inside	[insáid] n.	안쪽, 내부
14	outside	[autsáid] n.	바깥쪽, 외부
15	surface	[sə́ːrfis] n.	겉
16	between	[bitwíːn] prep.	사이
17	range	[reindʒ] n.	범위
18	direction	[dirékʃən] n.	방향, 방위
19	area	[ɛ́əriə] n.	면적
20	space	[speis] n.	공간
21	district	[dístrikt] n.	구역
22	both sides	[bouθ saidz] n.	양쪽
23	middle	[mídl] a.	한가운데
24	near	[niər] ad.	근처
25	far	[fɑːr] ad.	멀리
26	center	[séntər] n.	중심(중앙)
27	outer	[áutər] a.	밖의 / 외부의
28	inner	[ínər] a.	안의 / 내부의

Basic Ideas

39

···▸ Could you tell me where you are now?
현재 위치를 설명해주시겠습니까?

···▸ We moved next door.
우리는 옆집으로 이사했습니다.

···▸ Show me the insides of the product.
그 제품의 내부를 보여주세요.

···▸ There are trees planted on both sides of the road.
길 양쪽으로 가로수가 심어져 있습니다.

···▸ There is a bank opposite the post office.
우체국 맞은편에 은행이 있습니다.

✽ **core**	[kɔːr] n.	중심
✽ **head**	[hed] n.	향하다
✽ **broad**	[brɔːd] a.	넓은
✽ **eastern**	[íːstərn] a.	동쪽의
✽ **western**	[wéstərn] a.	서쪽의
✽ **northern**	[nɔ́ːrðərn] a.	북쪽의
✽ **southern**	[sʌ́ðərn] a.	남쪽의
✽ **southeast**	[sàuθíːst] a.	동남
✽ **northeast**	[nɔ̀ːrθíːst] a.	동북
✽ **northwest**	[nɔ̀ːrθwést] a.	북서
✽ **southwest**	[sàuθwést] a.	남서
✽ **underneath**	[ʌ̀ndərníːθ] prep.	아래에

2 Daily life

Part 012 Family 가족

A
- grandparents
- grandfather
- grandmother
- grandson/granddaughter
- parents
- mother/mom
- father/dad

B
- wife
- husband
- son
- daughter
- brother
- sister
- only child

C
- siblings
- uncle
- aunt
- relatives
- cousin
- nephew
- niece

D
- in-laws
- daughter-in-law
- son-in-law
- father-in-law
- mother-in-law
- get along with
- look like/resemble

Part 2

#	Word	Pronunciation	Meaning
1	grandparents	[grǽndpɛ̀ərənts] n.	조부모
2	grandfather	[grǽndfɑ́:ðər] n.	할아버지
3	grandmother	[grǽndmʌ́ðər] n.	할머니
4	grandson/granddaughter	[grǽndsʌn] /[grǽnddɔ̀:tər] n.	손자 / 손녀
5	parents	[pɛ̀ərənts] n.	양친 / 부모
6	mother/mom	[mʌ́ðər]/[mɑm] n.	어머니
7	father/dad	[fɑ́:ðər]/[dæd] n.	아버지
8	wife	[waif] n.	부인
9	husband	[hʌ́zbənd] n.	남편
10	son	[sʌn] n.	아들
11	daughter	[dɔ́:tər] n.	딸
12	brother	[brʌ́ðər] n.	남자 형제
13	sister	[sístər] n.	여자 형제
14	only child	[óunli tʃaild] n.	외동아이
15	siblings	[sibliŋz] n.	형제자매
16	uncle	[ʌ́ŋkl] n.	삼촌(숙부) / 아저씨
17	aunt	[ænt] n.	숙모(고모, 이모)아주머니
18	relatives	[rélətivz] n.	친척
19	cousin	[kʌ́zn] n.	사촌
20	nephew	[néfju:] n.	남자조카
21	niece	[ni:s] n.	여자조카
22	in-laws	[in lɔ:z]n.	시댁 / 처가 식구들
23	daughter-in-law	[dɔ́:tər in lɔ:] n.	며느리
24	son-in-law	[sʌn in lɔ:] n.	사위
25	father-in-law	[fɑ́:ðər in lɔ:] n.	시아버지 / 장인
26	mother-in-law	[mʌ́ðər in lɔ:] n.	시어머니 / 장모
27	get along with	[get əlɔ:ŋ wið]	–와 사이좋게 잘 지내다
28	look like/resemble	[luk laik] /[rizémbl] vt.	– 를 닮다

Daily Life

⋯▶ I have two younger sisters.
나에게는 여동생이 두 명 있습니다.

⋯▶ My grandfather traveled overseas alone.
할아버지는 혼자서 해외여행을 했습니다.

⋯▶ I look like my mom very much.
저는 엄마를 많이 닮았습니다.

⋯▶ He has a son and a daughter.
그는 아들과 딸이 한 명씩 있습니다.

⋯▶ The sisters get along very well.
저 자매는 사이가 좋다고 합니다.

⋯▶ Today is the wedding ceremony of my niece.
오늘은 조카딸의 결혼식입니다.

* **twins**	[twinz] n.	쌍둥이
* **older sister**	[ouldər sístər] n.	언니 / 누나
* **older brother**	[ouldər brʌ́ðər] n.	오빠 / 형
* **ancestor**	[ǽnsestər] n.	조상
* **descendant**	[diséndənt] n.	자손

Part 013 Daily Necessities
생활용품

A
- house chores
- garbage can
- dustpan
- duster
- floor cloth
- laundry
- broom

B
- carpet
- blanket
- bed cover
- curtain
- pillow
- hanger
- cushion

C
- hammer
- lamp
- ladder
- battery
- lights
- candle
- flashlight

D
- nail clipper
- toiletries
- toothpaste
- faucet
- bathtub
- detergent
- towel

Part 2

#	Word	Pronunciation	Meaning
1	**house chores**	[haus tʃɔːrz] n.	집안일
2	**garbage can**	[gáːrbidʒ kæn] n.	쓰레기통
3	**dustpan**	[dʌ́stpæn] n.	쓰레받기
4	**duster**	[dʌ́stər] n.	먼지 털이
5	**floor cloth**	[flɔːr klɔ(ː)θ] n.	걸레
6	**laundry**	[lɔ́ːndri] n.	세탁
7	**broom**	[bru(ː)m] n.	빗자루
8	**carpet**	[káːrpit] n.	융단
9	**blanket**	[blǽŋkit] n.	담요
10	**bed cover**	[bed kʌ́vər] n.	침대커버
11	**curtain**	[kə́ːrtən] n.	커튼
12	**pillow**	[pílou] n.	베개
13	**hanger**	[hǽŋər] n.	옷걸이
14	**cushion**	[kúʃən] n.	쿠션
15	**hammer**	[hǽmər] n.	망치
16	**lamp**	[læmp] n.	등불
17	**ladder**	[lǽdər] n.	사닥다리
18	**battery**	[bǽtəri] n.	건전지
19	**lights**	[laits] n.	형광등
20	**candle**	[kǽndl] n.	양초
21	**flashlight**	[flǽʃlait] n.	손전등
22	**nail clipper**	[neil klípər] n.	손톱깎이
23	**toiletries**	[tɔ́ilitriz] n.	목욕용품들
24	**toothpaste**	[túːθpèist] n.	치약
25	**faucet**	[fɔ́ːsit] n.	수도꼭지
26	**bathtub**	[bǽθtʌ̀b] n.	욕조
27	**detergent**	[ditə́ːrdʒənt] n.	세제
28	**towel**	[táuəl] n.	타월

Daily Life

⋯▸ I brush my teeth three times a day.
　　저는 하루에 세 번 이를 닦습니다.

⋯▸ Japanese take a shower everyday.
　　일본인은 매일 샤워를 합니다.

⋯▸ There is a mirror over the sink.
　　세면대 위에 거울이 걸려 있습니다.

⋯▸ You should make a bed for yourself.
　　침대는 스스로 정리하세요.

⋯▸ Recycling items must be sorted out separately.
　　재활용품들은 따로 분류해야 합니다.

* **shower**	[ʃóuər] n.		샤워
* **sink**	[siŋk] n.		세면기
* **dirt**	[dəːrt] n.		먼지
* **bubble**	[bʌ́bl] n.		거품
* **rub**	[rʌb] v.		문지르다 / 비비다
* **recycle**	[riːsáikl] v.		재활용하다
* **screw**	[skruː] n.		나사, 못
* **cassette tape**	[kæsét teip] n.		카세트 테이프
* **album**	[ǽlbəm] n.		앨범
* **lighter**	[láitər] n.		라이터
* **match**	[mætʃ] n.		성냥
* **earphone**	[íərfòun] n.		이어폰
* **bottle opener**	[bátl óupənər] n.		병따개

Part 014 Daily Activities
일상생활

A
- get up/wake up
- take a shower
- take a bath
- brush one's teeth
- floss one's teeth
- shave
- wash one's face

B
- comb the hair
- make the bed
- have breakfast
- wash the dishes
- take a nap
- go to work
- go to study

C
- clean the house
- listen to music
- listen to the radio
- meet friends
- dust
- vacuum
- watch TV

D
- go to the movies
- do the laundry
- cook dinner
- set a table
- clear a table
- go to bed

Part 2

1	get up/wake up	[get ʌ́p] /[weik ʌ́p] v.	일어나다
2	take a shower	[teikə ʃáuər] v.	샤워하다
3	take a bath	[teikə bæθ] v.	목욕하다
4	brush one's teeth	[brʌʃ wʌns tiːθ] v.	칫솔질하다
5	floss one's teeth	[flɔ(ː)s wʌns tiːθ] v.	치실을 사용하다
6	shave	[ʃeiv] v.	면도하다
7	wash one's face	[waʃ wʌns feis] v.	세수하다
8	comb the hair	[koum ðə hɛər] v.	머리를 빗다
9	make the bed	[meik ðə bed] v.	침대를 정리하다
10	have breakfast	[hæv brékfəst] v.	아침을 먹다
11	wash the dishes	[waʃ ðə diʃiz] v.	설거지 하다
12	take a nap	[teikə næp] v.	낮잠 자다
13	go to work	[gou tu wəːrk] v.	일하러 가다
14	go to study	[gou tu stʌ́di] v.	공부하러 가다
15	clean the house	[kliːn ðə haus] v.	집안을 청소하다
16	listen to music	[lisən tu mjúːzik] v.	음악을 듣다
17	listen to the radio	[lísən tu ðə réidiòu] v.	라디오를 듣다
18	meet friends	[miːt frendz] v.	친구를 만나다
19	dust	[dʌst] v.	먼지를 떨다
20	vacuum	[vǽkjuəm] v.	진공청소기를 돌리다
21	watch TV	[watʃ tíːvíː] v.	텔레비젼을 보다
22	go to the movies	[gou tu ðə múːviz] v.	영화 보러 가다
23	do the laundry	[du ðə lɔ́ːndri] v.	세탁하다
24	cook dinner	[kuk dínər] v.	저녁을 하다
25	set a table	[setə téibl] v.	상을 차리다
26	clear a table	[kliərə téibl] v.	상을 치우다
27	go to bed	[gou tu bed] v.	잠자리에 들다

Daily Life

···▸ What time did you get up this morning?
　　오늘 아침 몇 시에 일어났습니까?

···▸ I helped my mom with setting the dinner table.
　　저는 엄마가 저녁상 차리시는 것을 도와드렸습니다.

···▸ My sister always spends 30 minutes taking a shower.
　　여동생은 항상 30분씩 샤워를 합니다.

···▸ We decided to buy a dishwasher to reduce house chores.
　　우리는 집안일을 줄이기 위해 식기세척기를 사기로 결정했습니다.

···▸ I am doing homework while listening to the radio.
　　음악을 들으면서 숙제를 하고 있습니다.

* bleed	피흘리다
* boil	끓이다
* border	경계선
* borrow	빌리다
* bow	절하다
* break	깨뜨리다 / 고장 내다
* brief	잠시의 / 짤막한
* bring	가져오다 / 데려오다
* brush	솔
* bury	파묻다
* busy	바쁜 / 번화한
* call	부르다 / 전화하다

Part 015 Public Transportation
대중교통

A
- bus stop
- taxi stand
- train station
- parking lot
- gas station
- railroad crossing
- intersection

B
- traffic light
- street light
- crosswalk
- sidewalk
- one way street
- side street
- dirt road

C
- traffic law
- violate traffic law
- get a ticket
- speeding ticket
- fine
- be fined
- driving without a license

D
- pedestrian
- block
- shortcut
- underpass
- fasten the seat belt
- turn right(left)
- go straight

1	**bus stop**	[bʌs stɑp] n.	버스 정거장
2	**taxi stand**	[tǽksi stænd] n.	택시 타는 곳
3	**train station**	[trein stéiʃən] n.	철도역
4	**parking lot**	[páːrkiŋ lɑt] n.	주차장
5	**gas station**	[gæs stéiʃən] n.	주유소
6	**railroad crossing**	[réilròud krɔ́ːsiŋ] n.	건널목
7	**intersection**	[ìntərsékʃən] n.	십자로(교차로)
8	**traffic light**	[trǽfik lait] n.	신호등
9	**street light**	[striːt lait] n.	가로등
10	**crosswalk**	[krɔ́ːswɔːk] n.	횡단보도
11	**sidewalk**	[sáidwɔ̀ːk] n.	인도
12	**one way street**	[wʌn wei striːt] n.	일방통행로
13	**side street**	[said striːt] n.	골목
14	**dirt road**	[dəːrt roud] n.	비포장도로
15	**traffic law**	[trǽfik lɔː] n.	교통법규
16	**violate traffic law**	[váiəlèit trǽfik lɔː]	교통법규를 위반하다
17	**get a ticket**	[getə tíkit]	교통 딱지를 떼다
18	**speeding ticket**	[spíːdiŋ tíkit] n.	속도위반 딱지
19	**fine**	[fain] n.	벌금
20	**be fined**	[bi faind]	벌금을 내다
21	**driving without a license**	[dráiviŋ wiðáutə láisəns]	무면허 운전
22	**pedestrian**	[pədéstrin] n.	보행자
23	**block**	[blɑk] n.	블록
24	**shortcut**	[ʃɔːrtkʌ́t] n.	지름길
25	**underpass**	[ʌ́ndərpæ̀s] n.	지하도
26	**fasten the seat belt**	[fǽsn ðə siːt belt]	안전벨트를 착용하다
27	**turn right(left)**	[təːrn rait/left]	우(좌)회전하다
28	**go straight**	[gou streit]	곧장 가다

Daily Life

⋯▸ I was fined speeding.
　　속도위반으로 벌금을 냈습니다.

⋯▸ Show me a shortcut to the nearest subway station.
　　가장 가까운 전철역으로 가는 지름길을 알려주세요.

⋯▸ You must stop your car at a red light.
　　빨간 신호등 앞에서는 차를 세워야 합니다.

⋯▸ The tunnel construction is still underway.
　　터널 공사가 여전히 진행 중입니다.

⋯▸ There is a crosswalk.
　　저쪽에 횡단보도가 있군요.

✽ **national highway**	[nǽʃənəl háiwèi] n.	국도
✽ **boulevard**	[bú(:)ləvɑ̀:rd] n.	큰길
✽ **stop**	[stɑp] n.	정차
✽ **movement**	[mú:vmənt] n.	이동
✽ **transportation**	[trænspərtéiʃən] n.	수송
✽ **prohibition**	[pròuhəbíʃən] n.	금지
✽ **distant**	[dístənt] a.	(거리, 관계가) 먼
✽ **rapid**	[rǽpid] a.	빠른
✽ **across**	[əkrɔ́:s] ad.	가로질러서
✽ **slowly**	[slóuli] ad.	천천히
✽ **steering wheel**	[stíəriŋ hwi:l] n.	핸들
✽ **platform**	[plǽtfɔ̀:rm] n.	플랫폼

Part 016 Vehicles 탈것

A
- bus
- subway
- airplane
- automobile
- truck
- jeep
- ferry

B
- helicopter
- train
- bullet train
- freight train
- bicycle/bike
- motorcycle
- taxi

C
- ticket window
- turnstile
- express highway
- railroad
- driver's license
- seat belt
- seats for the elderly

D
- patrol car
- fare
- advance ticket
- commuter
- passenger
- wait in line
- median

Part 2

#	Word	Pronunciation	Korean
1	bus	[bʌs] n.	버스
2	subway	[sʌ́bwèi] n.	지하철
3	airplane	[ɛ́ərplèin] n.	비행기
4	automobile	[ɔ́:təməbì:l] n.	자동차
5	truck	[trʌk] n.	트럭
6	jeep	[dʒi:p] n.	지프
7	ferry	[féri] n.	배
8	helicopter	[hélikàptər] n.	헬리콥터
9	train	[trein] n.	기차
10	bullet train	[búlit trein] n.	고속철
11	freight train	[fréit trein] n.	화물열차
12	bicycle/bike	[báisikl] / [baik] n.	자전거
13	motorcycle	[móutərsàikl] n.	오토바이
14	taxi	[tǽksi] n.	택시
15	ticket window	[tíkit wíndou] n.	매표구
16	turnstile	[tə́:rnstàil] n.	회전식 개찰구
17	express highway	[iksprés háiwèi] n.	고속도로
18	railroad	[réilròud] n.	철도
19	driver's license	[dráivərz láisəns] n.	운전면허
20	seat belt	[si:t belt] n.	안전벨트
21	seats for the elderly	[si:ts fɔ:r ði éldərli] n.	경로석
22	patrol car	[pətróul ka:r] n.	순찰차
23	fare	[fɛər] n.	차비 / 운임
24	advance ticket	[ædvǽns tíkit] n.	예매권
25	commuter	[kəmjútər] n.	통근자
26	passenger	[pǽsəndʒər] n.	승객
27	wait in line	[wéitin lain] v.	줄서다
28	median	[mí:diən] n.	중앙 분리대

Daily Life

⋯› She drives at 150 kilometers an hour on the express way.
그녀는 고속도로에서 시속150킬로로 달리고 있습니다.

⋯› It takes only 2 hours to go to Busan from Seoul by bullet train.
서울에서 부산까지 고속철로 2시간밖에 안 걸립니다.

⋯› He came back home by taxi.
그는 택시를 타고 집으로 돌아왔습니다.

⋯› An airplane is much faster than subway.
비행기가 전철보다 훨씬 빠릅니다.

⋯› The policeman gave me a speeding ticket.
속도위반 딱지를 떼었습니다.

✻ **express**	[iksprés] n.	급행열차
✻ **arrive**	[əráiv] vi.	도착하다
✻ **land**	[lænd] n.	착륙하다
✻ **give up your seat to**		–에 자리를 양보하다
✻ **row**	[rou] v.	노를 젓다
✻ **fast**	[fæst] a.	빠른
✻ **aboard**	[əbɔ́:rd] ad.	(기차,버스,배,비행기)를 타고
✻ **transfer**	[trænsfə́r]	갈아타다
✻ **slow train**	[slou trein] n.	완행열차
✻ **convertible**	[kənvə́:rtəbl] n.	지붕을 접을 수 있는 차
✻ **camper**	[kǽmpər] n.	캠프용차
✻ **vending machine**	[vendiŋ məʃí:n] n.	자동판매기

Part 017 Telephone 전화

A
- pay phone/public phone
- cellular phone
- collect call
- international call
- domestic call
- local call
- long-distance call

B
- extension number
- text message
- Hold on the line please.
- Who's calling?
- Speaking.
- I'd like to talk to
- The line is busy.

C
- call/phone
- dial/ redial
- call back
- leave a message
- make a crank call
- pick up/get/answer the phone
- hang up the phone

D
- connect/transfer
- put through
- answering machine
- have a wrong number
- Lines are crossed.
- phone booth
- directory assistance

1	pay phone/public phone	[pei foun]/[pʌ́blik foun] n.	공중전화
2	cellular phone	[séljulər foun] n.	휴대전화
3	collect call	[kəlékt kɔːl] n.	수신자 부담 전화
4	international call	[ìntərnǽʃənəl kɔːl] n.	국제전화
5	domestic call	[douméstik kɔːl] n.	국내전화
6	local call	[lóukəl kɔːl] n.	시내전화
7	long-distance call	[lɔːŋ dístəns kɔːl] n.	장거리 전화
8	extension number	[iksténʃən nʌ́mbər] n.	내선 번호
9	text message	[tekst mésidʒ] n.	문자 메시지
10	Hold on the line please.	[hould ɔn ðə lain pliːz]	잠깐만 기다려 주세요
11	Who's calling?	[huːz kɔ́ːliŋ]	누구세요?
12	Speaking.	[spíːkiŋ]	말씀하세요
13	I'd like to talk to	[aid laik tu tɔːk tu]	- 와 통화하고 싶습니다
14	The line is busy.	[ðə lain iz bizi]	통화 중
15	call/phone	[kɔːl]/[foun] v.	전화하다
16	dial/ redial	[dáiəl]/[ridáiəl] v.	다이얼을 돌리다, 다시 걸다
17	call back	[kɔːl bæk] v.	다시 걸다
18	leave a message	[liːvə mésidʒ] v.	메시지를 남기다
19	make a crank call	[meikə kræŋk kɔːl] v.	장난 전화하다
20	pick up/get/answer the phone	[pik ʌ́p]/[get] /[ǽnsər ðə foun] v.	수화기를 들다
21	hang up the phone	[hæŋ ʌp ðə foun] v.	전화를 끊다
22	connect/transfer	[kənékt]/[trænsfə́r] v.	연결시키다
23	put through	[put θruː] v.	연결시키다
24	answering machine	[ǽnsəriŋ məʃíːn] n.	자동 응답기
25	have a wrong number	[hævə rɔːŋ nʌ́mbər] v.	잘못 걸다
26	Lines are crossed.	[lainz ɑːr krɔːst]	혼선되다
27	phone booth	[foun buːθ] n.	전화박스
28	directory assistance	[diréktəri əsistəns] n.	전화번호 안내

⋯ **Would you like to leave a message?**
메시지를 남기시겠습니까?

⋯ **I'd like to speak to your manager.**
과장님과 통화하고 싶습니다.

⋯ **You've got the wrong number.**
전화 잘못 거셨습니다.

⋯ **He hung up the phone abruptly.**
그는 갑자기 전화를 끊었습니다.

⋯ **Can you put me through to the Accounting Department?**
경리과로 연결시켜주시겠습니까?

✽ can opener	깡통따개
✽ canal	운하
✽ capable	유능한 / ~할 능력이 있는
✽ captain	선장 / 두령
✽ carefully	주의 깊게
✽ carry	나르다 / 휴대하다
✽ castle	성
✽ casual	우연히 / 평상복의
✽ cease	그만두다 / 그치다
✽ celebrate	축하하다
✽ cemetery	묘지
✽ cereal	곡물

P·a·r·t 018 Housing

주거

A
- build
- lodge
- move
- country
- city
- downtown
- suburb

B
- residential area
- commercial area
- house
- mansion
- apartment
- studio
- cottage

C
- residence
- address
- hometown
- population
- basement
- construction
- boarding house

D
- lighting
- rent
- deposit
- reward
- landowner
- tenant
- view

Part 2

1	**build**	[bild] v.	짓다 / 세우다
2	**lodge**	[lɑdʒ] v.	숙박하다
3	**move**	[muːv] v.	이사하다
4	**country**	[kʌ́ntri] n.	시골
5	**city**	[siti] n.	도시
6	**downtown**	[dauntáun] n.	번화가
7	**suburb**	[sʌ́bɔːrb] n.	교외
8	**residential area**	[rèzidénʃəl ɛ́əriə] n.	주택가
9	**commercial area**	[kəmə́ːrʃəl ɛ́əriə] n.	상업지구
10	**house**	[haus] n.	집
11	**mansion**	[mǽnʃən] n.	대저택
12	**apartment**	[əpάːrtmənt] n.	아파트
13	**studio**	[stjúːdiòu] n.	원룸
14	**cottage**	[kɑ́tidʒ] n.	(시골집 모양의) 별장
15	**residence**	[rézidəns] n.	주거지
16	**address**	[ədrés] n.	주소
17	**hometown**	[houmtáun] n.	고향
18	**population**	[pɑ́pjəléiʃən] n.	인구
19	**basement**	[béismənt] n.	지하실
20	**construction**	[kənstrʌ́kʃən] n.	건설
21	**boarding house**	[bɔ́ːrdiŋ haus] n.	하숙집
22	**lighting**	[láitiŋ] n.	채광
23	**rent**	[rent] n.	집세
24	**deposit**	[dipɑ́zit] n.	보증금
25	**reward**	[riwɔ́ːrd] n.	사례금
26	**landowner**	[lǽndòunər] n.	집주인
27	**tenant**	[ténənt] n.	세입자
28	**view**	[vjuː] n.	조망

Daily Life

⋯▸ **Where do you live ?**
사시는 곳은 어디입니까?

⋯▸ **It's very convenient to use public transportation if you live in a city**
도시에 살면 대중교통을 이용하기가 아주 편리합니다.

⋯▸ **This apartment building near the station is convenient to live in.**
역에서 가까운 이 아파트 건물은 살기에 좋습니다.

⋯▸ **This house has good lightening and low rent.**
이 집은 채광이 좋고, 집세도 쌉니다.

⋯▸ **It's very noisy outside because construction is going on.**
밖에서 공사가 진행되고 있어서 매우 시끄럽습니다.

∗ **furnished**	[fə́ːrnít] a.	가구가 구비된
∗ **unfurnished**	[ʌnfə́ːrnít] a.	가구가 구비되지 않은
∗ **environment**	[inváiərənmənt] n.	환경
∗ **pollution**	[pəlúːʃən] n.	오염
∗ **province**	[právins] n.	지방
∗ **tile**	[tail] n.	기와
∗ **paint**	[peint] n.	페인트
∗ **building**	[bildiŋ] n.	빌딩 / 건물

Part 019 House 집

A
- window
- front door
- garden
- grass
- yard
- basement
- garage

B
- rooftop
- wall
- wallpaper
- glass
- ceiling
- floor
- postbox

C
- living room
- bathroom
- bedroom
- parlor
- corridor
- stairs
- fireplace

D
- fence
- pillar
- attic
- study
- fire alarm
- doorbell
- utilities

#			
1	**window**	[windou] n.	창(문)
2	**front door**	[frʌnt dɔːr] n.	현관
3	**garden**	[gáːrdn] n.	정원
4	**grass**	[græs] n.	잔디
5	**yard**	[jɑːrd] n.	마당
6	**basement**	[béismənt] n.	지하실
7	**garage**	[gərɑ́ːʒ] n.	차고
8	**rooftop**	[rúːftɑ̀p] n.	옥상
9	**wall**	[wɔːl] n.	벽
10	**wallpaper**	[wɔ́ːlpèipər] n.	벽지
11	**glass**	[glæs] n.	유리
12	**ceiling**	[síːliŋ] n.	천장
13	**floor**	[flɔːr] n.	마루
14	**postbox**	[póustbɑ́ks] n.	우편함
15	**living room**	[liviŋ ruːm] n.	거실
16	**bathroom**	[bǽrùː(ː)m] n.	욕실
17	**bedroom**	[bédrùːm] n.	침실
18	**parlor**	[pɑ́ːrlər] n.	응접실
19	**corridor**	[kɔ́ːridər] n.	복도
20	**stairs**	[stéəz] n.	계단
21	**fireplace**	[fáiəplèis] n.	벽난로
22	**fence**	[fens] n.	담 / 울타리
23	**pillar**	[pilər] n.	기둥
24	**attic**	[ǽtik] n.	다락방
25	**study**	[stʌ́di] n.	서재
26	**fire alarm**	[faiər əlɑ́ːrm] n.	화재경보장치
27	**doorbell**	[dɔ́ːrbèl] n.	초인종
28	**utilities**	[juːtilətiz] n.	공공요금

Daily Life

⋯▶ My husband is in the study.
남편은 서재에 있습니다.

⋯▶ He repaired the roof.
그는 지붕을 고쳤습니다.

⋯▶ I want to change the wallpaper in my room.
저는 제 방의 벽지를 바꾸고 싶습니다.

⋯▶ Mom has her guests in the parlor.
엄마는 응접실에서 손님을 맞고 계십니다.

⋯▶ She bumped into a pillar.
그녀는 기둥에 부딪혔습니다.

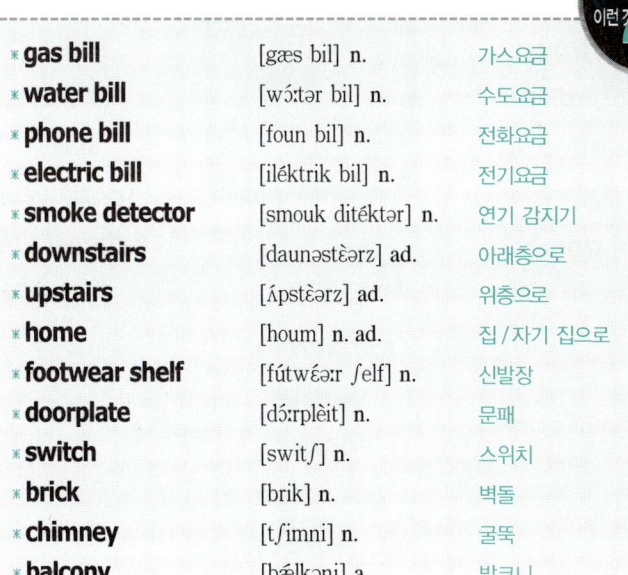

＊ **gas bill**	[gæs bil] n.	가스요금
＊ **water bill**	[wɔ́:tər bil] n.	수도요금
＊ **phone bill**	[foun bil] n.	전화요금
＊ **electric bill**	[iléktrik bil] n.	전기요금
＊ **smoke detector**	[smouk ditéktər] n.	연기 감지기
＊ **downstairs**	[daunstɛ́ərz] ad.	아래층으로
＊ **upstairs**	[ʌ́pstɛ̀ərz] ad.	위층으로
＊ **home**	[houm] n. ad.	집 / 자기 집으로
＊ **footwear shelf**	[fútwɛ́ər ʃelf] n.	신발장
＊ **doorplate**	[dɔ́:rplèit] n.	문패
＊ **switch**	[switʃ] n.	스위치
＊ **brick**	[brik] n.	벽돌
＊ **chimney**	[tʃímni] n.	굴뚝
＊ **balcony**	[bǽlkəni] a.	발코니

Part 020 Kitchen 부엌

A
- bowl
- dish
- chopstick
- spoon
- fork
- pot
- frying pan

B
- kitchen knife
- tablecloth
- tray
- kettle
- dish soap
- dish cloth
- apron

C
- cutting board
- rice scoop
- ladle
- ice tray
- sink
- cabinet
- exhaust fan

D
- refrigerator
- freezer
- toaster
- gas range
- microwave oven
- blender
- electric rice cooker

#	영어	발음	한국어
1	bowl	[boul] n.	그릇
2	dish	[diʃ] n.	접시 / 요리
3	chopstick	[tʃápstik] n.	젓가락
4	spoon	[spuːn] n.	숟가락
5	fork	[fɔːrk] n.	포크
6	pot	[pɑt] n.	냄비
7	frying pan	[fraiŋ pæn] n.	프라이팬
8	kitchen knife	[kítʃin naif] n.	식칼
9	tablecloth	[téibl klɔ̀(ː)θ] n.	식탁보
10	tray	[trei] n.	쟁반
11	kettle	[kétl] n.	주전자
12	dish soap	[diʃ soup] n.	설거지용 세제
13	dish cloth	[diʃ klɔ(ː)θ] n.	행주
14	apron	[éiprən] n.	앞치마
15	cutting board	[kʌ́tiŋ bɔːrd] n.	도마
16	rice scoop	[rais skuːp] n.	주걱
17	ladle	[léidl] n.	국자
18	ice tray	[ais trei] n.	얼음 만드는 틀
19	sink	[siŋk] n.	개수대
20	cabinet	[kǽbənit] n.	싱크대 찬장
21	exhaust fan	[igzɔ́ːst fæn] n.	환풍기
22	refrigerator	[rifrídʒərèitər] n.	냉장고
23	freezer	[fríːzər] n.	냉동고
24	toaster	[tóustər] n.	토스터기
25	gas range	[gæs reindʒ] v.	가스렌지
26	microwave oven	[máikrouwèiv ʌ́vən] n.	전자렌지
27	blender	[bléndər] n.	믹서
28	electric rice cooker	[iléktrik rais kúkər] n.	전기밥솥

Daily Life

···▶ Mom cooks dinner in the kitchen.
   엄마가 부엌에서 저녁을 만들고 계십니다.

···▶ I boiled water in the kettle.
   주전자로 물을 끓였습니다.

···▶ Chef beats the eggs.
   요리사가 달걀을 깨서 휘젓습니다.

···▶ There are spoons and forks on the table.
   테이블 위에 스푼과 포크가 놓여져 있습니다.

···▶ We put dirty plates into a dish washer.
   우리는 더러운 그릇들을 세척기에 넣었습니다.

* **coffee pot**	[kɔ́ːfi pɑt] n.	커피포트
* **teapot**	[tíːpɑ́t] n.	티포트
* **scrubber**	[skrʌ́bər] n.	수세미
* **egg beater**	[ég bíːtər] n.	달걀 거품기
* **iron pot**	[áiərn pɑt] n.	솥

Part 021 Electric Appliances
가전제품

A
television
stove
radio
camera
stereo
video
sewing machine

B
iron
humidifier
washer
drier
vacuum cleaner
electric blanket
dishwasher

가전제품

C
stand
outlet
photocopier
calculator
facsimile/fax
air conditioner
electric razor

D
coffee maker
fix/repair
turn on (off)
remote control
toaster
oven
CD player

#	영어	발음	한국어
1	**television**	[teləvíʒən] n.	텔레비젼
2	**stove**	[stouv] n.	난로
3	**radio**	[réidiòu] n.	라디오
4	**camera**	[kǽmərə] n.	카메라
5	**stereo**	[stériòu] n.	오디오
6	**video**	[vídiou] n.	비디오
7	**sewing machine**	[sóuiŋ məʃíːn] n.	미싱
8	**iron**	[áiərn] n.	다리미
9	**humidifier**	[hjuːmídəfàiər] n.	가습기
10	**washer**	[wáʃər] n.	세탁기
11	**drier**	[dráiər] n.	건조기
12	**vacuum cleaner**	[vǽkjuəm klíːnər] n.	진공 청소기
13	**electric blanket**	[iléktrik blǽŋkit] n.	전기 담요
14	**dishwasher**	[diʃwáʃər] n.	식기 세척기
15	**stand**	[stænd] n.	스탠드
16	**outlet**	[áutlet] n.	콘센트
17	**photocopier**	[fóutoukápiər] n.	복사기
18	**calculator**	[kǽlkjəlèitər] n.	전자계산기
19	**facsimile/fax**	[fæksíməli]/[fæks] n.	팩시밀리
20	**air conditioner**	[ɛər kəndiʃənər] n.	에어콘
21	**electric razor**	[iléktrik réizər] n.	전기면도기
22	**coffee maker**	[kɔ́ːfi méikər] n.	커피메이커
23	**fix/repair**	[fiks]/[ripɛ́ər] vt.	고치다 / 수선하다
24	**turn on(off)**	[təːrn ɔn]/[ɔːf] v.	스위치를 켜다 (끄다)
25	**remote control**	[rimóut kəntróul] n.	리모콘
26	**toaster**	[tóustər] n.	토스트
27	**oven**	[ʌ́vən] n.	오븐
28	**CD player**	[síːdi pléiər] n.	CD플레이어

- You can see a variety of electric appliances in a department store.
  백화점에 가면 다양한 가전제품을 볼 수 있습니다.
- Please turn off your cellular phone during the meeting.
  회의 동안에는 핸드폰의 전원을 꺼 주세요.
- I'm going to buy a brand-new digital camera.
  새로 나온 디지털 카메라를 살 예정입니다.
- Beers in the refrigerator are cold enough to drink.
  냉장고 안의 맥주는 마시기에 좋을 만큼 차갑습니다.
- Can you make three copies of this paper?
  이 서류를 3장씩 복사해 주세요.

✻ ceremony	의식
✻ certain	확실한 / 어떤
✻ chain	사슬
✻ challenge	도전 (하다)
✻ chance	기회
✻ charming	매력적인
✻ choice	선택
✻ cinema	영화
✻ clap	(손뼉을) 치다
✻ classify	분류하다
✻ clay	진흙
✻ clever	영리한

Part 022 Furniture 가구

A
- desk
- chair
- bookshelf
- dining room table
- coffee table
- nightstand

B
- clock
- alarm clock
- shelf
- couch/sofa
- armchair
- bench

C
- cushion
- mattress
- bed clothes/linens
- cradle
- single bed
- bunk bed

D
- dresser
- drawer
- wardrobe
- closet
- chandelier
- rug
- vase

#			
1	**desk**	[desk] n.	책상
2	**chair**	[tʃɛər] n.	의자
3	**bookshelf**	[búkʃèlf] n.	책장
4	**dining room table**	[dáiniŋ ruːm téibl] n.	식탁
5	**coffee table**	[kɔ́ːfi téibl] n.	커피 탁자
6	**nightstand**	[náitstǽnd] n.	침대 옆 탁자
7	**clock**	[klɑk] n.	벽시계
8	**alarm clock**	[əlάːrm klɑk] n.	자명종 시계
9	**shelf**	[ʃelf] n.	선반
10	**couch/sofa**	[kautʃ]/[sóufə] n.	소파
11	**armchair**	[άːrmtʃɛ̀ər] n.	안락의자
12	**bench**	[bentʃ] n.	벤치 / 긴 의자
13	**cushion**	[kúʃən] n.	방석
14	**mattress**	[mǽtris] n.	요
15	**bed clothes/linens**	[bed klouðz]/[linin] n.	이부자리
16	**cradle**	[kréidl] n.	요람
17	**single bed**	[siŋgl bed] n.	싱글 침대
18	**bunk bed**	[bʌŋk bed] n.	2층 침대
19	**dresser**	[drésər] n.	화장대
20	**drawer**	[drɔ́ːər] n.	서랍
21	**wardrobe**	[wɔ́ːrdròub] n.	양복장
22	**closet**	[klάzit] n.	옷장
23	**chandelier**	[ʃændəliər] n.	샹들리에
24	**rug**	[rʌg] n.	깔개
25	**vase**	[veis] n.	꽃병

⋯▸ There are books and notebooks on the table.
　　책상 위에 책과 노트가 놓여 있습니다.

⋯▸ Put it in the second drawer.
　　두 번째 서랍 속에 넣어두세요.

⋯▸ There was only one single bed in a room.
　　방에는 일인용 침대만 있었습니다.

⋯▸ My little sister wants to have her own bookshelf.
　　여동생은 책장을 갖고 싶어 합니다.

⋯▸ I set the alarm clock to get up early tomorrow.
　　내일 일찍 일어나기 위해 자명종을 맞춰두었습니다.

✻ cloth	천
✻ cloudy	흐린 / 구름이 많은
✻ club	곤봉 / 써클
✻ colony	식민지
✻ colorful	화려한
✻ combine	결합하다
✻ come	오다
✻ comedy	희극 / 코메디
✻ common	공통의 / 보통의
✻ communicate	(생각을) 전달하다
✻ community	지역사회
✻ compare	비교하다

Part 023 Clothes & Shoes
의복 및 신발

A
- suit
- jacket
- blouse
- coat
- sweater
- turtleneck
- cardigan

B
- vest
- skirt
- trousers/pants
- shorts
- underwear
- bra
- pajamas

C
- swimsuit
- overalls
- uniform
- jeans
- T-shirt
- tight
- loose

D
- stockings
- pantyhose
- high heels
- shoes
- sneakers
- sandals
- boots

#	영어	발음	한국어
1	**suit**	[suːt] n.	양복(한 벌 정장)
2	**jacket**	[dʒǽkit] n.	상의
3	**blouse**	[blaus] n.	블라우스
4	**coat**	[kout] n.	코트(웃옷)
5	**sweater**	[swétər] n.	스웨터
6	**turtleneck**	[tə́ːrtlnèk] n.	목 티
7	**cardigan**	[káːrdigən] n.	가디건
8	**vest**	[vest] n.	조끼
9	**skirt**	[skəːrt] n.	치마
10	**trousers/pants**	[tráuzərz]/[pænts] n.	바지
11	**shorts**	[ʃɔːrts] n.	반바지
12	**underwear**	[ʌ́ndərwɛ̀ər] n.	속옷
13	**bra**	[brɑː] n.	브래지어
14	**pajamas**	[pədʒɑ́məz] n.	잠옷
15	**swimsuit**	[swimsùːt] n.	수영복
16	**overalls**	[óuvərɔ̀ːlz] n.	멜빵바지
17	**uniform**	[júːnəfɔ̀ːrm] n.	유니폼
18	**jeans**	[dʒiːnz] n.	청바지
19	**T-shirt**	[tiːʃəːrt] n.	티셔츠
20	**tight**	[tait] a.	꼭 끼는
21	**loose**	[luːs] a.	헐거운
22	**stockings**	[stɑ́kiŋz] n.	스타킹
23	**pantyhose**	[pǽntihòuz] n.	팬티스타킹
24	**high heels**	[hai hiːlz] n.	하이힐
25	**shoes**	[ʃuːz] n.	구두
26	**sneakers**	[sniːkərz] n.	운동화
27	**sandals**	[sǽndlz] n.	샌들
28	**boots**	[buːts] n.	부츠

···▸ **A baggy style looks good on him.**
헐렁한 힙합 스타일은 그에게 잘 어울린다.

···▸ **Min-Young came to the party in jeans and a T-shirt.**
민영은 청바지와 티셔츠를 입고 파티에 나타났습니다.

···▸ **He goes jogging in red trainers every morning.**
그는 매일 아침 빨간색 운동복을 입고 조깅을 합니다.

···▸ **On what floor is the bathing suit corner?**
수영복 판매장은 몇 층에 있습니까?

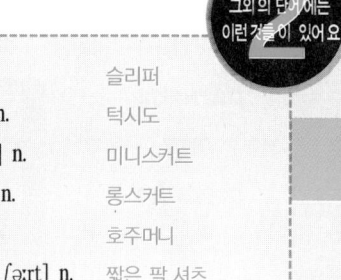

slippers	[slípərz] n.	슬리퍼
tuxedo	[tʌksíːdou] n.	턱시도
mini skirt	[mini skəːrt] n.	미니스커트
long skirt	[lɔːŋ skəːrt] n.	롱스커트
pocket	[pákit] n.	호주머니
short-sleeved shirt	[ʃɔːrt sliːvd ʃəːrt] n.	짧은 팔 셔츠
long-sleeved shirt	[lɔːŋ sliːvd ʃəːrt] n.	긴팔 셔츠
nightgown	[náitgàun] n.	여자용 잠옷
jumper	[dʒʌ́mpər] n.	점퍼
raincoat	[réinkòut] n.	비옷
down jacket	[daun dʒǽkit] n.	파카
shoe string	[ʃuː striŋ] n.	구두끈
jogging suit	[dʒágiŋ suːt] n.	조깅복

Part 024 Accessaries 악세서리

A
- real/genuine
- fake
- precious
- jewel
- diamond
- gold
- silver

B
- key ring
- perfume
- ring
- bracelet
- wrist watch
- beads
- purse/handbag

C
- brooch
- gloves
- tie clip
- scarf
- shawl
- earrings
- necklace

D
- treasure
- emerald
- ruby
- pearl
- coral
- crystal
- ivory

#	English	Pronunciation	Korean
1	real/genuine	[riːəl] / [dʒénjuin] a.	진짜의
2	fake	[feik] a.	가짜의
3	precious	[préʃəs] a.	귀중한 / 값비싼
4	jewel	[dʒúːəl] n.	보석
5	diamond	[dáiəmənd] n.	다이아몬드
6	gold	[gould] n.	금
7	silver	[sílvər] n.	은
8	key ring	[kiː riŋ] n.	열쇠고리
9	perfume	[pə́ːrfjuːm] n.	향수
10	ring	[riŋ] n.	반지
11	bracelet	[bréislit] n.	팔찌
12	wrist watch	[rist watʃ] n.	손목시계
13	beads	[biːdz] n.	구슬 장식
14	purse/handbag	[pəːrs] / [hǽndbæ̀g] n.	핸드백
15	brooch	[broutʃ] n.	브로우치
16	gloves	[glʌvz] n.	장갑
17	tie clip	[tai klip] n.	넥타이핀
18	scarf	[skɑːrf] n.	스카프
19	shawl	[ʃɔːl] n.	숄
20	earrings	[íəriŋz] n.	귀걸이
21	necklace	[néklis] n.	목걸이
22	treasure	[tréʒər] n.	보물
23	emerald	[émərəld] n.	에메랄드
24	ruby	[rúːbi] n.	루비
25	pearl	[pəːrl] n.	진주
26	coral	[kɔ́ːrəl] n.	산호
27	crystal	[kristl] n.	수정
28	ivory	[áivəri] n.	상아

Daily Life

···▶ It's a real diamond.
    이것은 진짜 다이아군요.

···▶ I bought this perfume in Paris.
    저는 파리에서 이 향수를 샀습니다.

···▶ I received an engagement ring from my fiance.
    약혼자에게 약혼반지를 받았습니다.

···▶ The price of the necklace is a million won.
    이 목걸이 가격은 백만원입니다.

···▶ She lost her earrings at the beach.
    그녀는 해변에서 귀걸이를 잃어버렸습니다.

* amethyst	[ǽməθist]	n.	자수정
* decorate	[dékərèit]	v.	장식하다
* fragrance	[fréigrəns]	n.	향기
* platina	[plǽtənə]	n.	백금
* sapphire	[sǽfaiəːr]	n.	사파이어

Part 025 General Goods 잡화

A
- bag
- hat
- cap
- glasses
- socks
- cigarette
- ashtray

B
- handkerchief
- umbrella
- parasol
- necktie
- necktie pin
- gloves

C
- wallet
- comb
- mirror
- suitcase
- muffler
- scarf

D
- fan
- belt
- contact lens
- ribbon
- sunglasses
- transportation card case
- thread

Part 2

#				
1	**bag**	[bæg] n.	가방
2	**hat**	[hæt] n.	(테가 있는)모자
3	**cap**	[kæp] n.	(테가 없는)모자
4	**glasses**	[glǽsiz] n.	안경
5	**socks**	[sɑks] n.	양말
6	**cigarette**	[sigərét] n.	담배
7	**ashtray**	[ǽʃtrèi] n.	재떨이
8	**handkerchief**	[hǽŋkərtʃif] n.	손수건
9	**umbrella**	[ʌmbrélə] n.	우산
10	**parasol**	[pǽrəsɔ̀ːl] n.	양산
11	**necktie**	[néktài] n.	넥타이
12	**necktie pin**	[néktài pin] n.	넥타이핀
13	**gloves**	[glʌvz] n.	장갑
14	**wallet**	[wálit] n.	지갑
15	**comb**	[koum] n.	빗
16	**mirror**	[mirər] n.	거울
17	**suitcase**	[súːtkèis] n.	여행가방
18	**muffler**	[mʌ́flər] n.	머플러
19	**scarf**	[skɑːrf] n.	스카프
20	**fan**	[fæn] n.	부채
21	**belt**	[belt] n.	벨트
22	**contact lens**	[kántækt lenz] n.	콘택트렌즈
23	**ribbon**	[ribən] n.	리본
24	**sunglasses**	[sʌ́nglǽsiz] n.	썬글라스
25	**transportation card case**	[trænspərtéiʃən kɑːrd keis] n.	교통카드 케이스
26	**thread**	[θred] n.	실

Daily Life

⋯ He is wearing a hat as well as gloves.
  그는 장갑뿐 아니라 모자도 쓰고 있습니다.

⋯ She was robbed of her handbag.
  그녀는 핸드백을 도난당했습니다.

⋯ Who's that person wearing glasses over there?
  저기에 안경을 쓴 사람이 누구죠?

⋯ These shoes are the same price as those boots.
  이 구두는 부츠와 같은 가격입니다.

⋯ I left my wallet at home so I couldn't buy anything.
  지갑을 집에 놓고 나와서 아무것도 살 수 없었습니다.

✳ complain	불평하다
✳ completely	완전히
✳ concern	우려 / 걱정
✳ conclude	끝내다 / 결론을 내리다
✳ condition	조건
✳ conflict	갈등
✳ congratulate	축하하다
✳ connect	연결하다 / 접속하다
✳ consist	~으로 이루어지다 / ~에 있다
✳ contain	포함하다
✳ continue	계속하다
✳ control	통제 / 조절(하다)

Part 026 Stationery
문구용품

A
- pen
- pencil
- ball-point pen
- eraser
- correction fluid
- fountain pen
- highlighter

B
- pencil case
- box
- organizer
- stapler
- brush
- ink
- envelope

C
- scissors
- rubber band
- ruler
- glue stick
- blackboard
- paper clip
- chalk

D
- Post-It note pad
- chinese ink
- scale
- compass
- stamp
- notebook
- business card

#	English	Pronunciation	Korean
1	**pen**	[pen] n.	펜
2	**pencil**	[pénsəl] n.	연필
3	**ball-point pen**	[bɔːl pɔint pen] n.	볼펜
4	**eraser**	[iréizər] n.	지우개
5	**correction fluid**	[kərékʃən flúːid] n.	수정액
6	**fountain pen**	[fáuntin pen] n.	만년필
7	**highlighter**	[háilàitər] n.	형광펜
8	**pencil case**	[pénsəl keis] n.	필통
9	**box**	[bɑks] n.	상자
10	**organizer**	[ɔ́ːrgənàizər] n.	수첩
11	**stapler**	[stéiplər] n.	호치키스
12	**brush**	[brʌʃ] n.	붓
13	**ink**	[iŋk] n.	잉크
14	**envelope**	[énvəlòup] n.	봉투
15	**scissors**	[sizərz] n.	가위
16	**rubber band**	[rʌ́bər bænd] n.	고무줄
17	**ruler**	[rúːlər] n.	자
18	**glue stick**	[gluː stik] n.	딱풀
19	**blackboard**	[blǽkbɔ̀ːrd] n.	칠판
20	**paper clip**	[péipər klip] n.	클립
21	**chalk**	[tʃɔːk] n.	분필
22	**Post-It note pad**	[poustit nout pæd] n.	포스트 메모장
23	**chinese ink**	[tʃainiːz iŋk] n.	먹
24	**scale**	[skeil] n.	저울
25	**compass**	[kʌ́mpəs] n.	컴퍼스
26	**stamp**	[stæmp] n.	도장
27	**notebook**	[nóutbùk] n.	공책
28	**business card**	[biznis kɑːrd] n.	명함

⋯▸ What's inside of the box?
저 상자 안에는 무엇이 들어 있습니까?

⋯▸ The teacher wrote questions on the blackboard with chalk.
선생님은 칠판에 분필로 문제를 썼습니다.

⋯▸ I received a fountain pen for a graduation gift.
졸업축하선물로 만년필을 받았습니다.

⋯▸ You'd better use big scissors in cutting that paper.
그 종이를 자를 때는 큰 가위를 사용하는 게 좋을 거예요.

⋯▸ Could you stamp this?
여기에 도장을 찍어 주시겠어요?

* **3-hole punch**	[θriː houl pʌntʃ] n.	3공 펀치
* **file cabinet**	[fail kǽbənit] n.	캐비넷
* **clip**	[klip] n.	클립
* **stamp pad**	[stæmp pæd] n.	도장 잉크
* **abacus**	[ǽbəkəs] n.	주판
* **needle**	[niːdl] n.	바늘
* **file**	[fail] n.	서류철
* **sharp pencil**	[ʃɑːrp pénsəl] n.	샤프
* **thumbtack**	[θʌ́mtæk] n.	압정
* **pad**	[pæd] n.	책받침
* **dice**	[dais] n.	주사위

Part 027 Stores 가게

A
- bookstore
- bakery
- florist
- drugstore/pharmacy
- department store
- fruit shop
- grocery

B
- shoe store
- butcher
- restaurant
- public bathroom
- traditional market
- furniture store
- stationery

C
- beauty salon
- Government office
- City Hall
- real estate agency
- toy shop
- karaoke room
- convenience store

D
- bar/pub
- Soju tent
- video rental shop
- dry cleaner's
- barber shop
- photo studio
- recreation room

Part 2

#	Word	Pronunciation	Korean
1	bookstore	[búkstɔ̀:r] n.	서점
2	bakery	[béikəri] n.	빵집
3	florist	[flɔ́(:)rist] n.	꽃집
4	drugstore/pharmacy	[drʌ́gstɔ̀:r] / [fá:rməsi] n.	약국
5	department store	[dipá:rtmənt stɔ:r] n.	백화점
6	fruit shop	[fru:t ʃɑp] n.	과일가게
7	grocery	[gróusəri] n.	야채가게
8	shoe store	[ʃu: stɔ:r] n.	신발가게
9	butcher	[bútʃər] n.	정육점
10	restaurant	[réstərənt] n.	레스토랑
11	public bathroom	[pʌ́blik bǽθrù(:)m] n.	목욕탕
12	traditional market	[trədíʃənəl má:rkit] n.	재래 시장
13	furniture store	[fə́:rnitʃər stɔ:r] n.	가구점
14	stationery	[stéiʃənèri] n.	문방구
15	beauty salon	[bjú:ti səlán] n.	미용실
16	Government office	[gʌ́vərnmənt ɔ́(:)fis] n.	구청
17	City Hall	[siti hɔ:l] n.	시청
18	real estate agency	[rí:əl istéit éidʒənsi] n.	부동산
19	toy shop	[tɔi ʃɑp] n.	완구점
20	karaoke room	[kæriɑ́uki ru:m] n.	노래방
21	convenience store	[kənví:njəns stɔ:r] n.	편의점
22	bar/pub	[bɑ:r] / [pʌb] n.	술집
23	Soju tent	[soudʒu: tent] n.	포장마차
24	video rental shop	[vídiou réntl ʃɑp] n.	비디오가게
25	dry cleaner's	[drai klí:nərz] n.	세탁소
26	barber shop	[bá:rbər ʃɑp] n.	이발소
27	photo studio	[fóutou stjú:diòu] n.	사진관
28	recreation room	[rèkriéiʃən ru:m] n.	오락실

Daily Life

⋯▸ **Koreans like to a go to karaoke room.**
   한국인은 노래방을 좋아합니다.

⋯▸ **I'll see you at Lotte department store at 3pm.**
   롯데 백화점 앞에서 3시에 만납시다.

⋯▸ **Soju tents are very popular in winter.**
   포장마차는 겨울에 아주 인기가 있습니다.

⋯▸ **Shall we go to Insa-dong to have traditional tea?**
   인사동에 전통차 마시러 갈까요?

⋯▸ **She goes to the beauty salon once a week.**
   그녀는 일주일에 한번 미용실에 갑니다.

✱	convenient	편안한
✱	cool	시원한 / 멋진
✱	corner	구석 / 모퉁이
✱	correct	고치다 / 수정하다
✱	correspond	교신하다 / 일치하다
✱	cowboy	카우보이
✱	crisis	위기
✱	crowded	붐비는
✱	crown	왕관 / 왕권
✱	cry	울다
✱	cube	입방체 / 정육면체
✱	cultural	문화적인

3 Human Body & Feeling

Part 028 Feeling (Nouns)
감정(명사)

A
- heart
- mood
- pleasure
- excitement
- happiness
- cheerfulness
- amusement

B
- kindness
- love
- imagination
- emotion
- hope
- relief
- comfort

C
- sympathy
- fear
- worries
- anxiety
- agony
- nervousness
- sadness

D
- anger
- shame
- hatred
- envy
- jealousy
- disappointment
- misunderstanding

Part 3

1	heart	[hɑːrt] n.	마음
2	mood	[muːd] n.	기분 / 분위기
3	pleasure	[pléʒər] n.	즐거움
4	excitement	[iksáitmənt] n.	흥분
5	happiness	[hǽpinis] n.	행복
6	cheerfulness	[tʃərfəlnis] n.	유쾌함
7	amusement	[əmjúːzmənt] n.	즐거움 / 재미 / 오락
8	kindness	[káindnis] n.	친절함
9	love	[lʌv] n.	사랑
10	imagination	[imæ̀dʒənéiʃən] n.	상상
11	emotion	[imóuʃən] n.	감정
12	hope	[houp] n.	희망
13	relief	[riliːf] n.	안심
14	comfort	[kʌ́mfərt] n.	편안함
15	sympathy	[símpəθi] n.	동정 / 연민
16	fear	[fiər] n.	두려움
17	worries	[wə́ːriz] n.	걱정
18	anxiety	[æŋzáiti] n.	불안
19	agony	[ǽgəni] n.	고민
20	nervousness	[nə́ːrvəsnis] n.	긴장
21	sadness	[sǽdnis] n.	슬픔
22	anger	[ǽŋgər] n.	화 / 노여움
23	shame	[ʃeim] n.	부끄러움 / 수치
24	hatred	[héitrid] n.	미움
25	envy	[énvi] n.	부러움
26	jealousy	[dʒéləsi] n.	질투
27	disappointment	[disəpɔ́intmənt] n.	실망
28	misunderstanding	[misʌ̀ndərstǽndiŋ] n.	오해

Human Body & Feeling

⋯▸ **It's my pleasure.**
　　천만에요.

⋯▸ **Life is full of worries.**
　　인생은 걱정 투성이이다.

⋯▸ **He shouted in excitement.**
　　그는 흥분해서 소리쳤습니다.

⋯▸ **Let's go to an amusement park next Sunday.**
　　다음주 일요일 놀이공원에 갑시다.

⋯▸ **We'll be together in joys and in sorrow.**
　　기쁠때나 슬플때나 우리는 함께 할 것입니다.

＊ **sentiment**	[séntəmənt] n.	감상
＊ **satisfaction**	[sæ̀tisfǽkʃən] n.	만족
＊ **dissatisfaction**	[dìssæ̀tisfǽkʃən] n.	불만
＊ **dream**	[driːm] n.	꿈
＊ **expectation**	[èkspektéiʃən] n.	기대
＊ **impression**	[impréʃən] n.	감명
＊ **admiration**	[æ̀dməréiʃən] n.	감탄
＊ **solitude/loneliness**	[sálitjùːd] / [lóunlinis] n.	고독

Part 029 Feeling(Verbs/Adjectives)
감정(동사 / 형용사)

A
- feel
- regret
- admire
- amaze
- annoy
- excite
- hate

B
- impress
- irritate
- laugh
- please
- disappoint
- satisfy
- offend

C
- ashamed
- afraid
- angry
- sad
- anxious
- stressed
- calm

D
- glad
- happy
- horrible
- awful
- funny, humorous
- lonely
- blue

1	feel	[fiːl] v.	느끼다
2	regret	[rigrét] v.	후회하다
3	admire	[ædmáiər] v.	감탄하다
4	amaze	[əméiz] vt.	몹시 놀라게 하다
5	annoy	[ənɔ́i] vt.	성가시게 굴다
6	excite	[iksáit] vt.	흥분시키다
7	hate	[heit] vt.	미워하다 / 증오하다
8	impress	[imprés] vt.	인상을 주다 / 감동시키다
9	irritate	[írətèit] vt.	짜증나게 하다 / 화나게 하다
10	laugh	[læf] v.	웃다 / 비웃다
11	please	[pliːz] vt.	기쁘게 하다
12	disappoint	[disəpɔ́int] vt.	실망시키다
13	satisfy	[sǽətisfài] vt.	만족시키다
14	offend	[əfénd] vt.	성내게 하다
15	ashamed	[əʃéimd] a.	부끄러워하는 / 수줍어하는
16	afraid	[əfréid] a.	두려워하는 / 걱정하는
17	angry	[ǽŋgri] a.	화난 / 성난
18	sad	[sæd] a.	슬픈
19	anxious	[ǽŋkʃəs] a.	걱정하는 / 열망하는
20	stressed	[strest] a.	압박을 받는
21	calm	[kɑːm] a.	침착한
22	glad	[glæd] a.	기쁜
23	happy	[hǽpi] a.	행복한 / 기쁜
24	horrible	[hɔ́ːrəbl] a.	무서운 / 끔찍한
25	awful	[ɔ́ːfəl] a.	무서운 / 대단한
26	funny / humorous	[fʌ́ni] / [hjúːmərəs] a.	재미있는 / 웃기는
27	lonely	[lóunli] a.	외로운
28	blue	[bluː] a.	우울한

···▶ **I feel happy today.**
  오늘 정말 행복합니다.

···▶ **He is always kind to me.**
  그는 저에게 항상 친절합니다.

···▶ **The movie was interesting.**
  그 영화 재미있었어요.

···▶ **Is there anything unsatisfactory about this item?**
  이 제품에 불만인 점은 없습니까?

···▶ **What's wrong? You look sad.**
  무슨 일이예요? 슬퍼 보이는군요.

⁂ **thrilled**	[θrild] a.	흥분되는
⁂ **unsatisfactory**	[ʌ̀nsætisfǽktəri] a.	불만스러운
⁂ **terrible**	[térəbl] a.	지독한
⁂ **interesting**	[íntəristiŋ] a.	재미있는
⁂ **disappointed**	[dìsəpɔ́intid] a.	낙심한

Part 030 Personality 성격

A
- liar
- dreamer
- naughty boy
- coward
- idler
- cold
- open-minded

B
- talkative
- moody
- patient
- jealous
- stubborn
- responsible
- outgoing

C
- brave
- wise
- careful
- curious
- diligent
- honest
- gentle

D
- lazy
- stupid
- modest
- polite
- shy
- rude
- selfish

#	Word	Pronunciation	Meaning
1	liar	[láiər] n.	거짓말쟁이
2	dreamer	[drí:mər] n.	몽상가
3	naughty boy	[nɔ́:ti bɔi] n.	개구쟁이
4	coward	[káuərd] n.	겁쟁이
5	idler	[áidlər] n.	게으름뱅이
6	cold	[kould] a.	차가운
7	open-minded	[óupən máindid] a.	개방적인
8	talkative	[tɔ́:kətiv] a.	수다스러운
9	moody	[mú:di] a.	변덕스러운
10	patient	[péiʃənt] a.	인내심이 많은
11	jealous	[dʒéləs] a.	질투심이 많은
12	stubborn	[stʌ́bə:rn] a.	고집센 완고한
13	responsible	[rispánsəbl] a.	책임감 있는
14	outgoing	[áutgòuiŋ] a.	활발한
15	brave	[breiv] a.	용감한
16	wise	[waiz] a.	슬기로운 / 현명한
17	careful	[kɛ́ərfəl] a.	주의 깊은 / 조심성 있는
18	curious	[kjúəríəs] a.	호기심이 강한
19	diligent	[dílədʒənt] a.	근면한 / 부지런한
20	honest	[ánist] a.	정직한
21	gentle	[dʒéntl] a.	점잖은 / 예의바른
22	lazy	[léizi] a.	게으른
23	stupid	[stjú:pid] a.	어리석은
24	modest	[mádist] a.	겸손한 / 정숙한
25	polite	[pəláit] a.	공손한
26	shy	[ʃai] a.	수줍은 / 부끄럼 타는
27	rude	[ru:d] a.	무례한
28	selfish	[sélfiʃ] a.	이기적인

···→ What is your ideal type?
　　당신의 이상형은 어떤 타입 입니까?

···→ What are your strong points?
　　당신의 장점은 무엇입니까?

···→ My class teacher is very kind and generous.
　　담임 선생님은 매우 상냥하고 관대합니다.

···→ You need courage to keep the secret.
　　비밀을 지키려면 용기가 필요합니다.

···→ My nephew is a naughty boy.
　　제 조카는 정말로 개구쟁이입니다.

✻ **typical**	[típikəl] a.	전형적인
✻ **serious**	[síəriəs] a.	진지한 / 중대한
✻ **silly**	[síli] a.	어리석은
✻ **sincere**	[sinsíəːr] a.	성실한
✻ **generous**	[dʒénərəs] a.	관대한
✻ **wicked**	[wíkid] a.	사악한 / 심술궂은
✻ **depressed**	[diprést] a.	의기소침한
✻ **delicate**	[délikit] a.	섬세한
✻ **careless**	[kɛ́ərlis] a.	부주의한
✻ **hardworking**	[hɑ́ːrdwə́ːrkiŋ] a.	부지런한 / 열심히 일하는
✻ **mild**	[maild] a.	부드러운 / 온화한
✻ **merry**	[méri] a.	상냥한
✻ **late riser**	[leit ráizər] n.	늦잠꾸러기
✻ **credible**	[krédəbl] a.	신뢰할 수 있는
✻ **active**	[ǽktiv] a.	활동적인 / 적극적인

Part 031 Human Body
신체 1

A
- head
- hair
- brain
- hand
- leg
- arm
- foot

B
- neck
- throat
- shoulder
- chest
- breast
- stomach
- back

신체 1

C
- rib
- waist
- elbow
- knee
- wrist
- ankle
- thigh

D
- navel
- palm
- finger
- thumb
- toe
- nail
- heel

Part 3

#	Word	Pronunciation	Meaning
1	head	[hed] n.	머리
2	hair	[hɛər] n.	머리카락
3	brain	[brein] n.	뇌
4	hand	[hænd] n.	손
5	leg	[leg] n.	다리
6	arm	[ɑːrm] n.	팔
7	foot	[fut] n.	발
8	neck	[nek] n.	목
9	throat	[θrout] n.	목구멍
10	shoulder	[ʃóuldər] n.	어깨
11	chest	[tʃest] n.	가슴
12	breast	[brest] n.	젖가슴
13	stomach	[stʌ́mək] n.	배
14	back	[bæk] n.	등
15	rib	[rib] n.	갈비뼈
16	waist	[weist] n.	허리
17	elbow	[élbou] n.	팔꿈치
18	knee	[niː] n.	무릎
19	wrist	[rist] n.	손목
20	ankle	[ǽŋkl] n.	발목
21	thigh	[θai] n.	넓적다리
22	navel	[néivəl] n.	배꼽
23	palm	[pɑːm] n.	손바닥
24	finger	[fíŋɡər] n.	손가락
25	thumb	[θʌm] n.	엄지손가락
26	toe	[tou] n.	발가락
27	nail	[neil] n.	손톱 / 발톱
28	heel	[hiːl] n.	발뒤꿈치

⋯▶ I have a headache.
두통으로 머리가 아픕니다.

⋯▶ My brother has a deep scar on his back.
제 남동생은 등에 깊은 상처가 있습니다.

⋯▶ I felt pain in my shoulder and went to the hospital.
어깨가 아파서 병원에 갔습니다.

⋯▶ He has a nice mustache.
그는 멋진 콧수염을 갖고 있습니다.

⋯▶ She has a long straight hair.
그녀는 긴 생머리를 갖고 있습니다.

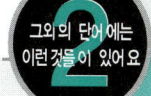

✽ **physical**	[fizikəl] a.	신체적인 / 물리적인
✽ **the nape of the neck**	[ðə neipɔv ðə nek] n.	목덜미
✽ **womb**	[wuːm] n.	자궁
✽ **fist**	[fist] n.	주먹
✽ **calf**	[kæf] n.	종아리
✽ **nipple**	[nipl] n.	젖꼭지
✽ **buttocks**	[bʌ́təks] n.	엉덩이

Part 032 Human Body

신체 2

A
- flesh
- blood
- bone
- muscle
- neuron
- skin
- tendon

B
- heart
- liver
- lung
- arteries
- vein
- spine
- kidney

C
- cell
- breath
- yawning
- sneeze
- tear
- nose dripping
- sweat

D
- saliva
- bowels
- small intestines
- large intestines
- appendix
- pancreas
- gall bladder

#	English	Pronunciation	Korean
1	**flesh**	[fleʃ] n.	살
2	**blood**	[blʌd] n.	피 / 혈액
3	**bone**	[boun] n.	뼈
4	**muscle**	[mʌ́sl] n.	근육
5	**neuron**	[njúərɑn] n.	신경
6	**skin**	[skin] n.	피부
7	**tendon**	[téndən] n.	힘줄
8	**heart**	[hɑːrt] n.	심장
9	**liver**	[lívər] n.	간장
10	**lung**	[lʌŋ] n.	폐 / 허파
11	**arteries**	[ɑ́ːrtəriz] n.	동맥
12	**vein**	[vein] n.	정맥
13	**spine**	[spain] n.	척추
14	**kidney**	[kídni] n.	신장
15	**cell**	[sel] n.	세포
16	**breath**	[breθ] n.	숨(호흡)
17	**yawning**	[jɔ́ːniŋ] a.	하품하는
18	**sneeze**	[sniːz] n. vi.	재채기(하다)
19	**tear**	[tiər] n.	눈물
20	**nose dripping**	[nouz dripiŋ] n.	콧물
21	**sweat**	[swet] n.	땀
22	**saliva**	[səláivə] n.	침
23	**bowels**	[báuəlz] n.	장
24	**small intestines**	[smɔːl intéstinz] n.	소장
25	**large intestines**	[lɑːrdʒ intéstinz] n.	대장
26	**appendix**	[əpéndiks] n.	맹장
27	**pancreas**	[pǽŋkriəs] n.	췌장
28	**gall bladder**	[gɔːl blǽdər] n.	담낭

Human Body & Feeling

⋯▶ I was in tears while watching movie.
영화를 보면서 눈물을 흘렸습니다.

⋯▶ He goes to a gym every day to tone his muscles.
그는 근육 단련을 위해 매일 체육관에 갑니다.

⋯▶ A baby's skin is very soft and smooth.
아기 피부는 정말로 부드럽고 매끈합니다.

⋯▶ My uncle underwent a heart operation.
삼촌은 심장 수술을 받았습니다.

⋯▶ I can't stop sneezing.
재채기를 멈출 수가 없습니다.

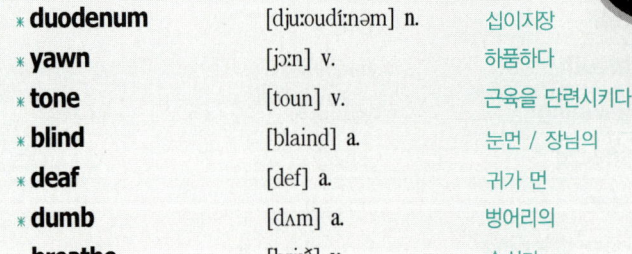

* **duodenum**	[djuːoudíːnəm] n.	십이지장
* **yawn**	[jɔːn] v.	하품하다
* **tone**	[toun] v.	근육을 단련시키다
* **blind**	[blaind] a.	눈먼 / 장님의
* **deaf**	[def] a.	귀가 먼
* **dumb**	[dʌm] a.	벙어리의
* **breathe**	[briːð] v.	숨쉬다

Part 033 Face
얼굴

A
- eye
- eyebrow
- eyelid
- double eyelid
- single eyelid
- eyelashes
- ear

B
- forehead
- nose
- nostril
- mouth
- lip
- tooth
- gum

C
- beard
- sideburns
- mustache
- wrinkle
- freckle
- discoloration
- chin

D
- cheek
- pimple
- temple
- dimple
- birthmark
- bald
- pale

#			
1	eye	[ai] n.	눈
2	eyebrow	[aíbráu] n.	눈썹
3	eyelid	[aílid] n.	눈꺼풀
4	double eyelid	[dʌ́bl aílid] n.	쌍꺼풀
5	single eyelid	[síŋgl aílid] n.	홑꺼풀
6	eyelashes	[aílǽʃiz] n.	속눈썹
7	ear	[iər] n.	귀
8	forehead	[fɔ́(:)rid] n.	이마
9	nose	[nouz] n.	코
10	nostril	[nástril] n.	콧구멍
11	mouth	[mauθ] n.	입
12	lip	[lip] n.	입술
13	tooth	[tuːθ] n.	이(치아)
14	gum	[gʌm] n.	잇몸
15	beard	[biərd] n.	턱수염
16	sideburns	[saidbə́ːrnz] n.	구레나룻
17	mustache	[mʌ́stæʃ] n.	콧수염
18	wrinkle	[ríŋkl] n.	주름
19	freckle	[frékl] n.	주근깨
20	discoloration	[diskʌ̀ləréiʃən] n.	기미
21	chin	[tʃin] n.	턱
22	cheek	[tʃiːk] n.	볼(뺨)
23	pimple	[pimpl] n.	여드름
24	temple	[témpl] n.	관자놀이
25	dimple	[dimpl] n.	보조개
26	birthmark	[bə́ːrθmáːrk] n.	점
27	bald	[bɔːld] a.	대머리의
28	pale	[peil] a.	창백한

⋯▸ **He has thick double eyelids.**
  그는 두꺼운 쌍꺼풀 눈을 갖고 있습니다.

⋯▸ **I went to the dental clinic due to a severe toothache.**
  심한 치통 때문에 치과에 갔습니다.

⋯▸ **This cosmetic prevents pimples on the face.**
  이것은 여드름을 방지하는 화장품입니다.

⋯▸ **I glanced at his profile.**
  그의 옆얼굴을 훔쳐봤습니다.

⋯▸ **My face blushed with cold.**
  추위로 볼이 빨게 졌습니다.

* **listen**	[lisɔn] v.	듣다
* **lick**	[lik] v.	핥다
* **beautiful**	[bjúːtəfəl] a.	아름다운
* **handsome**	[hǽnsəm] a.	잘생긴
* **nice**	[nais] a.	멋진
* **pretty**	[priti] a.	예쁜
* **ear-wax**	[iər wæks] n.	귓밥
* **eye-wax**	[ai wæks] n.	눈꼽
* **snot /nose wax**	[snɑt]/[nouz wæks] n.	꼬딱지
* **profile**	[próufail] n.	옆얼굴
* **complexion**	[kəmplékʃən] n.	안색

Part 034 Growth

성장

A
- boy
- girl
- man
- lady
- gentleman
- woman
- life

B
- fetus
- baby
- infant
- child
- puberty
- adolescent
- teenager

C
- minor
- young man
- adult
- senior citizen
- death
- funeral
- die/pass away

D
- pregnancy
- child birth
- have a baby
- adopt
- adoptee
- heir
- spouse

1	boy	[bɔi] n.	남자애
2	girl	[gəːrl] n.	여자애
3	man	[mæn] n.	남성
4	lady	[léidi] n.	숙녀
5	gentleman	[dʒéntlmən] n.	신사
6	woman	[wúmən] n.	여성
7	life	[laif] n.	인생
8	fetus	[fíːtəs] n.	태아
9	baby	[béibi] n.	갓난아이
10	infant	[ínfənt] n.	유아
11	child	[tʃaild] n.	어린이
12	puberty	[pjúːbərti] n.	사춘기
13	adolescent	[ædəlésənt] n.	청소년
14	teenager	[tíːnèidʒər] n.	십대
15	minor	[máinər] n.	미성년자
16	young man	[jʌŋ mæn] n.	젊은이
17	adult	[ədʌ́lt] n.	어른
18	senior citizen	[síːnjər sítəzən] n.	노인
19	death	[deθ] n.	사망
20	funeral	[fjúːnərəl] n.	장례식
21	die/pass away	[dai] / [pæs əwéi] v.	죽다
22	pregnancy	[prégnənsi] n.	임신
23	child birth	[tʃaild bəːrθ] n.	출산
24	have a baby	[hævə beibi] v.	아이를 낳다
25	adopt	[ədápt] v.	입양하다
26	adoptee	[ədɑpti] n.	입양아
27	heir	[ɛər] n.	후계자
28	spouse	[spauz] n.	배우자

- Children must behave like children.
  아이는 아이답게 행동해야 한다.
- My son enters elementary school this year.
  우리 아이는 올해 초등학생이 됩니다.
- She had a baby son.
  그녀는 아들을 낳았습니다.
- He was adopted to another country.
  그는 다른 나라로 입양되었습니다.
- Government encourages child birth these days.
  정부는 요즘 출산을 장려하고 있습니다.

* **accept**	[æksépt] v.	받아들이다
* **achieve**	[ətʃíːv] v.	성취하다
* **bear**	[bɛər] v.	낳다 / 견디다
* **become**	[bikʌ́m] v.	~이 되다
* **grow**	[grou] v.	자라다 / 기르다 / ~의 되다
* **dead**	[ded] a.	죽은
* **old**	[ould] a.	나이 든 / 오래된
* **young**	[jʌŋ] a.	젊은 / 어린
* **childhood**	[tʃáildhùd] n.	유년시절
* **university days**	[juːnəvə́ːrsəti deiz] n.	대학시절
* **young days**	[jʌŋ deiz] n.	청년시절
* **youth**	[juːθ] n.	청춘

4 Plants & Animals

Part 035 Grain

곡물

A
- rice
- rice plant
- wheat
- oat
- rye
- barley

B
- almond
- walnut
- chestnut
- peanut
- corn
- sesame

C
- bean
- soy bean
- red-bean
- unripe bean
- mung-bean
- kidney bean

D
- pea
- green pea
- German millet
- flour
- multi-grain bread
- whole wheat

#			
1	rice	[rais] n.	쌀
2	rice plant	[rais plænt] n.	벼
3	wheat	[hwiːt] n.	밀
4	oat	[out] n.	귀리
5	rye	[rai] n.	호밀
6	barley	[báːrli] n.	보리
7	almond	[áːmənd] n.	아몬드
8	walnut	[wɔ́ːlnʌt] n.	호두
9	chestnut	[tʃésnʌt] n.	밤
10	peanut	[píːnʌt] n.	땅콩
11	corn	[kɔːrn] n.	옥수수
12	sesame	[sésəmi] n.	참깨
13	bean	[biːn] n.	콩
14	soy bean	[sɔi biːn] n.	대두, 메주콩
15	red-bean	[red biːn] n.	팥
16	unripe bean	[ʌnráip biːn] n.	풋콩
17	mung-bean	[mʌŋ biːn] n.	녹두
18	kidney bean	[kídni biːn] n.	강낭콩
19	pea	[piː] n.	완두콩
20	green pea	[griːn piː] n.	껍질콩
21	German millet	[dʒə́ːrmən milit] n.	조
22	flour	[flauər] n.	밀가루
23	multi-grain bread	[mʌ́ltigrein bred] n.	잡곡빵
24	whole wheat	[houl hwiːt] n.	통밀

- Soy bean paste is made from soy beans.
  된장은 메주콩으로 만들어집니다.
- Butter roasted Corn is popular among young people these days.
  버터에 구운 옥수수가 요즘 젊은이들 사이에 유행입니다.
- I like barley bread.
  저는 보리빵을 좋아합니다.
- Peanut butter is my son's favorite.
  아들은 땅콩 버터를 가장 좋아합니다.
- Roasted chestnuts are a good snack in winter.
  군밤은 겨울에 좋은 간식거리입니다.

* cup	컵
* curl	(머리카락)곱슬거리게 하다
* curtain	커튼
* curve	곡선
* cut	자르다
* damage	피해 / 손상
* dare	감히~하다
* dash	돌진하다
* data	데이터 / 자료
* deep	깊은 / 깊게
* deliver	배달하다
* deny	부인하다 / 거절하다

Part 036 Plants / Trees
식물 / 나무

A
- leaf
- root
- stem
- branch
- fruit
- seed
- skin

B
- pine tree
- cherry tree
- palm tree
- ginkgo tree
- chestnut tree
- oak tree
- maple tree

C
- mulberry tree
- Japanese apricot tree
- Japanese cedar
- platanus
- poplar
- bamboo
- bush

D
- ivy
- rubber plant
- cotton plant
- magnolia
- seedling
- fallen leaves
- moss

#	단어	발음	뜻
1	**leaf**	[liːf] n.	잎
2	**root**	[ruːt] n.	뿌리
3	**stem**	[stem] n.	줄기
4	**branch**	[bræntʃ] n.	가지
5	**fruit**	[fruːt] n.	열매
6	**seed**	[siːd] n.	씨앗
7	**skin**	[skin] n.	껍질
8	**pine tree**	[pain triː] n.	소나무
9	**cherry tree**	[tʃéri triː] n.	벚나무
10	**palm tree**	[pɑːm triː] n.	야자수
11	**ginkgo tree**	[gíŋkou triː] n.	은행나무
12	**chestnut tree**	[tʃésnʌt triː] n.	밤나무
13	**oak tree**	[ouk triː] n.	떡갈나무
14	**maple tree**	[méipl triː] n.	단풍나무
15	**mulberry tree**	[mʌ́lbèri triː] n.	뽕나무
16	**Japanese apricot tree**	[dʒæpəníːz éiprəkàt triː] n.	매화나무
17	**Japanese cedar**	[dʒæpəníːz síːdər] n.	삼나무
18	**platanus**	[plǽtənəs] n.	플라타너스
19	**poplar**	[pɑ́plər] n.	미루나무
20	**bamboo**	[bæmbúː] n.	대나무
21	**bush**	[buʃ] n.	관목 / 덤불
22	**ivy**	[áivi] n.	담쟁이덩굴
23	**rubber plant**	[rʌ́bər plænt] n.	고무나무
24	**cotton plant**	[kátn plænt] n.	목화
25	**magnolia**	[mægnóuliə] n.	목련
26	**seedling**	[síːdliŋ] n.	모종
27	**fallen leaves**	[fɔ́ːlən líːvz] n.	낙엽
28	**moss**	[mɔ(ː)s] n.	이끼

Plants & Animals

⋯▸ Let's go to see the cherry blossoms.
   벚꽃 구경 갑시다.

⋯▸ There are still a few leaves left on the tree.
   나뭇가지에 잎이 몇 개 남아 있습니다.

⋯▸ ginkgo nuts are edible.
   은행열매는 먹을 수 있습니다.

⋯▸ Plants cover almost 80 percents of the planet.
   지구에는 식물이 80퍼센트 차지하고 있다.

⋯▸ There used be many pine trees in the mountains.
   이전에는 산에 소나무들이 많았었습니다.

* depend   믿다 / 의존하다
* destroy   파괴하다
* detect   발견하다
* devote   바치다 / 전념하다
* differ   다르다
* difficulty   어려움
* dirty   더러운
* disappear   사라지다
* discover   발견하다
* dislike   싫어하다
* distance   거리
* doll   인형

Part 037 Flowers

꽃

A
- petal
- bud
- pollen
- bulb
- vine
- bush

B
- flowerpot
- flowerbed
- rose
- cherry blossom
- lily
- sunflower

C
- tulip
- carnation
- azalea
- golden-bell
- chrysanthemum
- dandelion

D
- cosmos
- the rose of Sharon
- orchid
- daffodil
- cactus
- reed
- violet

#	Word	Pronunciation	Meaning
1	petal	[pétl] n.	꽃잎
2	bud	[bʌd] n.	꽃봉우리
3	pollen	[pálən] n.	꽃가루
4	bulb	[bʌlb] n.	알뿌리
5	vine	[vain] n.	덩굴
6	bush	[buʃ] n.	관목 / 덤블
7	flowerpot	[fláuər pɑt] n.	화분
8	flowerbed	[fláuər bed] n.	화단
9	rose	[rouz] n.	장미
10	cherry blossom	[tʃéri blásəm] n.	벚꽃
11	lily	[líli] n.	백합
12	sunflower	[sʌ́nflàuər] n.	해바라기
13	tulip	[tjúːlip] n.	튜울립
14	carnation	[kɑːrnéiʃən] n.	카네이션
15	azalea	[əzéiljə] n.	진달래
16	golden-bell	[góuldən bel] n.	개나리
17	chrysanthemum	[krisǽnθəməm] n.	국화
18	dandelion	[dǽndəlàiən] n.	민들레
19	cosmos	[kázməs] n.	코스모스
20	the rose of Sharon	[ðə rouzɔv ʃɛ́ərən] n.	무궁화
21	orchid	[ɔ́ːrkid] n.	난초
22	daffodil	[dǽfədil] n.	수선화
23	cactus	[kǽktəs] n.	선인장
24	reed	[riːd] n.	억새
25	violet	[váiəlit] n.	제비꽃

···▶ **Flowers blossoms when spring comes.**
　　봄이 되면, 꽃이 핍니다.

···▶ **A golden-bell is the symbol of spring**
　　개나리는 봄의 상징입니다.

···▶ **My favorite flower is red roses.**
　　내가 좋아하는 꽃은 붉은 장미입니다.

···▶ **The flower language of the lily is purity.**
　　백합의 꽃말은 순결입니다.

···▶ **Pollen causes allergic reactions to people these days.**
　　요즈음 꽃가루가 사람들에게 알레르기를 일으키고 있습니다.

✽ doubt	의심 하다
✽ dozen	12개
✽ drag	끌다
✽ drink	(술) 마시다
✽ drop	떨어뜨리다
✽ dry	건조 한
✽ dull	둔한 / 탁한
✽ during	~동안 / ~내내
✽ dye	염색(하다)
✽ early	일찍
✽ easily	쉽게
✽ easy	쉬운 / 편한

Part 038 Fruits 과일

A
- pick
- apple
- tangerine
- peach
- banana
- melon
- orange

B
- strawberries
- blueberries
- watermelon
- grapes
- pear
- persimmon
- kiwi fruit

C
- chinese date
- grapefruit
- pineapple
- cherries
- lime
- lemon
- plum

D
- apricot
- mango
- papaya
- coconut
- avocado
- pomegranate
- fig

#	단어	발음	뜻
1	**pick**	[pik] v.	(과일 등을)따다/고르다/줍다
2	**apple**	[ǽpl] n.	사과
3	**tangerine**	[tæ̀ndʒəríːn] n.	귤
4	**peach**	[piːtʃ] n.	복숭아
5	**banana**	[bənǽnə] n.	바나나
6	**melon**	[mélən] n.	멜론
7	**orange**	[ɔ́(ː)rindʒ] n.	오렌지
8	**strawberries**	[strɔ́ːbèriz] n.	딸기
9	**blueberries**	[blúːbèriz] n.	블루베리
10	**watermelon**	[wɔ́ːtərmèlən] n.	수박
11	**grapes**	[greips] n.	포도
12	**pear**	[pɛər] n.	배
13	**persimmon**	[pɔrsímən] n.	감
14	**kiwi fruit**	[kíːwi fruːt] n.	키위
15	**chinese date**	[tʃainíːz deit] n.	대추
16	**grapefruit**	[gréipfrùːt] n.	자몽
17	**pineapple**	[páinæ̀pl] n.	파인애플
18	**cherries**	[tʃériz] n.	버찌
19	**lime**	[laim] n.	라임
20	**lemon**	[lémən] n.	레몬
21	**plum**	[plʌm] n.	자두
22	**apricot**	[ǽprəkát] n.	살구
23	**mango**	[mǽŋgou] n.	망고
24	**papaya**	[pəpáːjə] n.	파파야
25	**coconut**	[kóukənʌ̀t] n.	코코넛
26	**avocado**	[æ̀vəkáːdou] n.	아보카도
27	**pomegranate**	[púməgræ̀nit] n.	석류
28	**fig**	[fig] n.	무화과

⋯ I eat fruit for breakfast every morning.
매일 아침식사로 과일을 먹고 있다.

⋯ Tangerine is sour, orange is sweet.
귤은 시고, 오렌지는 답니다.

⋯ Kiwi fruit and banana are usually exported.
키위와 바나나는 대체로 수입됩니다.

⋯ I used to play under a big chestnut tree.
커다란 밤나무 아래에서 놀곤 했습니다.

⋯ Mom peels off the skin of a persimmon with a knife.
칼로 감 껍질을 벗깁니다.

✽ elder	연장자의
✽ electric	전기의
✽ element	요소
✽ elementary	초보의 / 초등의
✽ else	그밖에
✽ embarrass	당황하게 하다
✽ empire	제국
✽ empty	빈
✽ enough	충분히
✽ entire	전체의 / 완전한
✽ equal	같은 / 동등한
✽ equip	갖추어 주다

Part 039 Vegetables
야채

A
- lettuce
- chinese cabbage
- cabbage
- onion
- green onion/scallion
- leek
- carrot

B
- cucumber
- pumpkin
- radish
- garlic
- ginger
- bell pepper
- bean sprout

C
- potato
- sweet potato
- tomato
- bamboo shoot
- spinach
- broccoli
- cauliflower

D
- mushroom
- eggplant
- ginseng
- celery
- asparagus
- lotus root
- parsley

1	lettuce	[létis] n.	(양)상추
2	chinese cabbage	[tʃainíːz kǽbidʒ] n.	배추
3	cabbage	[kǽbidʒ] n.	양배추
4	onion	[ʌ́njən] n.	양파
5	green onion/scallion	[griːn ʌ́njən] / [skǽljən] n.	파
6	leek	[liːk] n.	부추
7	carrot	[kǽrət] n.	당근
8	cucumber	[kjúːkəmbər] n.	오이
9	pumpkin	[pʌ́mpkin] n.	노란 호박
10	radish	[rǽdiʃ] n.	샐러드용 빨간 무
11	garlic	[gáːrlik] n.	마늘
12	ginger	[dʒindʒər] n.	생강
13	bell pepper	[bel pépər] n.	피망
14	bean sprout	[biːn spraut] n.	콩나물
15	potato	[pətéitou] n.	감자
16	sweet potato	[swiːt pətéitou] n.	고구마
17	tomato	[təméitou] n.	토마토
18	bamboo shoot	[bæmbúː ʃuːt] n.	죽순
19	spinach	[spinitʃ] n.	시금치
20	broccoli	[brákəli] n.	브로콜리
21	cauliflower	[kɔ́ːləflàuər] n.	콜리플라워
22	mushroom	[mʌ́ʃru(ː)m] n.	송이버섯
23	eggplant	[égplænt] n.	가지
24	ginseng	[dʒinseŋ] n.	인삼
25	celery	[séləri] n.	셀러리
26	asparagus	[əspǽrəgəs] n.	아스파라가스
27	lotus root	[lóutəs ruːt] n.	연근
28	parsley	[páːrsli] n.	파셀리

···▸ Wash the cabbage and boil it.
   배추를 씻어서 삶아두세요.

···▸ Mince the garlic.
   마늘을 잘게 다져주세요.

···▸ Raw ginger tastes bitter.
   생강은 그대로 먹으면 쓴맛이 납니다.

···▸ Can I please have mushroom soup?
   양송이 수프 있습니까?

···▸ Boil bean sprouts slightly.
   콩나물을 살짝 삶아주세요.

···▸ Broccoli has lots of vitamin B.
   브로콜리는 비타민 B가 많이 들어 있습니다.

＊ **yam**	[jæm] n.	마
＊ **crown daisy**	[kraun déizi] n.	쑥갓
＊ **taro**	[tá:rou] n.	토란
＊ **mugwort**	[mágwə̀:rt] n.	쑥
＊ **turnip**	[tə́:rnip] n.	순무
＊ **leaf mustard**	[li:f mástərd] n.	갓
＊ **burdock**	[bə́:rdák] n.	우엉

P·a·r·t 40 Animals

동물

A
- pet
- dog
- cat
- rabbit
- pig
- horse
- cow

B
- mouse
- rat
- lamb
- sheep
- goat
- donkey
- zebra

C
- elephant
- monkey
- deer
- bear
- camel
- tiger
- lion

D
- hyena
- koala
- giraffe
- lizard
- alligator
- fox
- gorilla

#	Word	Pronunciation	Meaning
1	**pet**	[pet] n.	애완동물
2	**dog**	[dɔ(:)g] n.	개
3	**cat**	[kæt] n.	고양이
4	**rabbit**	[rǽbit] n.	토끼
5	**pig**	[pig] n.	돼지
6	**horse**	[hɔːrs] n.	말
7	**cow**	[kau] n.	암소 / 젖소
8	**mouse**	[maus] n.	생쥐
9	**rat**	[ræt] n.	쥐
10	**lamb**	[læm] n.	새끼 양
11	**sheep**	[ʃiːp] n.	양
12	**goat**	[gout] n.	염소
13	**donkey**	[dáŋki] n.	당나귀
14	**zebra**	[zíːbrə] n.	얼룩말
15	**elephant**	[éləfənt] n.	코끼리
16	**monkey**	[mʌ́ŋki] n.	원숭이
17	**deer**	[dír] n.	사슴
18	**bear**	[bɛər] n.	곰
19	**camel**	[kǽməl] n.	낙타
20	**tiger**	[táigər] n.	호랑이
21	**lion**	[láiən] n.	사자
22	**hyena**	[haiíːnə] n.	하이에나
23	**koala**	[kouáːlə] n.	코알라
24	**giraffe**	[dʒrǽf] n.	기린
25	**lizard**	[lízərd] n.	도마뱀
26	**alligator**	[ǽligèitər] n.	악어
27	**fox**	[fɑks] n.	여우
28	**gorilla**	[gərílə] n.	고릴라

Plants & Animals

1 단어를 예문으로 만들어 볼까요?

···› We keep dogs in the house.
집에서 개를 기르고 있습니다.

···› I like to feed the cat.
저는 고양이에게 먹이 주는 것을 좋아합니다.

···› I saw hippos for the first time in a zoo.
저는 동물원에서 처음으로 하마를 보았습니다.

···› Monkeys resemble humans most.
원숭이는 가장 사람과 닮았습니다.

···› You can't swim in the lake because of alligators.
악어들 때문에 호수에서는 수영할 수 없습니다.

2 그외의 단어에는 이런것들이 있어요

* raccoon	[rækúːn]	n.	너구리
* chimpanzee	[tʃìmpænzíː]	n.	침팬지
* hump	[hʌmp]	n.	낙타혹
* dinosaur	[dáinəsɔ̀ːr]	n.	공룡
* female	[fíːmeil]	a.	암컷의
* whiskers	[hwískərz]	n.	고양이 수염
* tusk	[tʌsk]	n.	상아
* trunk	[trʌŋk]	n.	코끼리 코
* mane	[mein]	n.	사자갈기
* warthog	[wɔ́ːrthɔ̀ːg]	n.	멧돼지
* leopard	[lépərd]	n.	표범
* kangaroo	[kæ̀ŋgərúː]	n.	캥거루
* stripes	[strips]	n.	얼룩말 줄무늬
* polar bear	[póulər bɛər]	n.	북극곰

Part 041 Insects 곤충

A
- bee
- wasp
- butterfly
- dragonfly
- firefly
- fly
- maggot

B
- mosquito
- ant
- termite
- spider
- web
- earthworm
- silkworm

C
- grasshopper
- praying mantis
- flea
- scorpion
- beetle
- cricket
- ladybug

D
- moth
- caterpillar
- cocoon
- cockroach
- centipede
- snail
- slug

#	Word	Pronunciation	Meaning
1	**bee**	[biː] n.	꿀벌
2	**wasp**	[wɑsp] n.	말벌
3	**butterfly**	[bʌ́tərflài] n.	나비
4	**dragonfly**	[drǽgən flai] n.	잠자리
5	**firefly**	[fáiərflài] n.	반딧불
6	**fly**	[flai] n.	파리
7	**maggot**	[mǽgət] n.	구더기
8	**mosquito**	[məskíːtou] n.	모기
9	**ant**	[ænt] n.	개미
10	**termite**	[tə́ːrmait] n.	흰개미
11	**spider**	[spáidər] n.	거미
12	**web**	[web] n.	거미줄
13	**earthworm**	[ə́ːrθwə̀ːrm] n.	지렁이
14	**silkworm**	[silkwə́ːrm] n.	누에
15	**grasshopper**	[grǽshápər] n.	메뚜기
16	**praying mantis**	[preiŋ mǽntis] n.	사마귀
17	**flea**	[fliː] n.	벼룩
18	**scorpion**	[skɔ́ːrpiən] n.	전갈
19	**beetle**	[biːtl] n.	딱정벌레
20	**cricket**	[krikit] n.	귀뚜라미
21	**ladybug**	[léidibʌg] n.	무당벌레
22	**moth**	[mɔ(ː)θ] n.	나방
23	**caterpillar**	[kǽtərpilər] n.	유충
24	**cocoon**	[kəkúːn] n.	번데기
25	**cockroach**	[kákròutʃ] n.	바퀴벌레
26	**centipede**	[séntəpiːd] n.	지네
27	**snail**	[sneil] n.	달팽이
28	**slug**	[slʌg] n.	민달팽이

···▶ Bees collect honey from flowers.
　　 꿀벌은 꽃에서 벌꿀을 따옵니다.

···▶ I was bitten by a mosquito.
　　 모기에 물렸습니다.

···▶ Silkworm can be good medicine for some adult diseases.
　　 누에는 성인병에 잘 듣습니다.

···▶ I was surprised to find a cockroach in the kitchen.
　　 부엌에서 바퀴벌레를 발견하고 놀랐습니다.

···▶ Even a worm will turn.
　　 지렁이도 밟으면 꿈틀한다.

＊ error	실수
＊ especially	특히
＊ etc.	기타 등등
＊ even	~조차 / 더욱
＊ every	모든
＊ exact	정확한
＊ example	예 / 본보기
＊ excellent	우수한 / 뛰어난
＊ except	~을 제외하고 / ~이 외에는
＊ exhibit	전시하다
＊ exist	존재하다
＊ expect	기대하다

P·a·r·t

042 Fish & Sea Animals
물고기 및 바다생물

A
- shrimp
- squid
- octopus
- eel
- whale
- dolphin
- shark

B
- mackerel
- sardine
- saury
- crab
- trout
- salmon
- tuna

C
- sea horse
- turtle
- tortoise
- lobster
- frog
- tadpole
- snake

물고기

D
- sea slug
- sea urchin
- starfish
- oyster
- clam
- mussel
- seaweed

135

#	word	pronunciation	meaning
1	shrimp	[ʃrimp] n.	새우
2	squid	[skwíd] n.	오징어
3	octopus	[áktəpəs] n.	문어
4	eel	[iːl] n.	장어
5	whale	[hweil] n.	고래
6	dolphin	[dálfin] n.	돌고래
7	shark	[ʃɑːrk] n.	상어
8	mackerel	[mǽkərəl] n.	고등어
9	sardine	[sɑːrdíːn] n.	정어리
10	saury	[sɔ́ːri] n.	꽁치
11	crab	[kræb] n.	게
12	trout	[traut] n.	송어
13	salmon	[sǽmən] n.	연어
14	tuna	[tjúːnə] n.	다랑어
15	sea horse	[síː hɔːrs] n.	해마
16	turtle	[tə́ːrtl] n.	바다거북
17	tortoise	[tɔ́ːrtəs] n.	민물거북
18	lobster	[lábstər] n.	바다가재
19	frog	[frɔːg] n.	개구리
20	tadpole	[tǽdpòul] n.	올챙이
21	snake	[sneik] n.	뱀
22	sea slug	[síː slʌg] n.	해삼
23	sea urchin	[síː ə́ːrtʃin] n.	성게
24	starfish	[stáːrfíʃ] n.	불가사리
25	oyster	[ɔ́istər] n.	굴
26	clam	[klæm] n.	조개
27	mussel	[mʌ́səl] n.	홍합
28	seaweed	[síːwiːd] n.	김

Plants & Animals

⋯▶ There are beautiful carp in a pond.
　　연못에 아름다운 잉어들이 있습니다.
⋯▶ I had raw tuna fish for lunch.
　　점심으로 참치회를 먹었습니다.
⋯▶ We saw the famous dolphin show in an aquarium.
　　우리는 수족관에서 유명한 돌고래 쇼를 보았습니다.
⋯▶ I prefer clam chowder.
　　조개 크림 스프가 낫겠네요.
⋯▶ Rattlesnakes are very poisonous.
　　방울뱀은 맹독성이다.

＊ **rattlesnake**	[rǽtlsnèik] n.	방울뱀
＊ **shell**	[ʃel] n.	거북 등껍질
＊ **pollack**	[pάlək] n.	명태
＊ **claw**	[klɔː] n.	가재 집게
＊ **algae**	[ǽldʒiː] n.	해초
＊ **brown seaweed**	[braun síːwiːd] n.	미역
＊ **kelp**	[kelp] n.	다시마
＊ **green layer**	[griːn léiər] n.	파래
＊ **abalone**	[æ̀bəlóuni] n.	전복
＊ **puffer**	[pʌ́fər] n.	복어
＊ **carp**	[kɑːrp] n.	잉어
＊ **flatfish**	[flǽtfiʃ] n.	넙치
＊ **red snapper**	[red snǽpər] n.	도미

Part 043 Birds

새

A
- cage
- nest
- hair
- tail
- wing
- hatch
- duck

B
- hen
- chick
- goose
- wild goose
- sparrow
- swallow
- pigeon

C
- hawk
- eagle
- crow
- magpie
- pheasant
- skylark
- owl

D
- seasonal bird
- resident bird
- parrot
- crane
- swan
- peacock
- ostrich

1	**cage**	[keidʒ] n.	새장(우리)
2	**nest**	[nest] n.	둥지 / 보금자리
3	**hair**	[hɛər] n.	털
4	**tail**	[teil] n.	꼬리
5	**wing**	[wiŋ] n.	날개
6	**hatch**	[hætʃ] v.	알을 깨다 / 부화하다
7	**duck**	[dʌk] n.	오리
8	**hen**	[hen] n.	암탉
9	**chick**	[tʃik] n.	병아리
10	**goose**	[guːs] n.	거위
11	**wild goose**	[waild guːs] n.	기러기
12	**sparrow**	[spǽrou] n.	참새
13	**swallow**	[swálou] n.	제비
14	**pigeon**	[pídʒən] n.	비둘기
15	**hawk**	[hɔːk] n.	매
16	**eagle**	[íːgl] n.	독수리
17	**crow**	[krou] n.	까마귀
18	**magpie**	[mǽgpài] n.	까치
19	**pheasant**	[fézənt] n.	꿩
20	**skylark**	[skáilàːrk] n.	종달새
21	**owl**	[aul] n.	올빼미
22	**seasonal bird**	[síːzənəl bəːrd] n.	철새
23	**resident bird**	[rézidənt bəːrd] n.	텃새
24	**parrot**	[pǽrət] n.	앵무새
25	**crane**	[krein] n.	두루미(학)
26	**swan**	[swɑn] n.	백조
27	**peacock**	[píːkàk] n.	공작
28	**ostrich**	[ɔ́(ː)stritʃ] n.	타조

⋯▸ Cranes fly together in a group.
학이 무리를 이루며 날고 있습니다.

⋯▸ Are you a lark type or owl type?
당신은 종달새 형인가요? 아니면 올빼미 형인가요?

⋯▸ It is said to be lucky to hear magpie sing in the morning.
아침에 까치우는 소리를 들으면 운이 좋다고 합니다.

⋯▸ We keep ducks and hens in the house.
집에서 오리와 닭을 기르고 있습니다.

⋯▸ He's a wild goose father, that is, his son and wife are in Canada.
그는 기러기 아빠입니다. 즉 아들과 아내가 캐나다에 있습니다.

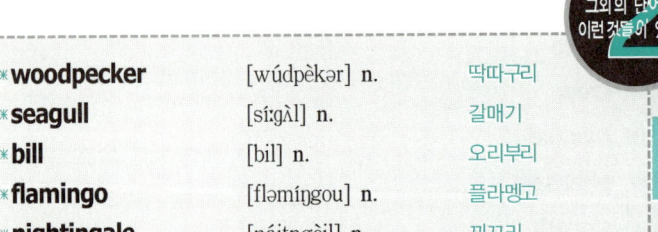

✽ **woodpecker**	[wúdpèkər] n.	딱따구리
✽ **seagull**	[síːgʌ̀l] n.	갈매기
✽ **bill**	[bil] n.	오리부리
✽ **flamingo**	[fləmíŋgou] n.	플라멩고
✽ **nightingale**	[náitngèil] n.	꾀꼬리
✽ **pelican**	[pélikən] n.	펠리칸
✽ **quail**	[kweil] n.	메추라기
✽ **penquin**	[péŋgwin] n.	펭귄

5 Food

Part 044 Cooking 요리

A
- recipe
- menu
- eat out
- pay the bill
- go Dutch
- chef's special

B
- Korean food
- Korean style barbecue
- rib meat
- curry and rice
- rice and soup
- red pepper paste

C
- cold noodle dish
- Chinese food
- dumpling
- dumpling soup
- fried rice
- sweet and sour pork

D
- fast food
- instant food
- instant cup noodles
- French fries
- self-service
- way of cooking

#			
1	recipe	[résəpiː] n.	조리법
2	menu	[ménjuː] n.	메뉴
3	eat out	[iːt áut] v.	외식하다
4	pay the bill	[pei ðə bil] v.	계산하다
5	go Dutch	[gou dʌtʃ] v.	각자부담하다
6	chef's special	[ʃefs spéʃəl] n.	추천요리
7	Korean food	[kəríːən fuːd] n.	한국요리
8	Korean style barbecue	[kəríːən stail báːrbikjùː] n.	불고기
9	rib meat	[rib miːt] n.	갈비
10	curry and rice	[kə́ːri ən rais] n.	카레라이스
11	rice and soup	[rais ən suːp] n.	국밥
12	red pepper paste	[red pépər peist] n.	고추장
13	cold noodle dish	[kould núːdl diʃ] n.	냉면
14	Chinese food	[tʃainíːz fuːd] n.	중화요리
15	dumpling	[dʌ́mpliŋ] n.	만두
16	dumpling soup	[dʌ́mpliŋ suːp] n.	만두국
17	fried rice	[fraid rais] n.	볶음밥
18	sweet and sour pork	[swiːt ən sáuər pɔːrk] n.	탕수육
19	fast food	[fæst fuːd] n.	패스트푸드
20	instant food	[ínstənt fuːd] n.	인스턴트 음식
21	instant cup noodles	[ínstənt kʌp núːdlz] n.	컵라면
22	French fries	[frentʃ fráiz] n.	감자 튀김
23	self-service	[self sə́ːrvis] n.	셀프서비스
24	way of cooking	[wei ɔv kúkiŋ] n.	조리법

⋯› I had a cup noodles at a convenience store.
편의점에서 컵라면을 먹었습니다.

⋯› My favorite food is Kimchi fried rice.
김치 볶음밥이 제일 좋습니다.

⋯› What is the chef's special in this restaurant?
이 식당의 특별요리가 뭡니까?

⋯› How about going to a buffet restaurant this Sunday?
이번 일요일에 뷔페 식당에 가는 거 어때요?

⋯› We enjoy dumpling rice cake soup on New Year's Day.
설날에는 떡만두국을 먹습니다.

＊ **grate**	[greit] v.	(강판에) 갈다
＊ **chop**	[tʃɑp] v.	잘게 썰다
＊ **mince**	[mins] v.	다지다
＊ **dice**	[dais] v.	깍둑썰기하다
＊ **slice**	[slais] v.	얇게 썰다
＊ **pan fry/stir fry**	[pæn frai]/[stər frai] v.	볶다
＊ **deep fry**	[diːp frai] v.	튀기다
＊ **chill**	[tʃil] v.	차갑게 하다
＊ **roast**	[roust] v.	굽다
＊ **defrost**	[diːfrɔ́ːst] vt.	해동시키다
＊ **peel off**	[piːl ɔf] v.	껍질을 벗기다
＊ **barbecue**	[báːrbikjùː] v.	직접 불에 굽다
＊ **strain**	[strein] v.	거르다

Part 045 Seasonings 조미료

A
- salt
- sugar
- brown sugar
- sugar cube
- soy sauce
- soy bean paste

B
- red pepper paste
- pepper
- vinegar
- oil
- sauce
- spices

C
- ketchup
- mayonnaise
- dressing
- red pepper powder
- sesame oil
- sesame salt

D
- shredded pepper
- potato powder
- bitter
- spicy
- sour
- mild
- salty

#			
1	**salt**	[sɔːlt] n.	소금
2	**sugar**	[ʃúgər] n.	설탕
3	**brown sugar**	[braun ʃúgər] n.	흑설탕
4	**sugar cube**	[ʃúgər kjuːb] n.	각설탕
5	**soy sauce**	[sɔi sɔːs] n.	간장
6	**soy bean paste**	[sɔ́ibiːn peist] n.	된장
7	**red pepper paste**	[red pépər peist] n.	고추장
8	**pepper**	[pépər] n.	후추
9	**vinegar**	[vínigər] n.	식초
10	**oil**	[ɔil] n.	기름
11	**sauce**	[sɔːs] n.	소스
12	**spices**	[spaisiz] n.	양념
13	**ketchup**	[kétʃəp] n.	케찹
14	**mayonnaise**	[mèiɔnéiz] n.	마요네즈
15	**dressing**	[drésiŋ] n.	드레싱
16	**red pepper powder**	[red pépər páudər] n.	고추가루
17	**sesame oil**	[sésəmi ɔil] n.	참기름
18	**sesame salt**	[sésəmi sɔːlt] n.	깨소금
19	**shredded pepper**	[ʃredid pépər] n.	실고추
20	**potato powder**	[pətéitou páudər] n.	감자가루
21	**bitter**	[bítər] a.	쓴 / 쓰라린
22	**spicy**	[spáisi] a.	매운
23	**sour**	[sáuər] a.	맛이 신
24	**mild**	[maild] a.	담백한
25	**salty**	[sɔ́ːlti] a.	짠 / 소금기 있는

⋯▸ They put Italian dressing on the top of green salad.
그들은 야채 샐러드에 이탈리안 드레싱을 뿌렸습니다.

⋯▸ It tastes better to have dried squid dipped in mayo.
말린 오징어에 마요네즈를 묻혀서 먹으면 더 맛있습니다.

⋯▸ Vinegar is good for health.
식초는 건강에 좋습니다.

⋯▸ I need more sugar in my coffee.
커피에 설탕이 좀 더 필요합니다.

⋯▸ She sprinkled salt and pepper in cream soup.
그녀는 크림스프에 소금과 후추를 뿌렸습니다.

⋯▸ Please give me some honey mustard sauce on the side.
허니 겨자 소스는 따로 갖다 주세요.

* explain	설명하다
* extend	뻗다 / 늘이다
* extra	여분의 / 특별한
* extreme	극도의 / 과격한
* fact	사실
* fair	공정한 / 맑은
* fairy	요정
* fall	떨어지다
* false	잘못된 / 거짓의 / 가짜의
* familiar	친숙한
* famous	유명한
* fasten	단단히 고정시키다 / 매다

Part 046 Meal

식사

A
- meat
- beef
- pork
- chicken
- mutton
- lamb

B
- turkey
- horse meat
- boiled egg
- cooked rice
- side dishes
- broth/soup

식사(재료)

C
- porridge
- breakfast
- lunch
- dinner
- supper
- coffee break

D
- chew
- starve
- delicious
- full/ stuffed
- hungry
- thirsty

Part 5

#	Word	Pronunciation	Meaning
1	**meat**	[miːt] n.	(식용)고기
2	**beef**	[biːf] n.	소고기
3	**pork**	[pɔːrk] n.	돼지고기
4	**chicken**	[tʃíkin] n.	닭고기
5	**mutton**	[mʌ́tn] n.	양고기
6	**lamb**	[læm] n.	새끼 양고기
7	**turkey**	[tə́ːrki] n.	칠면조
8	**horse meat**	[hɔːrs miːt] n.	말고기
9	**boiled egg**	[bɔild eg] n.	삶은 달걀
10	**cooked rice**	[kukt rais] n.	밥
11	**side dishes**	[said diʃiz] n.	반찬
12	**broth/soup**	[brɔ(ː)θ] / [suːp] n.	국
13	**porridge**	[pɔ́ːridʒ] n.	죽
14	**breakfast**	[brékfəst] n.	아침식사
15	**lunch**	[lʌntʃ] n.	점심식사
16	**dinner**	[dínər] n.	저녁
17	**supper**	[sʌ́pər] n.	간단한 저녁
18	**coffee break**	[kɔ́ːfi breik] n.	잠깐의 휴식
19	**chew**	[tʃuː] v.	씹다
20	**starve**	[stáːrv] v.	굶주리다
21	**delicious**	[dilíʃəs] a.	맛있는
22	**full/ stuffed**	[ful]/[stʌft] a.	배부른
23	**hungry**	[hʌ́ŋgri] a.	배고픈
24	**thirsty**	[θə́ːrsti] a.	목마른

Food

⋯▸ I always have rice and miso soup for breakfast.
아침식사는 항상 밥과 된장국을 먹고 있습니다.

⋯▸ We went out for lunch.
우리는 점심에 외식을 했습니다.

⋯▸ Which one do you prefer, beef or pork?
소고기와 돼지고기 어느 쪽을 좋아하니?

⋯▸ I tried cooking chicken soup.
치킨 스프를 만들어 봤습니다.

⋯▸ I'm starved to death.
배가 고파 죽을 지경입니다.

✻ fat	지방 / 뚱뚱한
✻ fault	실수 / 잘못
✻ favor	호의
✻ favorite	마음에 드는 것
✻ fee	요금 / 수수료
✻ feed	먹이를 주다 / 기르다
✻ female	암컷의
✻ few	거의 없는
✻ field	들판 / 밭
✻ fight	싸우다
✻ film	필름
✻ finally	마침내 / 결국

Part 047 Dessert & Alcohol
후식 및 술

A
- alcoholic beverage
- non-alcoholic beverage
- soft drink / cold drink
- green tea
- black tea
- barley tea
- herb tea

B
- snacks between meals
- korean traditional candy
- milk
- coke
- cider
- juice
- hot chocolate

C
- cookie
- cake
- ice cream
- chocolate
- pudding
- yogurt
- chewing gum

D
- draft beer
- brandy
- cocktail
- champagne
- plum wine
- Cheers !
- Bottoms up!

#	English	Pronunciation	Korean
1	alcoholic beverage	[ǽlkəhɔ́(:)lik bévəridʒ] n.	술
2	non-alcoholic beverage	[nɑnǽlkəhɔ́(:)lik bévəridʒ] n.	음료수
3	soft drink / cold drink	[sɔ(:)ft driŋk]/[kould driŋk] n.	음료수
4	green tea	[gríːn tiː] n.	녹차
5	black tea	[blǽk tiː] n.	홍차
6	barley tea	[báːrli tiː] n.	보리차
7	herb tea	[həːrb tiː] n.	허브차
8	snacks between meals	[snǽks bitwíːn miːlz]	간식
9	korean traditional candy	[kəríːən trədíʃənəl kǽndi] n.	엿
10	milk	[mílk] n.	우유
11	coke	[kóuk] n.	콜라
12	cider	[sáidər] n.	사이다
13	juice	[dʒúːs] n.	쥬스
14	hot chocolate	[hɑt tʃɔ́kəlit] n.	코코아
15	cookie	[kúki] n.	쿠키
16	cake	[kéik] n.	케익
17	ice cream	[áis kriːm] n.	아이스크림
18	chocolate	[tʃɔ́ːkəlit] n.	쵸콜릿
19	pudding	[púdiŋ] n.	푸딩
20	yogurt	[jóugərt] n.	요구르트
21	chewing gum	[tʃúːiŋ gʌm] n.	껌
22	draft beer	[drǽft biər] n.	생맥주
23	brandy	[brǽndi] n.	브랜디
24	cocktail	[káktèil] n.	칵테일
25	champagne	[ʃæmpéin] n.	샴페인
26	plum wine	[plʌm wain] n.	매실주
27	Cheers !	[tʃíəz]	건배!
28	Bottoms up!	[bátəmz ʌ́p]	원샷!

Food

- If you have cake everyday, you will gain weight.
  매일 케이크를 먹으면 살이 찝니다.
- I always enjoy dessert after a meal.
  저는 언제나 식 후 디저트를 즐깁니다.
- Drinking too much coke is a bad habit.
  콜라를 많이 마시는 것은 나쁜 습관입니다.
- How about going for cold beer after work?
  퇴근 후에 시원한 맥주 한잔 어때요?
- It's homemade ice cream.
  집에서 직접 만든 아이스크림입니다.

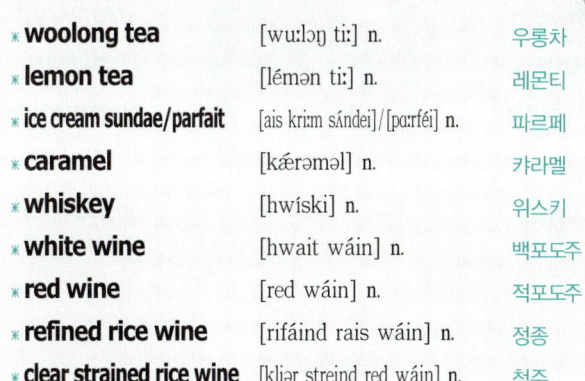

woolong tea	[wuːlɔŋ tiː] n.	우롱차
lemon tea	[lémən tiː] n.	레몬티
ice cream sundae/parfait	[ais kriːm sʌ́ndei]/[pɑrféi] n.	파르페
caramel	[kǽrəməl] n.	캬라멜
whiskey	[hwíski] n.	위스키
white wine	[hwait wáin] n.	백포도주
red wine	[red wáin] n.	적포도주
refined rice wine	[rifáind rais wáin] n.	정종
clear strained rice wine	[kliər streind red wáin] n.	청주
wine glass	[wáin glæs] n.	와인잔

Part 048 Restaurants & Western Food
식당 및 양식

A
- cafeteria
- drive-in restaurant
- fast food restaurant
- all-you-can-eat restaurant
- appetizer
- entree
- dessert

B
- steak
- well-done
- medium
- rare
- pork cutlet
- spaghetti
- curry

C
- salad bar
- biscuit
- croissant
- pizza
- hamburger
- toast
- sandwich

D
- hot dog
- fried egg
- bacon
- sausage
- margarine
- butter
- cheese

#	Word	Pronunciation	Meaning
1	**cafeteria**	[kæfitíəriə] n.	간이 식당
2	**drive-in restaurant**	[draivin réstərənt] n.	드라이브인(차안에서 주문)
3	**fast food restaurant**	[fæst fuːd réstərənt] n.	패스트 푸드 레스토랑
4	**all-you-can-eat restaurant**		뷔페 식당
5	**appetizer**	[ǽpitàizər] n.	전채요리
6	**entree**	[ɑ́ːntrei] n.	주요리
7	**dessert**	[dizə́ːrt] n.	후식
8	**steak**	[steik] n.	스테이크
9	**well-done**	[wel dʌ́n] a.	푹 익힌
10	**medium**	[míːdiəm] a.	중간 정도로 익힌
11	**rare**	[rɛəːr] a.	살짝 익힌
12	**pork cutlet**	[pɔːrk kʌ́tlit] n.	돈까스
13	**spaghetti**	[spəgéti] n.	스파게티
14	**curry**	[kə́ːri] n.	카레
15	**salad bar**	[sǽləd bɑːr] n.	샐러드 부페
16	**biscuit**	[bískit] n.	비스켓
17	**croissant**	[krəsɑ́ːnt] n.	크로아상
18	**pizza**	[píːtsə] n.	피자
19	**hamburger**	[hǽmbə̀rgər] n.	햄버거
20	**toast**	[toust] n.	토스트
21	**sandwich**	[sǽndwitʃ] n.	샌드위치
22	**hot dog**	[hɑ́t dɔ(ː)g] n.	핫도그
23	**fried egg**	[fraid ég] n.	계란 후라이
24	**bacon**	[béikən] n.	베이컨
25	**sausage**	[sɔ́ːsidʒ] n.	소시지
26	**margarine**	[mɑ́ːrdʒərin] n.	마가린
27	**butter**	[bʌ́tər] n.	버터
28	**cheese**	[tʃíːz] n.	치즈

Food

···▸ **Spicy curry and rice in this restaurant is the best.**
　　이 레스토랑의 매콤한 카레라이스는 최고입니다.

···▸ **How would you like the steak?**
　　스테이크는 어느 정도로 해 드릴까요?

···▸ **Well-done, please.**
　　바싹 익혀주세요.

···▸ **What is today's special?**
　　오늘의 특별요리는 무엇입니까?

···▸ **Could you bring me a house salad?**
　　샐러드를 가져다 주시겠습니까?

＊ find	발견하다 / 찾아내다 / 알아내다
＊ flag	깃발
＊ flash	번쩍이다
＊ flat	납작한 / (타이어)구멍난
＊ flight	비행(기)
＊ float	띄우다 / 뜨다
＊ flow	흐르다
＊ foe	적 / 원수
＊ fold	접다
＊ follow	따르다
＊ food	음식
＊ foolish	어리석은

6 Health & Disease

P·a·r·t 049 Health

건강

A
- fever
- nutrition
- digestion
- breath
- absorption
- tear
- blood pressure

B
- sanitation
- cough
- dizziness
- feel dizzy
- disgusting
- healthy
- weak

C
- sweat
- pulse
- feces
- urine
- pass gas
- constipation

D
- have a sore throat
- have (catch) a cold
- have a flu
- have an injection (shot)
- have a bloody nose
- have a runny nose

#	영어	발음	한글
1	**fever**	[fíːvər] n.	열 / 열병
2	**nutrition**	[njuːtríʃən] n.	영양
3	**digestion**	[didʒéstʃən] n.	소화
4	**breath**	[breθ] n.	호흡
5	**absorption**	[æbsɔ́ːrpʃən] n.	흡수
6	**tear**	[tiər] n.	눈물
7	**blood pressure**	[blʌd préʃər] n.	혈압
8	**sanitation**	[sænətéiʃən] n.	위생
9	**cough**	[kɔ(ː)f] n.	기침
10	**dizziness**	[dizinis] a.	현기증
11	**feel dizzy**	[fiːl dizi]	현기증이 나다
12	**disgusting**	[disɡʌ́stiŋ] a.	메스꺼운
13	**healthy**	[hélθi] a.	건강한
14	**weak**	[wiːk] a.	약한
15	**sweat**	[swet] n.	땀
16	**pulse**	[pʌls] n.	맥
17	**feces**	[fíːsiːz] n.	대변
18	**urine**	[júərin] n.	소변
19	**pass gas**	[pæs ɡæs] n.	방귀
20	**constipation**	[kɑ̀nstəpéiʃən] n.	변비
21	**have a sore throat**	[hævə sɔːr θrout]	목이 아프다
22	**have (catch) a cold**	[hævə kould]	감기에 걸리다
23	**have a flu**	[hævə fluː]	독감에 걸리다
24	**have an injection(shot)**	[hævən indʒékʃən] ([ʃɑt])	주사를 맞다
25	**have a bloody nose**	[hævə blʌ́di nouz]	코피 나다
26	**have a runny nose**	[hævə rʌ́ni nouz]	콧물 흘리다

- He is very sensitive to the cold(heat).
  그는 추위(더위)를 잘 탑니다.
- It contains enough nutrition.
  이것은 영양이 충분히 포함되어 있습니다.
- Her blood pressure is getting higher.
  그녀의 혈압이 점점 올라갑니다.
- I try to stay healthy.
  저는 건강을 유지하려고 노력합니다.
- My friend had the flu.
  내 친구는 심한 독감에 걸렸습니다.
- I felt dizzy when I stood up suddenly.
  갑자기 일어서자 현기증이 났습니다.

*	force	힘 / 세력
*	form	형성하다
*	fortunately	다행히도
*	fortune	재산 / 행운
*	found	설립하다
*	frame	뼈대 / 구조
*	frankly	솔직하게
*	free	자유로운 / 한가한 / 공짜의
*	fresh	신선한
*	friend	친구
*	fry	튀기다
*	fun	즐거운 생각 / 장난

Part 050 Disease 질병

A
- symptom
- scar
- vomiting
- fracture
- headache
- high blood pressure
- burn

B
- diabetes
- heart disease
- heart attack
- stroke
- cancer
- lung cancer
- asthma

C
- diarrhea
- chicken pox
- measles
- athlete's foot
- allergy
- obesity
- morning sickness

D
- hiccups
- chill
- bruise
- bleeding
- overwork
- stress
- cavity

#	영어	발음	뜻
1	**symptom**	[símptəm] n.	증상
2	**scar**	[skɑːr] n.	상처
3	**vomiting**	[vɔ́mitiŋ] n.	구토
4	**fracture**	[frǽktʃər] n.	골절
5	**headache**	[hédèik] n.	두통
6	**high blood pressure**	[hai blʌd préʃər] n.	고혈압
7	**burn**	[bəːrn] n.	화상
8	**diabetes**	[dàiəbíːtiz] n.	당뇨병
9	**heart disease**	[hɑːrt dizíːz] n.	심장병
10	**heart attack**	[hɑːrt ətǽk] n.	심장 발작
11	**stroke**	[strouk] n.	뇌졸중
12	**cancer**	[kǽnsər] n.	암
13	**lung cancer**	[lʌŋ kǽnsər] n.	폐암
14	**asthma**	[ǽzmə] n.	천식
15	**diarrhea**	[dàiəríːə] n.	설사
16	**chicken pox**	[tʃikin pɑks] n.	수두
17	**measles**	[míːzlz] n.	홍역
18	**athlete's foot**	[ǽθliːts fut] n.	무좀
19	**allergy**	[ǽlərdʒi] n.	알레르기
20	**obesity**	[oubíːsəti] n.	비만
21	**morning sickness**	[mɔ́ːrniŋ síknis] n.	입덧
22	**hiccups**	[híkʌps] n.	딸꾹질
23	**chill**	[tʃil] n.	오한
24	**bruise**	[bruːz] n.	멍
25	**bleeding**	[blíːdiŋ] n.	출혈
26	**overwork**	[òuvərwə́ːrk] n.	과로
27	**stress**	[stres] n.	스트레스
28	**cavity**	[kǽvəti] n.	썩은 이빨

- Finally I recovered from the severe flu.
  마침내 지독한 독감이 나았습니다.
- My son is suffering from a high fever.
  아들이 고열에 시달리고 있습니다.
- I had an operation in the hospital.
  병원에서 수술을 받았습니다.
- Thanks to the medicine, I could have sleep soundly.
  약 덕분에 푹 잘 수 있었습니다.
- She got over the disease, but still suffers somewhat from the aftermath.
  그녀는 병은 이겨냈지만 여전히 얼마간의 후유증에 시달리고 있습니다.

swollen	[swóulən] a.	부어오른
itchy	[ítʃi] a.	가려운
stomach ulcer	[stʌ́mək ʌ́lsər] n.	위궤양
rash	[ræʃ] n.	발진, 뾰루지
pneumonia	[njumóunjə] n.	폐렴
gastric cancer	[gǽstrik kǽnsər] n.	위암
gastritis	[gætráitis] n.	위염
tuberculosis	[tjubərkjəlóusis] n.	결핵
sequela	[sikwíːlə] n.	후유증
vomit/throw up	[vɔ́mit]/[θrou ʌp] v.	구토하다
the handicapped	[ðə hǽndikæpt] n.	장애인
the blind	[ðə blaind] n.	장님
suppuration	[sʌ̀pjəréiʃən] n.	화농
sunburn	[sʌ́nbə̀ːrn] n.	(햇볕에) 탐

Part 051 Hospital

병원 1

A
- clinic
- patient
- hospital gown
- drug
- medicine
- ointment
- vitamins

B
- medical check-up
- medical examination
- blood test
- physical therapy
- operation
- shot / injection
- blood type

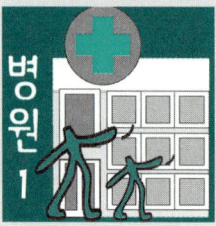

C
- bandage
- sling
- cast
- disinfection
- treatment
- narcotism
- X-rays

D
- nasal spray
- heating pad
- ice pack
- visit a sick person
- enter a hospital
- leave the hospital
- examine

Part 6

#	Word	Pronunciation	Meaning
1	clinic	[klínik] n.	개인(전문)병원
2	patient	[péiʃənt] n.	환자
3	hospital gown	[háspitl gaun] n.	환자복
4	drug	[drʌg] n.	약
5	medicine	[médəsən] n.	(주로) 내복약
6	ointment	[ɔ́intmənt] n.	연고
7	vitamins	[váitəminz] n.	비타민제
8	medical check-up	[médikəl tʃekʌp] n.	건강 진단
9	medical examination	[médikəl igzæmənéiʃən] n	검사
10	blood test	[blʌd test] n.	피검사
11	physical therapy	[físikəl θérəpi] n.	물리치료
12	operation	[àpəréiʃən] n.	수술
13	shot/injection	[ʃat]/[indʒékʃən] n.	주사
14	blood type	[blʌd taip] n.	혈액형
15	bandage	[bǽndidʒ] n.	붕대
16	sling	[sliŋ] n.	어깨에 맨 붕대
17	cast	[kæst] n.	기브스
18	disinfection	[dìsinfékʃən] n.	소독
19	treatment	[tríːtmənt] n.	치료
20	narcotism	[náːrkətìzəm] n.	마취
21	X-rays	[eks reiz] n.	엑스레이
22	nasal spray	[néizəl sprei] n.	코 스프레이
23	heating pad	[híːtiŋ pæd] n.	열 패드
24	ice pack	[ais pæk] n.	얼음주머니
25	visit a sick person	[vízitə sik páːrsən] v.	문병가다
26	enter a hospital	[éntərə háspitl] v.	입원하다
27	leave the hospital	[liːvə háspitl] v.	퇴원하다
28	examine	[igzǽmin] v.	검사하다 / 진찰하다

Health & Disease

⋯ I left the hospital.
병원에서 퇴원했습니다.

⋯ My blood type is A.
나의 혈액형은 A형입니다.

⋯ He was conveyed to the emergency room in an ambulance.
구급차로 응급실에 실려 갔습니다.

⋯ What is the room number at the hospital?
병실은 몇 호실입니까?

⋯ She keeps entering and leaving the hospital.
계속 입원과 퇴원을 반복했습니다.

✽	function	기능
✽	fund	자금 / 기금
✽	furious	성난 / 격노한
✽	gain	얻다 / 획득하다
✽	gap	틈 / 차이 / 간격
✽	garbage	(부엌) 쓰레기
✽	gate	대문
✽	gather	모으다 / 모이다
✽	gay	명랑한 / 즐거운
✽	generally	일반적으로
✽	genuine	진짜의
✽	get	얻다 / ~의 상태가 되다

Part 052 Hospital

병원 2

A
- pharmacy
- pharmacist
- medical insurance
- health insurance
- medical chart
- prescription

B
- plastic surgery
- counseling
- internal medicine
- surgery
- pediatrics
- oriental medicine
- oriental medicine doctor

C
- liquid medicine
- powder
- tablet
- pill
- capsule
- eye-drops
- cough syrup

D
- sleeping pill
- painkiller
- ward
- ambulance
- emergency room
- delivery room
- wheelchair

1	**pharmacy**	[fáːrməsi] n.	약국
2	**pharmacist**	[fáːrməsist] n.	약사
3	**medical insurance**	[médikəl inʃúrəns] n.	의료보험
4	**health insurance**	[helθinʃúrəns] n.	건강보험
5	**medical chart**	[médikəl tʃɑːrt] n.	진료차트
6	**prescription**	[priskrípʃən] n.	처방전
7	**plastic surgery**	[plǽstik sə́ːrdʒəri] n.	성형외과
8	**counseling**	[káunsəliŋ] n.	정신과 상담
9	**internal medicine**	[intə́ːrnl médəsən] n.	내과
10	**surgery**	[sə́ːrdʒəri] n.	외과
11	**pediatrics**	[pìːdiǽtriks] n.	소아과
12	**oriental medicine**	[ɔ̀ːriéntl médəsən] n.	한방약
13	**oriental medicine doctor**	[ɔ̀ːriéntl médəsən daktər] n.	한의사
14	**liquid medicine**	[líkwid médəsən] n.	물약
15	**powder**	[páudər] n.	가루약
16	**tablet**	[tǽblit] n.	정제
17	**pill**	[pil] n.	알약
18	**capsule**	[kǽpsjul] n.	캡슐
19	**eye-drops**	[ai drɑps] n.	안약
20	**cough syrup**	[kɔ(ː)f sírəp] n.	감기약
21	**sleeping pill**	[slíːpiŋ pil] n.	수면제
22	**painkiller**	[péinkilər] n.	진통제
23	**ward**	[wɔːrd] n.	병실, 병동
24	**ambulance**	[ǽmbjuləns] n.	구급차
25	**emergency room**	[imə́ːrdʒənsi ruːm] n.	응급실
26	**delivery room**	[dilívəri ruːm] n.	분만실
27	**wheelchair**	[hwíːltʃɛər] n.	휠체어

⋯ She can't sleep without sleeping pills.
그녀는 수면제 없이는 잠을 못 이룹니다.

⋯ Where is the ramp for wheelchairs?
휠체어를 위한 경사로가 어디 있습니까?

⋯ I received a prescription from the doctor.
의사에게서 처방전을 받았습니다.

⋯ I went to an oriental medicine doctor to have my sprained ankle treated.
삔 발목을 치료하기 위해 한의사에게 갔습니다.

⋯ Mom put a bandage on my finger.
엄마가 손가락에 반창고를 붙여주었습니다.

* **dermatology**	[də̀ːrmətálədʒi] n.	피부과
* **ophthalmology**	[àfθəlmálədʒi] n.	안과
* **gynecology**	[gàinikálədʒi] n.	부인과
* **orthopedics**	[ɔ̀ːrθoupíːdiks] n.	정형외과
* **neurology**	[njuərálədʒi] n.	신경과

7 Education

P·a·r·t 053 Education

교육

A
- student
- teacher
- study abroad
- enter the school
- graduate from school
- drop out of school
- join a club

B
- kindergarten/pre-school
- elementary school
- middle school
- high school
- two-year college
- university
- graduate school

C
- cram school
- child-care facilities
- academy/institute
- foreign languages school
- lifelong education
- teaching method

D
- entrance ceremony
- graduation ceremony
- bachelor's degree
- master's degree
- doctorate
- professor
- instructor

1	student	[stjúːdənt] n.	학생
2	teacher	[tíːtʃər] n.	선생님
3	study abroad	[stʌ́di əbrɔ́ːd] v.	유학하다
4	enter the school	[éntər ðə skuːl] v.	입학하다
5	graduate from school	[grǽdʒuèit frʌm skuːl] v.	졸업하다
6	drop out of school	[drɑp autəv skuːl] v.	중퇴하다
7	join a club	[dʒɔinə klʌb] v.	서클에 가입하다
8	kindergarten/pre-school	[kíndərgàːrtn] / [pri skuːl] n.	유치원
9	elementary school	[èləméntəri skuːl] n.	초등학교
10	middle school	[mídl skuːl] n.	중학교
11	high school	[hai skuːl] n.	고등학교
12	two-year college	[tuːjiər kɑ́lidʒ] n.	전문학교
13	university	[jùːnəvə́ːrsəti] n.	대학교
14	graduate school	[grǽdʒuət skuːl] n.	대학원
15	cram school	[kræm skuːl] n.	입시학원
16	child-care facilities	[tʃaildkɛər fəsílətiz] n.	보육원
17	academy/institute	[əkǽdəmi] / [ínstətjùːt] n.	학원
18	foreign languages school	[fɔ́(ː)rin lǽŋgwidʒz skuːl] n.	어학원
19	lifelong education	[láiflɔ̀(ː)ŋ èdʒukéiʃən] n.	평생교육
20	teaching method	[tíːtʃiŋ méθəd] n.	교수법
21	entrance ceremony	[éntrəns sérəmòuni] n.	입학식
22	graduation ceremony	[grædʒuéiʃən sérəmòuni] n.	졸업식
23	bachelor's degree	[bǽtʃələrz digríː] n.	학사학위
24	master's degree	[mǽstərz digríː] n.	석사학위
25	doctorate	[dɑ́ktərit] n.	박사학위
26	professor	[prəfésər] n.	교수
27	instructor	[instrʌ́ktər] n.	강사

Part 7

Education

⋯▶ Are you preparing for studying abroad?
유학 준비를 하고 있습니까?

⋯▶ I've been to my daughter's graduation ceremony in high school.
딸의 고등학교 졸업식에 다녀왔습니다.

⋯▶ I send my son to a music academy after school.
저는 방과 후에 아이를 음악학원에 보내고 있습니다.

⋯▶ My dream is to teach English at a university.
제 꿈은 대학에서 영어를 가르치는 것입니다.

⋯▶ I went to the same high school with her.
우리는 고등학교 동창입니다.

✽ giant	거인
✽ gift	선물 / 재능
✽ give	주다
✽ glory	영광
✽ good	좋은 / 잘하는
✽ grace	우아함 / 품위
✽ gradual	점차적인
✽ grammar	문법
✽ grand	웅장한 / 위대한
✽ grant	승인하다 / 주다
✽ grateful	고마워하는
✽ great	큰 / 위대한 / 멋진

Part 054 School 학교

A
- grade
- credit
- semester/term
- major in
- minor in
- double major
- sign up for a class

B
- freshman
- sophomore
- junior
- senior
- classmate
- graduate
- dropout

C
- school cafeteria
- classroom
- library
- gym
- dormitory
- auditorium
- playground

D
- school reunion
- alumni
- Foundation Day
- college entrance exam
- on-campus
- off-campus
- bullying

#	Word	Pronunciation	Meaning
1	grade	[greid] n.	학년
2	credit	[krédit] n.	학점
3	semester/term	[siméstər]/[təːrm] n.	학기
4	major in	[méidʒər in] v.	전공하다
5	minor in	[máəinər in] v.	부전공하다
6	double major	[dʌ́bl méidʒər] n.	복수전공
7	sign up for a class	[sainʌp fərə klæs] v.	수강신청하다
8	freshman	[fréʃmən] n.	대학 1학년
9	sophomore	[sáfəmɔ̀ːr] n.	대학 2학년
10	junior	[dʒúːnjər] n.	3학년 / 후배
11	senior	[síːnjər] n.	4학년 / 선배
12	classmate	[klǽsmèit] n.	반 친구(급우)
13	graduate	[grǽdʒuit] n.	졸업생
14	dropout	[drápaut] n.	중퇴자
15	school cafeteria	[skuːl kæ̀fitíəriə] n.	식당
16	classroom	[klǽsrù(ː)m] n.	교실
17	library	[láibrèri] n.	도서관
18	gym	[dʒim] n.	체육관
19	dormitory	[dɔ́ːrmətɔ̀ːri] n.	기숙사
20	auditorium	[ɔ̀ːditɔ́ːriəm] n.	강당
21	playground	[pléigràund] n.	운동장 / 놀이터
22	school reunion	[skuːl riːjúːnjən] n.	동창회
23	alumni	[əlʌ́mnai] n.	동창생
24	Foundation Day	[faundéiʃən dei] n.	개교기념일
25	college entrance exam	[kálidʒ éntrəns igzǽm] n.	대입시험
26	on-campus	[ɔn kǽmpəs] a.	학교내부의
27	off-campus	[ɔf kǽmpəs] a.	학교외부의
28	bullying	[búliŋ] n.	괴롭힘, 이지메

⋯▸ We're going to have winter vacation soon.
　　겨울방학이 막 시작될 겁니다.

⋯▸ I stay in a dormitory.
　　저는 기숙사에 살고 있습니다.

⋯▸ My sister passed the college entrance exam.
　　언니는 대학 입학시험에 합격했습니다.

⋯▸ How is the food in the university cafeteria?
　　대학식당의 음식은 어떻습니까?

⋯▸ I go to English academy to learn speaking fluently.
　　저는 유창하게 영어를 말하고 싶어서 영어학원에 다니고 있습니다.

✽ **teasing**	[tíːziŋ] n.	장난
✽ **academic**	[ækədémik] a.	대학의 / 학구적인
✽ **spring vacation**	[spriŋ veikéiʃən] n.	봄방학
✽ **summer vacation**	[sʌ́mər veikéiʃən] n.	여름방학
✽ **winter vacation**	[wíntər veikéiʃən] n.	겨울방학

Part 055 Academic Subjects
교과목 / 학문

A
- English
- Korean
- Mathematics
- History
- Ethics
- Physical education
- Chinese character

B
- Literature
- Economics
- Education
- Philosophy
- Psychology
- Anthropology
- Business administration

C
- Science
- Chemistry
- Biology
- Physics
- Genetics
- Medical Science
- astronomy

D
- Fine art
- Music
- Sociology
- scholar
- discovery
- invention
- research

#	English	Pronunciation	Korean
1	English	[íŋgliʃ] n.	영어
2	Korean	[kəríːən] n.	국어
3	Mathematics	[mæθəmǽtiks] n.	수학
4	History	[hístəri] n.	역사
5	Ethics	[éθiks] n.	윤리
6	Physical education	[fízikəl èdʒukéiʃən] n.	체육
7	Chinese character	[tʃainíːz kǽriktər] n.	한자
8	Literature	[lítərətʃər] n.	문학
9	Economics	[ìːkənámiks] n.	경제학
10	Education	[èdʒukèiʃən] n.	교육학
11	Philosophy	[filásəfi] n.	철학
12	Psychology	[saikálədʒi] n.	심리학
13	Anthropology	[ænθrəpálədʒi] n.	인류학
14	Business administration	[bíznis ædmìnəstréiʃən] n.	경영학
15	Science	[sáiəns] n.	과학
16	Chemistry	[kémistri] n.	화학
17	Biology	[baiálədʒi] n.	생물
18	Physics	[fíziks] n.	물리학
19	Genetics	[dʒinétiks] n.	유전학
20	Medical Science	[médikəl sáiəns] n.	의학
21	astronomy	[əstránəmi] n.	천문학
22	Fine art	[fain ɑːrt] n.	미술
23	Music	[mjúːzik] n.	음악
24	Sociology	[sòusiálədʒi] n.	사회학
25	scholar	[skálər] n.	학자
26	discovery	[diskʌ́vəri] n.	발견
27	invention	[invénʃən] n.	발명
28	research	[risə́ːrtʃ] n.	연구

Education

⋯▸ In the end my brother received a master's degree.
　　형은 드디어 석사학위를 땄습니다.
⋯▸ Let's look it up in a dictionary.
　　사전을 찾아봅시다.
⋯▸ There are some ways to solve the problem.
　　문제를 해결하기 위한 몇 가지 방법이 있습니다.
⋯▸ We played soccer during physical education.
　　체육시간에 축구를 했습니다.
⋯▸ I'm majoring in Chemistry.
　　화학을 전공하고 있습니다.
⋯▸ We have a Genetics final test after this.
　　이 시간 끝나고 나서 우리는 유전학 기말 고사가 있습니다.

✼ **physiology**	[fìziálədʒi] n.	생리학
✼ **ecology**	[i:kálədʒi]	생태학
✼ **Korean literature**	[kərí:ən lítərətʃər] n.	국문학
✼ **English literature**	[íŋgliʃ lítərətʃər] n.	영문학
✼ **observe**	[əbzə́:rv] v.	관찰하다
✼ **scientific**	[sàiəntífik] a.	과학의 / 과학적인
✼ **develop**	[divéləp] v.	개발하다
✼ **dictionary**	[díkʃənèri] n.	사전
✼ **ability**	[əbíləti] n.	능력
✼ **goal/aim**	[goul] / [eim] n.	목표
✼ **method**	[méθəd] n.	방법
✼ **knowledge**	[nálidʒ] n.	지식
✼ **effort**	[éfərt] n.	노력
✼ **talent/gift**	[tǽlənt] / [gift] n.	재능
✼ **genius**	[dʒí:njəs] n.	천재
✼ **devise**	[diváiz] v.	고안하다
✼ **investigate**	[invéstəgèit] v.	조사하다 / 연구하다
✼ **understand**	[ʌ̀ndərstǽnd] v.	이해하다

Part 056 History 역사

A
- culture
- civilization
- anthropology
- archaeology
- historical
- situation

B
- development
- preservation
- change
- maintenance
- improvement
- leave one's mark

C
- period
- the Middle Ages
- the modern times
- the present times
- the ancient times
- remains

D
- the first World War
- Cold War
- prosperity
- inheritance
- destruction
- collapse
- fighting

1	culture	[kʌ́ltʃər] n.	문화
2	civilization	[sìvəlizéiʃən] n.	문명
3	anthropology	[æ̀nθrəpálədʒi] n.	인류학
4	archaeology	[à:rkiálədʒi] n.	고고학
5	historical	[histɔ́(:)rikəl] a.	역사학적인
6	situation	[sìtʃuéiʃən] n.	상황
7	development	[divéləpmənt] n.	발달
8	preservation	[prèzərvéiʃən] n.	보존
9	change	[tʃeindʒ] n. v.	변화(하다)
10	maintenance	[méintənəns] n.	유지
11	improvement	[imprú:vmənt] n.	개선
12	leave one's mark	[li:v wʌns mɑ:rk] v.	발자취를 남기다
13	period	[píəriəd] n.	시대
14	the Middle Ages	[ðə mídl eidʒz] n.	중세
15	the modern times	[ðə mádə:rn taimz] n.	근대
16	the present times	[ðə prézənt taimz] n.	현대
17	the ancient times	[ði éinʃənt taimz] n.	고대
18	remains	[riméinz] n.	유적
19	the first World War	[ðə fə:rst wə:rld wɔ:r] n.	제 1차 세계대전
20	Cold War	[kould wɔ:r] n.	냉전
21	prosperity	[praspérəti] n.	번영
22	inheritance	[inhèritəns] n.	유산
23	destruction	[distrʌ́kʃən] n.	파멸
24	collapse	[kəlǽps] n. v.	멸망(하다)
25	fighting	[fáitiŋ] n.	투쟁

- We must not forget about our history.
  역사는 잊어서는 안됩니다.
- Don't miss the changes of the period.
  시대의 변화를 놓치지 말 것
- Cultural exchanges among other countries are increasing.
  타국간의 문화교류가 증가되고 있습니다.
- He specialized in Linguistics.
  그는 언어학을 전공했습니다.

✱ greedy	탐욕스러운
✱ greenhouse	온실
✱ grill	그릴에 굽다
✱ ground	운동장
✱ group	단체
✱ hamster	햄스터
✱ handicap	장애
✱ handle	손잡이 / 처리하다
✱ handshake	악수
✱ hang	매달다 / 걸다

Part 057 Classes 수업

A
- class teacher
- class monitor
- attendance
- absence
- homework
- preview
- review

B
- tuitions and fees
- scholarship
- quiz
- mid-term
- final
- do good on the exam
- fail in an exam

C
- write an essay
- attend a class
- skip a class
- pass the test
- be late for class
- leave earlier
- transfer to a school

D
- lecture
- thesis
- textbook
- reference book
- report card
- club activity
- after school

#	English	Pronunciation	Korean
1	class teacher	[klæs tíːtʃər] n.	담임 선생님
2	class monitor	[klæs mánitər] n.	반장
3	attendance	[əténdəns] n.	출석
4	absence	[ǽbsəns] n.	결석
5	homework	[hóumwə̀rk] n.	숙제
6	preview	[príːvjùː] n.	예습
7	review	[rivjúː] n.	복습
8	tuitions and fees	[tjuːíʃənz æn fiːz] n.	수업료
9	scholarship	[skálərʃìp] n.	장학금
10	quiz	[kwiz] n.	쪽지 시험
11	mid-term	[mid təːrm] n.	중간고사
12	final	[fáinəl] n.	기말고사
13	do good on the exam	[du gud ən ði igzǽm] v.	시험을 잘 치르다
14	fail in an exam	[feilin ən igzǽm] v.	시험을 실패하다
15	write an essay	[rait ən ései] v.	레포트를 쓰다
16	attend a class	[əténdə klæs] v.	출석하다
17	skip a class	[skipə klæs] v.	수업을 빼먹다
18	pass the test	[pæs ðə test] v.	합격하다
19	be late for class	[bi leit fəːr klæs] v.	지각하다
20	leave earlier	[liːv ə́ːrliər] v.	조퇴하다
21	transfer to a school	[trǽsfər tu ə skuːl] v.	전학가다
22	lecture	[léktʃəːr] n.	강의
23	thesis	[θíːsis] n.	논문
24	textbook	[tékstbùk] n.	교과서
25	reference book	[réfərəns buk] n.	참고서
26	report card	[ripɔ́ːrt kɑːrd] n.	성적표
27	club activity	[klʌb æktívəti] n.	클럽활동
28	after school	[ǽftər skuːl] ad.	방과 후

⋯▶ History class is still going on in the classroom.
　　교실에서는 여전히 역사 수업이 진행되고 있습니다.

⋯▶ When do I have to summit the report?
　　레포트는 언제까지 내면 됩니까?

⋯▶ I'm very happy to get a good score on an exam.
　　시험에서 좋은 점수를 받아서 무척 기쁩니다.

⋯▶ You should brush up on the subject little by little everyday.
　　매일 조금씩 복습해야만 합니다.

⋯▶ What is your major ?
　　당신의 전공은 무엇입니까?

✻ required subject	[rikwáiərd sʌ́bdʒikt] n.	필수과목
✻ concentrate	[kánsəntrèit] v.	집중하다
✻ teach	[tiːtʃ] v.	가르치다
✻ absent	[ǽbsənt] a.	결석한 / 없는
✻ submission	[səbmíʃən] n.	제출
✻ scholarship recipient	[skálərʃip risípiənt] n.	장학생
✻ syllabus	[síləbəs] n.	강의 계획표
✻ teachers' room	[tíːtʃərz ruːm] n.	교무실

Part 058 Mathematics
수학

A
- circle
- line
- angle
- triangle
- square
- rectangle
- oval

B
- add
- subtract
- multiply
- divide
- concept
- vertical
- horizontal

C
- amount
- account
- score points
- statistics
- distribution
- mental calculation
- ratio

D
- solve
- fraction
- quarter
- one third
- half
- two thirds
- calculate

1	**circle**	[sə́ːrkl] n.	원
2	**line**	[lain] n.	선
3	**angle**	[ǽŋgl] n.	각
4	**triangle**	[tráiæ̀ŋgl] n.	삼각형
5	**square**	[skwɛəːr] n.	정사각형
6	**rectangle**	[réktæ̀ŋgl] n.	직사각형
7	**oval**	[óuvəl] n.	타원형
8	**add**	[æd] v.	더하다
9	**subtract**	[səbtrǽkt] v.	빼다
10	**multiply**	[mʌ́ltəplài] v.	곱하다
11	**divide**	[diváid] v.	나누다
12	**concept**	[kánsept] n.	개념
13	**vertical**	[və́ːrtikəl] a.	수직의
14	**horizontal**	[hɔ̀ːrəzántl] n.	수평의
15	**amount**	[əmáunt] n.	양 / 총계
16	**account**	[əkáunt] n.	계산
17	**score points**	[skɔːr pɔints] n.	채점하다
18	**statistics**	[stətítiks] n.	통계
19	**distribution**	[dìtrəbjúːʃən] n.	분포
20	**mental calculation**	[méntl kæ̀lkjuléiʃən] n.	암산
21	**ratio**	[réiʃou] n.	비율
22	**solve**	[salv] vt.	풀다 / 해결하다
23	**fraction**	[frǽkʃən] n.	(수학) 분수
24	**quarter**	[kwɔ́ːrtər] n.	4분의 1
25	**one third**	[wʌn θəːrd] n.	3분의 1
26	**half**	[hæf] n.	2분의 1
27	**two thirds**	[tuː θə́ːrdz] n.	3분의 2
28	**calculate**	[kǽlkjulèit] v.	계산하다

Education

⋯▸ I am poor at mathematics.
　　저는 수학을 못합니다.
⋯▸ More than half of the students passed the test.
　　학생 과반수가 시험에 통과했습니다.
⋯▸ A triangle shape has three straight lines and three angles.
　　삼각형은 세 개의 선과 세 개의 각을 갖습니다.
⋯▸ Seven is an odd number.
　　7은 홀수입니다.
⋯▸ What is the rectangular thing for over there?
　　저쪽에 있는 직사각형 물건은 무슨 용도로 쓰입니까?

✻ harbor	항구
✻ hard	어려운 / 단단한
✻ hardly	거의 ~않다
✻ harmful	해로운
✻ harsh	거친
✻ hastily	서둘러서
✻ have	가지다
✻ hay	건초
✻ hear	듣다
✻ helpful	도움이 되는 / 유익한
✻ herb	풀잎 / 약초
✻ hero	영웅

⑧ Economics, Business, Media & Government Institutions

Part 059 Economy
경제

A
- production
- technology
- demand
- supply
- consumption
- expenditure
- cost of living

B
- enterprise
- depression
- prosperity
- profit
- goods
- income
- payment

C
- capital
- discount
- labor
- quality
- subcontract
- wholesale
- retail sale

D
- bargain
- deal
- compete
- fail
- succeed
- produce
- waste

#			
1	**production**	[prədʌ́kʃən] n.	생산
2	**technology**	[teknálədʒi] n.	과학기술
3	**demand**	[dimǽnd] n.	수요
4	**supply**	[səplái] n.	공급
5	**consumption**	[kənsʌ́mpʃən] n.	소비
6	**expenditure**	[ikspéndit∫ər] n.	지출
7	**cost of living**	[kɔːst ɔv líviŋ] n.	물가
8	**enterprise**	[éntərpràiz] n.	기업
9	**depression**	[dipréʃən] n.	불경기
10	**prosperity**	[prɑspérəti] n.	호황
11	**profit**	[prɑ́fit] n.	이익
12	**goods**	[gudz] n.	상품
13	**income**	[íŋkʌm] n.	수입 / 소득
14	**payment**	[péimənt] n.	지불
15	**capital**	[kǽpitl] n.	자본
16	**discount**	[dískaunt] n.	할인
17	**labor**	[léibər] n.	노동
18	**quality**	[kwɑ́ləti] n.	품질 / 질
19	**subcontract**	[sʌbkɑ́ntrækt] n.	하청
20	**wholesale**	[hóulsèil] n.	도매
21	**retail sale**	[ríːteil seil] n.	소매
22	**bargain**	[bɑ́ːrgən] n. v.	흥정(하다)
23	**deal**	[diːl] v.	거래(하다)
24	**compete**	[kəmpíːt] vi.	경쟁하다
25	**fail**	[feil] v.	실패하다
26	**succeed**	[səksíːd] v.	성공하다
27	**produce**	[prədjúːs] v.	생산하다 / 제작하다
28	**waste**	[weist] n. v.	낭비(하다)

- There is more supply than demand.
  수요에 비해 공급이 너무 많습니다.
- How would you like to pay?
  지불은 어떻게 하시겠습니까?
- We broke off business relations with that company.
  그 회사와의 거래를 끊었습니다.
- Import companies must mark the place of origin on their products.
  수입 상사들은 상품에 반드시 원산지 표시를 해야 합니다.
- The cost of living in Seoul is on the increase.
  서울의 물가는 계속 상승중입니다.

✱ **needy**	[níːdi]	a.	매우 가난한
✱ **poor**	[puər]	a.	가난한
✱ **wealthy/rich**	[wélθi]/[ritʃ]	a.	부유한
✱ **spend**	[spend]	v.	쓰다 / 보내다
✱ **successful**	[səksésfəl]	a.	성공한
✱ **success**	[səksés]	n.	성공
✱ **failure**	[féiljər]	n.	실패

Part 060 Business

비즈니스

A
- work
- value
- deficit
- surplus
- organization
- sold-out
- bankrupt

B
- investment
- transaction
- business partner
- supplier
- distributor
- debt
- monopoly

C
- regular price
- high price
- employer
- employee
- receipt
- changes
- structure

D
- system
- go into bankruptcy
- corporation
- product
- guest
- customer
- income and expenditure

Part 8

#	Word	Pronunciation	Meaning
1	work	[wəːrk] n.	일
2	value	[vǽljuː] n.	가치
3	deficit	[défəsit] n.	적자
4	surplus	[sə́ːrplʌs] n.	흑자
5	organization	[ɔ̀ːrgənizéiʃən] n.	조직
6	sold-out	[souldaut] n.	매진
7	bankrupt	[bǽŋkrʌpt] n. a.	파산자, 파산한
8	investment	[invéstmənt] n.	투자
9	transaction	[trænsǽkʃən] n.	거래
10	business partner	[bíznis páːrtnər] n.	거래처
11	supplier	[səpláiər] n.	공급자
12	distributor	[distríbjutər] n.	유통업자
13	debt	[det] n.	부채
14	monopoly	[mənápəli] n.	독점
15	regular price	[régjulər prais] n.	정가
16	high price	[hai prais] n.	고가
17	employer	[emplɔ́iər] n.	고용주
18	employee	[implɔiíː] n.	종업원
19	receipt	[risíːt] n.	영수증
20	changes	[tʃeindʒiz] n.	거스름돈
21	structure	[strʌ́ktʃər] n.	구조
22	system	[sístəm] n.	제도
23	go into bankruptcy	[gou intu bǽŋkrʌptsi] v.	도산하다
24	corporation	[kɔ̀ːrpəréiʃən] n.	주식회사
25	product	[prádəkt] n.	상품
26	guest	[gest] n.	손님
27	customer	[kʌ́stəmər] n.	단골손님
28	income and expenditure	[íŋkʌm ən ikspénditʃər] n.	수지

Economics, Business

⋯ Could you give me a discounted rate?
   가격을 좀 깎아줄 수 있습니까?
⋯ There are various kinds of products in the shop.
   이 가게에는 다양한 종류의 상품이 있습니다.
⋯ This bar has many regular customers.
   이 술집은 단골손님들이 많습니다.
⋯ Mom buys clothes at a department store only when they're on sale.
   엄마는 세일 기간 중에만 백화점에서 옷을 삽니다.
⋯ Let's go forward without worrying about failure.
   실패를 두려워하지 말고, 힘냅시다.
⋯ The products sold out quickly.
   그 제품은 금방 매진되었습니다.

∗ **on sale**	[ɔn seil] n.	세일 중
∗ **purchase**	[pə́ːrtʃəs] n. vt.	구입(하다)
∗ **merchant**	[mə́ːrtʃənt] n.	상인
∗ **sell**	[sel] v.	팔다
∗ **have a great success in life**	[hævə greit səksés in laif] v.	출세하다
∗ **choose**	[tʃuːz] v.	고르다 / 선택하다
∗ **cheap**	[tʃiːp] a.	싼
∗ **expensive**	[ikspénsiv] a.	비싼

Part 061 Company 회사1

A
- headquarter
- branch
- chairman
- president
- secretary
- manager
- assistant manager

B
- director
- executive
- overtime
- meeting
- day off
- merger
- stock

C
- bonus/allowance
- payday
- stockholder
- work place
- labor union
- seniority system

D
- go to work
- finish the work
- go on a business trip
- get a job
- leave the office
- get a raise
- retire

#	Word	Pronunciation	Meaning
1	headquarter	[hédkwɔ̀ːrtər] n.	본사
2	branch	[brætʃ] n.	지사
3	chairman	[tʃɛ́əmən] n.	회장
4	president	[prézidənt] n.	사장
5	secretary	[sékrətèri] n.	비서
6	manager	[mǽnidʒər] n.	과장
7	assistant manager	[əsístənt mǽnidʒər] n.	대리
8	director	[diréktər] n.	중역 임원
9	executive	[igzékjutiv] n.	간부급
10	overtime	[óuvərtàim] n.	잔업
11	meeting	[míːtiŋ] n.	회의
12	day off	[dei ɔf] n.	휴가
13	merger	[mə́ːrdʒər] n.	합병
14	stock	[stɑk] n.	주식
15	bonus/allowance	[bóunəs]/[əláuəns] n.	보너스 / 수당
16	payday	[péidèi] n.	월급날
17	stockholder	[stɑ́khòuldər] n.	주주
18	work place	[wəːrk pleis] n.	직장
19	labor union	[léibər júːnjən] n.	노동조합
20	seniority system	[siːnjɔ́ːrəti sístəm] n.	연공서열
21	go to work	[gou tə wəːrk] v.	출근하다
22	finish the work	[fíniʃ ðə wəːrk] v.	퇴근하다
23	go on a business trip	[gou ɔn ə bíznis trip] v.	출장가다
24	get a job	[getə dʒɑb] v.	취직하다
25	leave the office	[liːv ðə ɔ́(ː)fis] v.	퇴직하다
26	get a raise	[getə reiz] v.	월급이 오르다
27	retire	[ritáiər] v.	은퇴하다

- I work at a trading company.
  저는 무역회사에 근무하고 있습니다.
- He always finishes work at 6pm.
  그는 항상 오후 6시에 퇴근합니다.
- Can I get paid for the overtime?
  잔업 수당을 받을 수 있나요?
- She's in a meeting now.
  그녀는 지금 회의 중입니다.

✱ hide	숨다 / 숨기다
✱ high	높은 / 비싼
✱ hike	하이킹하다
✱ hint	힌트 / 요령
✱ hold	잡고있다 / 지니다 / 개최하다
✱ hole	구멍
✱ hollow	속이 빈
✱ homesick	향수병에 걸린
✱ honey	꿀
✱ honor	영예
✱ hood	두건
✱ hook	갈고리

Part 062 Company

회사 2

A
- personnel
- managing director
- general manager
- department
- section
- supervisor
- subordinate

B
- tax affairs
- wage/salary
- pension
- promotion
- workaholic
- retirement
- resignation

C
- clerk / junior level
- reception desk
- vice president
- nine-to-five job
- general affairs Dept
- unemployment
- Accounting Dept.

D
- cooperate
- earn
- establish
- employ
- manage
- lay off
- fire
- be in charge of

#	英語	発音	韓国語
1	personnel	[pə̀:rsənél] n.	인사
2	managing director	[mǽnidʒiŋ diréktər] n.	상무
3	general manager	[dʒénərəl mǽnidʒər] n.	부장
4	department	[dipá:rtmənt] n.	부
5	section	[sékʃən] n.	과
6	supervisor	[sú:pərvàizər] n.	상사
7	subordinate	[səbɔ́:rdənit] n.	부하
8	tax affairs	[tæks əfέərz] n.	세무
9	wage/salary	[weidʒ]/[sǽləri] n.	임금
10	pension	[pénʃən] n.	연금
11	promotion	[prəmóuʃən] n.	승진
12	workaholic	[wə̀:rkəhɔ́:lik] n.	일벌레
13	retirement	[ritáiərmənt] n.	은퇴
14	resignation	[rèzignéiʃən] n.	사직
15	clerk/ junior level	[klə:rk]/[dʒú:njər lévəl] n.	평사원
16	reception desk	[risépʃən desk] n.	접수처
17	vice president	[vais prézidənt] n.	부회장
18	nine-to-five job	[nain tu faiv dʒɑb] n.	사무직
19	general affairs Dept.	[dʒénərəl əfέərz dipá:rtmənt] n.	총무과
20	unemployment	[ʌ̀nemplɔ́imənt] n.	실업
21	Accounting Dept.	[əkáuntiŋ dipá:rtmənt] n.	경리과
22	cooperate	[kouápərèit] v.	협력하다 / 협동하다
23	earn	[ə:rn] vt.	벌다
24	establish	[istǽbliʃ] vt.	설립하다
25	employ	[emplɔ́i] vt.	고용하다
26	manage	[mǽnidʒ] v.	경영하다
27	lay off	[lei ɔf] v.	(회사 사정으로)감원되다
28	fire	[faiər] v.	(자신의 잘못으로)해고 당하다
29	be in charge of	[bi in tʃɑ:rdʒ əv] v.	담당하다

- I got promoted thanks to good performance.
  좋은 실적 덕택에 승진했습니다.
- She is in charge of the project.
  그녀가 그 프로젝트 담장자입니다.
- Many people got laid off due to the bad economy.
  많은 사람들이 불경기로 회사에서 해고되었습니다.
- This company was established in 1971.
  이 회사는 1971년에 설립되었습니다.

* horn	뿔
* hot	더운
* how	어떻게 / 얼마나
* howl	(개, 이리) 짖다
* huge	거대한
* human	인간의
* humor	유머
* hurrah	만세
* hurry	서두르다
* hurt	상처내다 / 아프다
* hut	오두막집
* ice	얼음

Part 063 Industry

산업

A
- mining
- coal mine
- vein of ore
- fishing
- fisherman
- fishing boat
- agriculture

B
- farmer
- farm land
- rice farming
- harvest
- rice planting
- agricultural chemicals
- fertilizer

C
- farm
- crop
- forestry
- ranch
- livestock farming
- livestock/domestic animal
- seed

D
- breeding
- orchard
- shipment
- factory
- process
- salt farm
- log

산업

Part 8

#	Word	Pronunciation	Korean
1	**mining**	[máiniŋ] n.	광업
2	**coal mine**	[koul main] n.	탄광
3	**vein of ore**	[vein əv ɔːr] n.	광맥
4	**fishing**	[fíʃiŋ] n.	어업
5	**fisherman**	[fíʃərmən] n.	어부
6	**fishing boat**	[fíʃiŋ bout] n.	어선
7	**agriculture**	[ǽgrikʌ̀ltʃər] n.	농업
8	**farmer**	[fáːrmər] n.	농민
9	**farm land**	[fɑːrm lænd] n.	농경지
10	**rice farming**	[rais fáːrmiŋ] n.	벼농사
11	**harvest**	[háːrvist] n.	추수, 수확
12	**rice planting**	[rais plǽntiŋ] n.	모내기
13	**agricultural chemicals**	[ǽgrikʌ̀ltʃərəl kémikəlz] n.	농약
14	**fertilizer**	[fəːrtəlàizər] n.	비료
15	**farm**	[fɑːrm] n.	농장
16	**crop**	[krɑp] n.	농작물 / 수확
17	**forestry**	[fɔ́(ː)ristri] n.	임업
18	**ranch**	[ræntʃ] n.	목장
19	**livestock farming**	[láivstɑ̀k fáːrmiŋ] n.	축산
20	**livestock/domestic animal**	[láivstɑ̀k] / [douméstik ǽnəməl] n.	가축
21	**seed**	[siːd] n.	종자
22	**breeding**	[bríːdiŋ] n.	양식
23	**orchard**	[ɔ́ːrtʃərd] n.	과수원
24	**shipment**	[ʃípmənt] n.	출하
25	**factory**	[fǽktəri] n.	공장
26	**process**	[práses] v.	가공(하다)
27	**salt farm**	[sɔːlt fɑːrm] n.	염전
28	**log**	[lɔ(ː)g] n.	통나무

Economics, Business

⋯▸ My Dad is a fisherman, and his brother is a farmer.
아빠는 어부이고, 삼촌은 농민입니다.

⋯▸ I used to pick fruit in an orchard for a part-time job in Australia.
호주에 있을 때 아르바이트로 과수원에서 과일을 따곤 했습니다.

⋯▸ It's time for harvest.
추수 시기가 왔습니다.

⋯▸ The coal mine has collapsed suddenly.
탄광이 갑자기 무너졌습니다.

* image	이미지
* immediately	즉시
* important	중요한
* impossible	불가능한
* improve	개선하다 / 나아지다
* include	포함하다
* increase	증가하다
* indeed	정말 / 사실은
* independent	독립적인
* indicate	가리키다 / 나타내다
* individual	개인의 / 개개의
* indoor	집 안의 / 실내의

Part 064 Trade

무역 / 거래

A
- export
- import
- sample
- order
- price
- cost

B
- friction
- customs
- fare
- tax
- estimate
- confiscation

C
- introduction
- commission
- shipping
- exchange rate
- offer
- the time for payment
- claim

D
- smuggling
- freight
- the place of origin
- sales
- inferior goods
- sign a contract

1	**export**	[íkspɔːrt] n.	수출 / 수출품
2	**import**	[ímpɔːrt] n.	수입
3	**sample**	[sǽmpl] n.	견본
4	**order**	[ɔ́ːrdər] n. v.	주문(하다)
5	**price**	[prais] n.	가격
6	**cost**	[kɔːst] n.	비용
7	**friction**	[fríkʃən] n.	마찰
8	**customs**	[kʌ́stəmz] n.	세관
9	**fare**	[fɛər] n.	운임
10	**tax**	[tæks] n.	관세
11	**estimate**	[éstəmèit] n.	견적
12	**confiscation**	[kɑ́nfiskèiʃən] n.	몰수
13	**introduction**	[ìntrədʌ́kʃən] n.	도입
14	**commission**	[kəmíʃən] n.	수수료
15	**shipping**	[ʃípiŋ] n.	선적
16	**exchange rate**	[ikstʃéindʒ reit] n.	환율
17	**offer**	[ɔ́(ː)fər] n.	제의 / 제안
18	**the time for payment**	[ðə taim fɔːr péimənt] n.	납기
19	**claim**	[kleim] v.	클레임
20	**smuggling**	[smʌ́gliŋ] n.	밀수
21	**freight**	[freit] n.	화물
22	**the place of origin**	[ðə pleisəv ɔ́ːrədʒin] n.	원산지
23	**sales**	[seilz] n.	매상
24	**inferior goods**	[infíəríər gudz] n.	불량품
25	**sign a contract**	[sainə kɑ́ntrækt] v.	계약하다

…▸ I'm here to discuss the contract.
　　이번 계약 건을 상의하려고 왔습니다.

…▸ We have to finish the shipping by the end of this month.
　　이달 말까지 선적을 마쳐야 합니다.

…▸ We completed the sample for shipping.
　　선적할 견본이 완성되었습니다.

…▸ The high exchange rate put our company in trouble.
　　높은 환율 때문에 회사가 어려움에 처했습니다.

…▸ He was accused of smuggling.
　　밀수 혐의로 그는 고소되었습니다.

＊ inferior	하위의 / 열등한
＊ inform	알리다
＊ informal	비공식의 / 약식의
＊ information	정보
＊ insist	주장하다 / 우기다
＊ instead	그 대신에
＊ instruct	가르치다
＊ intend	~할 작정이다 / 의도하다
＊ interrupt	가로막다
＊ invade	침입하다
＊ invent	발명하다
＊ involve	포함하다 / 끌어내다

Part 065 Politics 정치

A
- vote
- voter
- voting right
- candidate
- elect
- election
- election campaign

B
- win an election
- support
- pass a bill
- Assembly
- Congress
- Senator
- Parliament

C
- power
- policy
- choice
- right
- obligation
- responsibility
- cooperation

D
- political party
- ruling party
- opposition party
- political power
- conservative
- liberal
- politician

#			
1	vote	[vout] n. v.	투표(하다)
2	voter	[vóutər] n.	유권자
3	voting right	[vóutiŋ rait] n.	선거권
4	candidate	[kǽndidit] n.	후보자
5	elect	[ilékt] v.	선출하다 / 선거하다
6	election	[ilékʃən] n.	선거
7	election campaign	[ilékʃən kæmpéin] n.	선거운동
8	win an election	[win ən ilékʃən] v.	당선되다
9	support	[səpɔ́ːrt] n. v.	지지(하다)
10	pass a bill	[pæs ə bil] v.	법안을 통과시키다
11	Assembly	[əsémbli] n.	국회
12	Congress	[káŋgris] n.	미 국회
13	Senator	[sénətər] n.	미 상원의원
14	Parliament	[páːrləmənt] n.	영국 의회
15	power	[páuər] n.	권력
16	policy	[páləsi] n.	정책
17	choice	[tʃɔis] n.	선택
18	right	[rait] n.	권리
19	obligation	[àbləgéiʃən] n.	의무
20	responsibility	[rispànsəbíləti] n.	책임
21	cooperation	[kouàpəréiʃən] n.	협력
22	political party	[pəlítikəl páːrti] n.	정당
23	ruling party	[rúːliŋ páːrti] n.	여당
24	opposition party	[àpəziʃən páːrti] n.	야당
25	political power	[pəlítikəl páuər] n.	정권
26	conservative	[kənsʌ́ːrvətiv] n. a.	보수파, 보수적인
27	liberal	[líbərəl] n. a.	진보파, 진보적인
28	politician	[pàlətíʃən] n.	정치가

⋯▸ I voted for him.
그에게 지지표를 던졌다.

⋯▸ The ruling party became opposition party as a result of general election.
총선거의 결과로 여당이 야당이 되었습니다.

⋯▸ The candidate raised lots of money during the election campaign.
선거 운동 기간 중에 그 후보는 거액을 모금하였습니다.

⋯▸ Five candidates are competing in one area.
한 지역에서 5명의 후보자가 경쟁하고 있습니다.

⋯▸ Everyone can have the right to vote when they reach 20.
20살이 되면 투표권을 가집니다.

∗ **corruption**	[kərʌ́pʃən] n.	부패
∗ **lawmaker/representative**	[lɔ́ːmèikər]/[rèprizéntətiv] n.	국회의원
∗ **candidacy**	[kǽndidəsi] n.	입후보
∗ **political**	[pəlítikəl] a.	정치적인

Part 066 Occupations
직업 1

A
- banker
- accountant
- lawyer
- driver
- company employee
- civil officer
- businessman

B
- entertainer
- comedian
- singer
- actor
- actress
- model
- announcer

C
- pilot
- stewardess
- designer
- worker
- detective
- policeman
- professor

D
- work part-time
- work full-time
- fireman
- athlete
- chef/cook
- waiter
- waitress

#			
1	**banker**	[bǽŋkər] n.	은행가
2	**accountant**	[əkáuntənt] n.	회계사
3	**lawyer**	[lɔ́:jər] n.	변호사
4	**driver**	[dráivər] n.	운전수
5	**company employee**	[kʌ́mpəni implɔíi:] n.	회사원
6	**civil officer**	[sívəl ɔ́(:)fisər] n.	공무원
7	**businessman**	[bíznismæ̀n] n.	사업가
8	**entertainer**	[èntərtéinər] n.	연예인
9	**comedian**	[kəmí:diən] n.	코메디언
10	**singer**	[síŋər] n.	가수
11	**actor**	[ǽktər] n.	배우
12	**actress**	[ǽktris] n.	여배우
13	**model**	[mádl] n.	모델
14	**announcer**	[ənáunsər] n.	아나운서
15	**pilot**	[páilət] n.	파일럿
16	**stewardess**	[stjú:ərdis] n.	스튜어디스
17	**designer**	[dizáinər] n.	디자이너
18	**worker**	[wə́:rkər] n.	노동자
19	**detective**	[ditéktiv] n.	형사
20	**policeman**	[pəlí:smən] n.	경찰
21	**professor**	[prəfésər] n.	교수
22	**work part-time**	[wə:rk pɑ:rt taim] v.	아르바이트를 하다
23	**work full-time**	[wə:rk ful taim] v.	정규직으로 근무하다
24	**fireman**	[fáiərmən] n.	소방수
25	**athlete**	[ǽθli:t] n.	운동선수
26	**chef/cook**	[ʃef] / [kuk] n.	요리사
27	**waiter**	[wéitər] n.	웨이터
28	**waitress**	[wéitris] n.	웨이트레스

⋯▶ There are a variety of jobs in the world.
세상에는 다양한 직업들이 있습니다.

⋯▶ I wanted to be a singer but had to give up because of my parents objection.
가수가 되고 싶었습니다만, 부모님의 반대로 포기했습니다.

⋯▶ Please call the police.
경찰을 불러 주세요.

⋯▶ A famous TV station recruits announcers now.
한 유명 방송국에서 지금 아나운서를 모집합니다.

⋯▶ He studied very hard, and became a professor.
그는 열심히 공부해서 교수가 되었습니다.

⋯▶ I want to be a famous actress.
저는 커서 유명한 배우가 되고 싶습니다.

✻ item	항목
✻ jar	단지, 항아리
✻ jewelry	보석
✻ join	결합하다 / 참가하다
✻ journey	(육상의)여행
✻ jump	뛰다
✻ just	바로 / 막 / 오직
✻ keep	보존하다 / 지키다 / 계속하다
✻ key	열쇠
✻ kick	(발로)차다
✻ kind	친절한
✻ kite	연

Part 067 Occupations
직업 2

A
- doctor
- surgeon
- physician
- dentist
- oriental medicine doctor
- pharmacist
- nurse

B
- novelist
- writer/author
- journalist
- reporter
- editor
- translator
- interpreter

C
- musician
- composer
- painter/artist
- sculptor
- architect
- carpenter

D
- physicist
- astronaut
- chemist
- engineer
- barber
- hair designer
- baby-sitter

#	Word	Pronunciation	Meaning
1	**doctor**	[dáktər] n.	의사
2	**surgeon**	[sə́:rdʒən] n.	외과의사
3	**physician**	[fizíʃən] n.	내과의사
4	**dentist**	[déntist] n.	치과의사
5	**oriental medicine doctor**	[ɔ̀:riéntl médəsən dáktər] n.	한의사
6	**pharmacist**	[fá:rməsist] n.	약사
7	**nurse**	[nə:rs] n.	간호원
8	**novelist**	[návəlist] n.	소설가
9	**writer/author**	[ráitər]/[ɔ́:θər] n.	작가
10	**journalist**	[dʒə́:rnəlist] n.	저널리스트
11	**reporter**	[ripɔ́:rtər] n.	기자
12	**editor**	[édətər] n.	편집자
13	**translator**	[trænsléitər] n.	번역가
14	**interpreter**	[intə́:rprətər] n.	통역사
15	**musician**	[mju:zíʃən] n.	음악가
16	**composer**	[kəmpóuzər] n.	작곡가
17	**painter/artist**	[péintər]/[á:rtist] n.	화가
18	**sculptor**	[skʌ́lptər] n.	조각가
19	**architect**	[á:rkitèkt] n.	건축가
20	**carpenter**	[ká:rpəntər] n.	목수
21	**physicist**	[fízəsist] n.	물리학자
22	**astronaut**	[ǽstrənɔ̀:t] n.	우주비행사
23	**chemist**	[kémist] n.	화학자
24	**engineer**	[èndʒəníər] n.	엔지니어(기사)
25	**barber**	[bá:rbər] n.	이발사
26	**hair designer**	[hɛər dizáinər] n.	미용사
27	**baby-sitter**	[béibisitər] n.	보모

⋯ My dream is to be a interpreter.
　내 장래 꿈은 통역사입니다.

⋯ A reporter from a fashion magazine visited my house this afternoon.
　오늘 오후에 패션 잡지 기자가 우리 집을 방문했습니다.

⋯ She is an amateur singer as well as lawyer.
　그녀는 변호사이면서 아마츄어 가수입니다.

⋯ I am a part-time babysitter.
　저는 시간제로 애기 보는 일을 합니다.

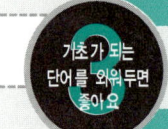

✽ knock	치다 / 두드리다
✽ know	알다
✽ large	큰 / 넓은
✽ last	지속하다
✽ lawn	잔디
✽ lay	눕히다 / (알을)낳다
✽ leave	떠나다 / 남기다 / ～한 상태로 두다
✽ lesson	교훈
✽ let	～시키다 / ～하게 하다
✽ lifelong	일생/평생의
✽ little	작은 / 적은 / 어린
✽ local	지역의

Part 068 Post Office
우체국

A
- letter
- envelope
- letter paper
- stamp
- postcard
- money order
- postmark

B
- mailman
- zip code
- mailbox
- window
- postal worker
- return address
- address

C
- registered letter
- airmail
- sea mail
- surface mail
- overnight mail
- express mail
- junk mail

D
- arrival date
- shipping date
- telegram
- parcel
- scale
- send email

#	Word	Pronunciation	Meaning
1	letter	[létər] n.	편지
2	envelope	[énvəlòup] n.	봉투
3	letter paper	[létər péipər] n.	편지지
4	stamp	[stæmp] n.	우표
5	postcard	[póustkà:rd] n.	엽서
6	money order	[máni ɔ́:rdər] n.	우편환
7	postmark	[póustmà:rk] n.	소인
8	mailman	[méilmæ̀n] n.	우편배달부
9	zip code	[zip koud] n.	우편번호
10	mailbox	[méilbàks] n.	우체통
11	window	[wíndou] n.	창구
12	postal worker	[póustəl wə́:rkər] n.	우체국 직원
13	return address	[ritə́:rrn ədrés] n.	보내는 이 주소
14	address	[ədrés] n.	받는 이 주소
15	registered letter	[rédʒəstərd létər] n.	등기
16	airmail	[ɛ́ərmèil] n.	항공편
17	sea mail	[si: meil] n.	배편
18	surface mail	[sə́:rfis meil] n.	육로편
19	overnight mail	[óuvərnàit meil] n.	하룻밤에 배달되는 빠른 우편
20	express mail	[iksprés meil] n.	속달
21	junk mail	[dʒʌŋk meil] n.	광고성 우편
22	arrival date	[əráivəl deit] n.	도착 날짜
23	shipping date	[ʃípiŋ deit] n.	선적 날짜
24	telegram	[téləgræ̀m] n.	전보
25	parcel	[pá:rsəl] n.	소포
26	scale	[skeil] n.	저울
27	send email	[send í:mèil] v.	전자 우편을 보내다

⋯→ **I was about to go to the post office to send a letter.**
편지를 부치러 막 우체국에 갈 참이었습니다.

⋯→ **Put stamps on a postcard.**
엽서에 우표를 붙여주세요.

⋯→ **How often do you pick up mails each day?**
하루에 몇 번이나 편지를 수거하십니까?

⋯→ **I dropped a letter into a postbox.**
우체통에 편지를 넣었습니다.

⋯→ **I'd like to send a parcel to my friend in Canada.**
캐나다에 있는 친구에게 소포를 보내려고 합니다.

* **lock** 자물쇠
* **lose** 잃다
* **loud** 소리가 큰 / 시끄러운
* **low** 낮은
* **lucky** 행운의
* **mad** 미친 / 열광한
* **major** 주요한
* **male** 수컷의
* **mammal** 포유류
* **mankind** 인류
* **marble** 대리석
* **mask** 탈 / 복면

Part 069 Bank

은행

A
- money
- bank account
- bank account number
- bank note
- exchange rate
- cash
- coin

B
- loan
- credit
- security
- installment savings
- save money
- send money

C
- check
- draft
- currency
- interest
- exchange money
- deposit money
- withdraw money

D
- credit card
- cash card
- traveler's check
- automatic teller machine (ATM)
- security guard
- PIN number
- money rates

Part 8

#	Word	Pronunciation	Korean
1	**money**	[mʌ́ni] n.	돈
2	**bank account**	[bæŋk əkáunt] n.	은행 구좌
3	**bank account number**	[bæŋk əkáunt nʌ́mbər] n.	구좌번호
4	**bank note**	[bæŋk nout] n.	통장
5	**exchange rate**	[ikstʃéindʒ reit] n.	환율
6	**cash**	[kæʃ] n.	현금
7	**coin**	[kɔin] n.	동전
8	**loan**	[loun] n.	대출
9	**credit**	[krédit] n.	신용
10	**security**	[sikjúəriti] n.	보증, 증권
11	**installment savings**	[instɔ́ːlmənt séiviŋz] n.	적금
12	**save money**	[seiv mʌ́ni] v.	저축하다
13	**send money**	[send mʌ́ni] v.	송금하다
14	**check**	[tʃek] n.	수표
15	**draft**	[dræft] n.	어음
16	**currency**	[kə́ːrənsi] n.	화폐
17	**interest**	[íntərist] n.	이자
18	**exchange money**	[ikstʃéindʒ mʌ́ni] v.	환전하다
19	**deposit money**	[dipázit mʌ́ni] v.	입금하다
20	**withdraw money**	[wiðdrɔ́ː mʌ́ni] v.	출금하다
21	**credit card**	[krédit kaːrd] n.	신용카드
22	**cash card**	[kæʃ kaːrd] n.	현금카드
23	**traveler's check**	[trǽvlərz tʃek] n.	여행자 수표
24	**automatic teller machine (ATM)**	[ɔ̀ːtəmǽtik télər məʃíːn] n.	현금 자동 지급기
25	**security guard**	[sikjúəriti gaːrd] n.	경비원
26	**PIN number**	[pin nʌ́mbər] n.	비밀번호
27	**money rates**	[mʌ́ni reits] n.	금리

Economics, Business

⋯▶ I'll go back to a bank.
　　은행에 갔다 오겠습니다.

⋯▶ He withdrew some money.
　　그는 얼마간의 돈을 인출했습니다.

⋯▶ We decided to take out a bank loan to buy a house.
　　우리는 집을 사기 위해 은행대출을 결심했습니다.

⋯▶ I transferred money to the account of my friend.
　　친구의 구좌로 송금했습니다.

⋯▶ She exchanged all the money to dollars before departure.
　　그녀는 출국 전에 모든 돈을 달러로 환전했습니다.

*owe	[ou] v.	빚지다
*due	[djuː] a.	지불기일이 된
*financial	[finǽnʃəl] a.	재정상의 / 금융상의
*yen	[jen] n.	엔
*won	[wʌn] n.	원
*dollar	[dálər] n.	달러
*remittance	[rimítəns] n.	송금

P·a·r·t 070 War

전쟁

A
- military
- soldier
- army
- navy
- air force
- weapon
- enemy

B
- attack
- defend
- rule
- independence
- battle
- victory
- defeat

C
- warship
- bomb
- cannon
- direction
- injury
- allied nations
- allied forces

D
- terrorist
- spy
- guerilla
- coup
- ambush
- surrender
- cease-fire

#			
1	**military**	[mílitèri] n.	군대
2	**soldier**	[sóuldʒər] n.	군인
3	**army**	[ɑ́ːrmi] n.	육군
4	**navy**	[néivi] n.	해군
5	**air force**	[ɛər fɔːrs] n.	공군
6	**weapon**	[wépən] n.	무기
7	**enemy**	[énəmi] n.	적
8	**attack**	[ətǽk] n. v.	공격(하다)
9	**defend**	[difénd] v.	방어하다
10	**rule**	[ruːl] n. v.	지배(하다)
11	**independence**	[ìndipéndəns] n.	독립
12	**battle**	[bǽtl] n.	전투
13	**victory**	[víktəri] n.	승리
14	**defeat**	[difíːt] n.	패배
15	**warship**	[wɔ́ːrʃip] n.	군함
16	**bomb**	[bɑm] n.	폭탄
17	**cannon**	[kǽnən] n.	대포
18	**direction**	[dirékʃən] n.	방위
19	**injury**	[índʒəri] n.	부상
20	**allied nations**	[ǽlaid néiʃənz] n.	동맹국들
21	**allied forces**	[ǽlaid fɔːrsiz] n.	아군
22	**terrorist**	[térərist] n.	테러리스트
23	**spy**	[spai] n.	간첩
24	**guerilla**	[gərílə] n.	게릴라
25	**coup**	[kuː] n.	쿠데타
26	**ambush**	[ǽmbuʃ] n.	기습공격
27	**surrender**	[səréndər] n. v.	항복(하다)
28	**cease-fire**	[síːs fáiər] n.	휴전, 종전

- War must not break out.
  전쟁은 절대로 일어나서는 안 됩니다.
- I joined the army after finishing the first semester.
  1학기를 마치고 군 입대를 하였습니다.
- He turned out to be a spy later.
  나중에 그가 스파이로 밝혀졌습니다.
- I never surrender.
  절대로 항복하지 않아.
- The allied nations occupy the region.
  동맹국들이 그 지역을 점령하고 있습니다.

* **missile**	[mísəl] n.	미사일
* **secret**	[síːkrit] n.	기밀
* **admiral**	[ǽdmərəl] n.	해군장성
* **general**	[dʒénərəl] n.	장군
* **join the army**	[dʒɔin ði ɑ́ːrmi] v.	군입대하다
* **struggle**	[strʌ́gl] n. v.	투쟁(하다) / 분투(하다)
* **team spirit training**	[tiːm spírit tréiniŋ] n.	팀스피리트(합동) 훈련
* **discharge from the military service**	[distʃɑ́ːrdʒ frəm ðə mílitèri sə́ːrvis] v.	제대하다

Part 071 Mass Media
매스미디어

A
- magazine
- publish
- interview
- reporter
- anchor
- sponsor
- producer

B
- journalism
- broadcast
- television station
- radio station
- documentary
- news
- drama

C
- live coverage
- pre-recorded
- simulcast
- re-run
- satellite
- cable
- commercial

D
- newspaper
- newspaper office
- morning paper
- evening paper
- article
- editorial
- advertisement

1	**magazine**	[mǽgəzíːn] n.	잡지
2	**publish**	[pʌ́bliʃ] v.	출판하다
3	**interview**	[íntərvjùː] n. v.	인터뷰(하다)
4	**reporter**	[ripɔ́ːrtər] n.	기자
5	**anchor**	[ǽŋkər] n.	방송앵커
6	**sponsor**	[spánsər] n.	스폰서
7	**producer**	[prədjúːsər] n.	프로듀서(PD)
8	**journalism**	[dʒə́ːrnəlìzəm] n.	언론
9	**broadcast**	[brɔ́ːdkæ̀st] n.	방송
10	**television station**	[teləvíʒən stéiʃən] n.	TV방송국
11	**radio station**	[réidiòu stéiʃən] n.	라디오방송국
12	**documentary**	[dákjumèntəri] n.	다큐멘터리
13	**news**	[njuːz] n.	뉴스 / 소식 / 보도
14	**drama**	[dráːmə] n.	드라마
15	**live coverage**	[laiv kʌ́vəridʒ] n.	생방송
16	**pre-recorded**	[pri rekɔ́ːrdid] n.	녹화 방송
17	**simulcast**	[sáiməlkæ̀st] n.	동시중계
18	**re-run**	[rirʌn] n.	재방송
19	**satellite**	[sǽtəlàit] n.	위성 방송
20	**cable**	[kéibl] n.	케이블 방송
21	**commercial**	[kəmə́ːrʃəl] n.	방송 광고
22	**newspaper**	[njúːzpèipər] n.	신문
23	**newspaper office**	[njúːzpèipər ɔ́(ː)fis] n.	신문사
24	**morning paper**	[mɔ́ːrniŋ péipər] n.	조간
25	**evening paper**	[íːvniŋ péipər] n.	석간
26	**article**	[áːrtikl] n.	기사
27	**editorial**	[èdətɔ́ːriəl] n.	사설
28	**advertisement**	[ǽdvərtáizmənt] n.	광고

⋯▸ A reporter interviewed my friend on the street.
  기자가 거리에서 내 친구를 인터뷰했습니다.
⋯▸ I often watch the Discovery channel.
  저는 디스커버리 채널을 자주 시청합니다.
⋯▸ You should read the editorial pages everyday.
  여러분은 신문 사설을 매일 읽는게 좋겠어요.
⋯▸ A famous athlete announced his marriage in a press conference.
  한 유명 스포츠 선수가 기자 회견에서 결혼 발표를 했습니다.
⋯▸ She filmed a documentary on wild animals.
  그녀는 야생동물에 관한 다큐멘터리를 촬영했습니다.

∗ **monthly magazine**	[mʌ́nθli mæ̀gəzíːn] n.	월간지
∗ **weekly magazine**	[wíːkli mæ̀gəzíːn] n.	주간지
∗ **lines**	[lainz] n.	대사
∗ **acting**	[ǽktiŋ] n.	연기
∗ **channel**	[tʃǽnl] n.	채널
∗ **cover the story**	[kʌ́vər ðə stɔ́ːri] v.	내용을 보도하다
∗ **collect data**	[kəlékt déitə] v.	자료를 모으다
∗ **announcement**	[ənáunsmənt] n.	발표
∗ **criticize**	[krítisàiz] vt.	비평하다 / 비판하다
∗ **antenna**	[ænténə] n.	안테나

Part 072 Crime 범죄

A
- violence
- theft
- criminal
- suspect
- robber
- thief
- pickpocket

B
- suicide
- murder
- arson
- fraud
- kidnap
- rape
- ransom

C
- bribery
- hostage
- arrest
- chase
- evidence
- fingerprint
- clue

D
- drug
- patrol car
- pistol
- handcuffs
- Freeze!
- prison/jail
- jail break

1	**violence**	[váiələns] n.	폭력
2	**theft**	[θeft] n.	절도
3	**criminal**	[krímənl] n.	범인
4	**suspect**	[səspékt] n.	용의자
5	**robber**	[rábər] n.	강도
6	**thief**	[θi:f] n.	도둑
7	**pickpocket**	[píkpàkit] n.	소매치기
8	**suicide**	[sú:əsàid] n.	자살
9	**murder**	[mə́:rdər] n.	살인
10	**arson**	[á:rsn] n.	방화
11	**fraud**	[frɔ:d] n.	사기
12	**kidnap**	[kídnæp] n. v.	납치(하다)
13	**rape**	[reip] n.	강간
14	**ransom**	[rǽnsəm] n.	몸값
15	**bribery**	[bráibəri] n.	뇌물
16	**hostage**	[hástidʒ] n.	인질
17	**arrest**	[ərést] n. vt.	체포(하다)
18	**chase**	[tʃeis] v.	추적(하다)
19	**evidence**	[évidəns] n.	증거
20	**fingerprint**	[fíŋgərprìnt] n.	지문
21	**clue**	[klu:] n.	단서
22	**drug**	[drʌg] n.	마약
23	**patrol car**	[pətróul kɑ:r] n.	순찰차
24	**pistol**	[pístl] n.	권총
25	**handcuffs**	[hǽndkʌfs] n.	수갑
26	**Freeze!**	[fri:z]	멈춰!
27	**prison/jail**	[prízn]/[dʒeil] n.	감옥 / 교도소
28	**jail break**	[dʒeil breik] n.	탈옥

- Police just arrested the criminal.
  경찰이 범인을 막 체포했습니다.
- He committed a crime.
  그가 범행을 저질렀습니다.
- They found the evidence in his house.
  그들은 그의 집에서 증거를 발견하였습니다.
- She got the order to assassinate the enemy.
  그녀는 적을 암살하라는 명령을 받았습니다.
- Fingerprints left on the cup were the proof that clinched the case.
  컵에 남겨진 지문이 사건을 종결짓는 증거가 되었습니다.

* **escape**	[iskéip] v.	도망(가다)
* **accuse**	[əkjúːz] v.	고발하다 / 비난하다
* **deceive**	[disíːv] v.	속이다 / 기만하다
* **commit**	[kəmít] vt.	범하다 / 위탁하다
* **flee**	[fliː] v.	도망치다
* **kill**	[kil] v.	죽이다
* **prove**	[pruːv] v.	증명하다 / 판명하다
* **steal**	[stiːl] v.	훔치다
* **guilty**	[gílti] a.	유죄의
* **innocent**	[ínəsnt] a.	무죄의
* **assassination**	[əsæsənéiʃən] n.	암살
* **prosecutor**	[prásəkjùːtər] n.	검찰
* **confess**	[kənfés] v.	자백하다

Part 073 Accident & Disasters
사건 및 재난

A
- human disaster
- natural disaster
- earthquake
- aftershock
- fire
- wildfire

B
- storm
- flood
- landslide
- storm waves
- cold wave
- drought
- crash

C
- refuge
- shelter
- run away from home
- prevention
- deviation
- drunk driving
- car accident

D
- burn
- drown
- explode
- happen
- danger
- contact

Part 8

#				
1	human disaster	[hjú:mən dizǽstər] n.	인재
2	natural disaster	[nǽtʃərəl dizǽstər] n.	천재
3	earthquake	[ə́:rθkwèik] n.	지진
4	aftershock	[ǽftərʃɑ̀k] n.	여진
5	fire	[faiər] n.	화재 / 불
6	wildfire	[wáildfàiə:r] n.	산불
7	storm	[stɔ:rm] n.	폭풍
8	flood	[flʌd] n.	홍수 / 범람
9	landslide	[lǽndslàid] n.	산사태
10	storm waves	[stɔ:rm weivz] n.	해일
11	cold wave	[kould weiv] n.	한파
12	drought	[draut] n.	가뭄
13	crash	[kræʃ] n.	추락 / 충돌
14	refuge	[réfju:dʒ] n.	피난
15	shelter	[ʃéltər] n.	피난처
16	run away from home	[rʌnəwéi frəm houm] v.	가출하다
17	prevention	[privénʃən] n.	예방
18	deviation	[dì:viéiʃən] n.	탈선
19	drunk driving	[drʌŋk dráiviŋ] n.	음주 운전
20	car accident	[kɑ:r ǽksidənt] n.	교통사고
21	burn	[bə:rn] v.	불타다 / 불태우다
22	drown	[draun] v.	익사하다 / 익사시키다
23	explode	[iksplóud] v.	폭발하다
24	happen	[hǽpən] vi.	일이일어나다 / 우연히 ~하다
25	danger	[déindʒər] n.	위험
26	contact	[kántækt] n. v.	연락(하다)

Economics, Business

⋯▸ **Earthquakes often occur in Japan.**
　　일본은 지진 다발국입니다.

⋯▸ **There was a car accident this morning.**
　　오늘 아침 교통사고가 발생했습니다.

⋯▸ **Wildfire spread to the village in a minute.**
　　순식간에 산불이 마을로 번졌다.

⋯▸ **Big storm waves were caused by an earthquake.**
　　지진으로 해일이 일어났습니다.

⋯▸ **We can save life and property by preventing human disasters.**
　　인재를 예방함으로써 생명과 재산을 보호할 수 있습니다.

✽ master	주인 / 명수
✽ matter	중요하다
✽ maybe	어쩌면 / 아마 / 아마도
✽ mean	의미하다 / ~할 작정이다
✽ melt	녹다 / 녹이다
✽ member	회원
✽ mild	부드러운 / 온화한
✽ mind	마음 / 정신
✽ minor	작은 / 미성년자
✽ mistake	실수 (하다)
✽ mix	섞다 / 섞이다
✽ modern	현대의

P·a·r·t 074 Law

법률

A
- trial
- Constitution
- approval
- disapproval
- court
- Supreme Court
- family court

B
- counseling
- judge
- prosecutor
- defendant
- plaintiff
- juror

C
- verdict
- proof/evidence
- testimony
- acquit
- convict
- innocent
- guilty

D
- interrogation
- file a suit
- misjudgment
- sentence
- capital punishment
- life imprisonment
- break the law

Part 8

1	trial	[tráiəl] n.	재판
2	Constitution	[kànstətjúːʃən] n.	헌법
3	approval	[əprúːvəl] n.	찬성
4	disapproval	[dìsəprúːvəl] n.	반대
5	court	[kɔːrt] n.	법원
6	Supreme Court	[səpríːm kɔːrt] n.	대법원
7	family court	[fǽməli kɔːrt] n.	가정법원
8	counseling	[káunsəliŋ] n.	상담
9	judge	[dʒʌdʒ] n.	판사
10	prosecutor	[práəsəkjùːtər] n.	검사
11	defendant	[diféndənt] n.	피고인
12	plaintiff	[pléintif] n.	원고
13	juror	[dʒúərər] n.	배심원
14	verdict	[vɜ́ːrdikt] n.	(배심원) 평결
15	proof/evidence	[pruːf] / [évidəns] n.	증거 / 증명
16	testimony	[téstəmòuni] n.	증언
17	acquit	[əkwít] vt.	무죄 석방되다
18	convict	[kənvíkt] vt.	유죄 판결이 나다
19	innocent	[ínəsnt] a.	무죄의
20	guilty	[gílti] a.	유죄의
21	interrogation	[intèrəgèiʃən] n.	심문
22	file a suit	[failə suːt] v.	기소하다
23	misjudgment	[misdʒʌ́dʒmənt] n.	오판
24	sentence	[séntəns] n. v.	구형(받다)
25	capital punishment	[kǽpitl pʌ́niʃmənt] n.	사형
26	life imprisonment	[laif imprízənmənt] n.	종신형
27	break the law	[breik ðə lɔː] v.	법을 어기다

Economics, Business

···▸ He was acquitted of murder.
살인 혐의에 대해 그는 무죄 판결을 받았습니다.

···▸ The trial was postponed.
재판이 연기되었습니다.

···▸ I met a lawyer to discuss this matter.
이번 문제에 대해 의논하기 위해 변호사를 만났습니다.

···▸ She attended the trial as a witness.
그녀는 목격자로서 재판에 참석했습니다.

···▸ The judge sentenced him to 2 years in prison.
판사는 그에게 징역 2년형을 선고하였습니다.

* moist	축축한
* mostly	대체로
* motion	동작
* mug	원통형 찻잔
* mystery	신비 / 불가사의
* name	이름
* napkin	냅킨
* narrow	좁은
* native	출생의 / 토착민의
* nearly	거의 / 가까스로
* neat	깔끔한
* necessary	필요한 / 없어서는 안될

9 Hobbies & Leisure

Part 075 Hobbies 취미

A
- listening to music
- movie theater
- going to the movies
- play
- concert
- musical
- dance

B
- comics
- cartoon
- animation
- stamp collecting
- coin collecting
- collection
- model building

C
- bird watching
- photography
- drive
- hiking
- taking a walk
- mountain climbing
- fishing

D
- knitting
- sewing
- embroidery
- calligraphy
- painting
- sculpting
- pottery

#	English	Pronunciation	Korean
1	listening to music	[lísniŋ tə mjúːzik] n.	음악 감상
2	movie theater	[múːvi θíːətər] n.	영화관
3	going to the movies	[gou tə ðə múːviz]	영화 보러 가기
4	play	[plei] n.	연극
5	concert	[kánsəːrt] n.	콘서트 / 연주회
6	musical	[mjúːzikəl] n.	뮤지컬
7	dance	[dæns] n. v.	춤(추다)
8	comics	[kámiks] n.	단행본 만화책
9	cartoon	[kɑːrtúːn] n.	만화
10	animation	[ǽnəméiʃən] n.	만화영화
11	stamp collecting	[stæmp kəléktiŋ] n.	우표수집
12	coin collecting	[kɔin kəléktiŋ] n.	동전수집
13	collection	[kəlékʃən] n.	수집 / 수집물
14	model building	[mádl bíldiŋ] n.	모형 조립
15	bird watching	[bəːrd wɑtʃiŋ] n.	조류관찰
16	photography	[fətágrəfi] n.	사진
17	drive	[draiv] n.	드라이브
18	hiking	[háikiŋ] n.	도보여행
19	taking a walk	[teikə wɔːk]	산책
20	mountain climbing	[máuntən kláimiŋ] n.	등산
21	fishing	[fíʃiŋ] n.	낚시
22	knitting	[nítiŋ] n.	뜨게질
23	sewing	[sóuiŋ] n.	바느질
24	embroidery	[embrɔ́idəri] n.	자수
25	calligraphy	[kəlígrəfi] n.	서예
26	painting	[péintiŋ] n.	그림그리기
27	sculpting	[skʌ́lptiŋ] n.	조각하기
28	pottery	[pátəri] n.	도자기 공예

Hobbies & Leisure

- ⋯→ What are your hobbies?
  취미는 무엇입니까?
- ⋯→ Let's play paduk.
  바둑을 둡시다.
- ⋯→ I wish I could go fishing.
  낚시하러 가면 좋겠는데.
- ⋯→ Let's go to a mountain if the weather is fine tomorrow.
  내일 날씨가 좋으면 등산하러 갑시다.
- ⋯→ Grandma spends all day knitting.
  할머니는 뜨개질을 하시면서 하루를 보내십니다.

✱ reading	[rídiŋ] n.	독서
✱ chess	[tʃes] n.	장기
✱ mah-jong	[máːdʒɔ́ːŋ] n.	마작
✱ opera	[ápərə] n.	오페라
✱ puppet show	[pʌ́pit ʃou] n.	인형극
✱ leisure	[líːʒəːr] n.	여가 / 틈
✱ adventure	[ædvéntʃər]	모험
✱ draw	[drɔː] v.	그리다
✱ enjoy	[endʒɔ́i] vt.	즐기다
✱ entertain	[èntərtéin] v.	즐겁게 하다
✱ play	[plei] v.	놀다 / 경기를 하다 / 연주하다
✱ relax	[rilǽks] v.	편하게 하다 / 편히 쉬다

076 Travel

여행

A
- day trip
- backpacking
- backpacker
- package tour
- sightseeing
- honeymoon
- school excursion

B
- hotel
- inn
- baggage
- map
- reservation
- airport
- hot spring

C
- vacation
- tourist
- traveler
- tourist attractions
- historic sites
- domestic travel
- overseas travel

D
- airlines
- travel agency
- itinerary
- souvenir
- non-smoking area
- smoking area

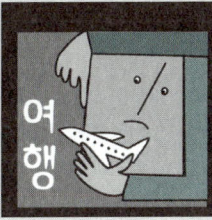

1	day trip	[dei trip] n.	당일치기 여행
2	backpacking	[bǽkpæ̀kiŋ] n.	배낭여행
3	backpacker	[bǽkpæ̀kər] n.	배낭 여행자
4	package tour	[pǽkidʒ tuər] n.	패키지여행
5	sightseeing	[sáitsìːiŋ] n.	관광
6	honeymoon	[hʌ́nimùːn] n.	신혼여행
7	school excursion	[skuːl ikskə́ːrʒən] n.	수학여행
8	hotel	[houtél] n.	호텔
9	inn	[in] n.	여관
10	baggage	[bǽgidʒ] n.	짐
11	map	[mæp] n.	지도
12	reservation	[rèzəːrvéiʃən] n.	예약
13	airport	[ɛ́rpɔ̀ːrt] n.	공항
14	hot spring	[hɑt spriŋ] n.	온천
15	vacation	[veikéiʃən] n.	휴가
16	tourist	[túərist] n.	관광객
17	traveler	[trǽvlər] n.	여행자
18	tourist attractions	[túərist ətrǽkʃənz] n.	관광지
19	historic sites	[histɔ́(ː)rik sait] n.	역사 고적지
20	domestic travel	[douméstik trǽvəl] n.	국내여행
21	overseas travel	[óuvərsìː(z) trǽvəl] n.	해외여행
22	airlines	[ɛ́ərlàinz] n.	항공사
23	travel agency	[trǽvəl éidʒənsi] n.	여행사
24	itinerary	[aitínərèri] n.	여행 일정
25	souvenir	[sùːvəníər] n.	기념물
26	non-smoking area	[nɑn smóukiŋ ɛ́əriə] n.	금연석
27	smoking area	[smóukiŋ ɛ́əriə] n.	흡연석

⋯▸ We're going to stay at a five-star hotel.
우리는 특급 호텔에 묵을 예정입니다.

⋯▸ I bought a souvenir in a tourist spot.
관광 명소에서 기념품을 샀습니다.

⋯▸ I'll go to Hawaii for my honeymoon.
신혼여행으로 하와이에 갈 겁니다.

⋯▸ You can enjoy a day trip to the East Coast.
동해로 가는 당일 여행을 즐겨보세요.

⋯▸ Hot springs in Japan are the most famous .
일본의 온천이 가장 유명합니다.

⋯▸ I traveled to Australia for a month as a backpacker.
저는 한 달간 호주 배낭여행을 떠났었습니다.

* course	[kɔːrs] n.	관광코스
* camp	[kæmp] n.	캠프(야영지)
* passenger	[pǽsəndəʒər] n.	승객
* voyage	[vɔ́idʒ] n.	항해 / 여행
* decide	[disáid] v.	결정하다 / 결심하다
* cancel	[kǽnsəl] v.	취소하다
* exploration	[èkspləréiʃən] n.	탐험

Part 077 Sightseeing 관광

A
- city sightseeing
- cruise
- art gallery
- painting
- statue
- works of art
- museum

B
- ancient palace
- aquarium
- memorial
- zoo
- botanical garden
- Folk Village
- water parks

C
- visitor
- pond
- bridge
- original
- censorship
- observation platform
- exhibition

D
- traditional tea shop
- festival
- tour guide
- seasickness
- carsickness
- infirmary
- cable car

1	city sightseeing	[sáitsiːiŋ] n.	시내관광
2	cruise	[kruːz] n.	선박여행
3	art gallery	[ɑːrt gǽləri] n.	화랑
4	painting	[péintiŋ] n.	그림
5	statue	[stǽtʃuː] n.	동상
6	works of art	[wəːrks əv ɑːrt] n.	예술 작품들
7	museum	[mjuːzíːəm] n.	박물관
8	ancient palace	[éinʃənt pǽlis] n.	고궁
9	aquarium	[əkwɛ́əriəm] n.	수족관
10	memorial	[mimɔ́ːriəl] n.	기념비
11	zoo	[zuː] n.	동물원
12	botanical garden	[bətǽnikəl gɑ́ːrdn] n.	식물원
13	Folk Village	[fouk vílidʒ] n.	민속촌
14	water parks	[wɔ́ːtər pɑːrks] n.	물놀이 공원
15	visitor	[vízitər] n.	방문객
16	pond	[pɑnd] n.	연못
17	bridge	[bridʒ] n.	다리
18	original	[ərídʒənəl] n.	원본
19	censorship	[sénsərʃip] n.	검열
20	observation platform	[ɑ̀bzərvéiʃən plǽtfɔ̀ːrm] n.	전망대
21	exhibition	[èksəbíʃən] n.	전시회
22	traditional tea shop	[trədíʃənəl tiː ʃɑp] n.	전통찻집
23	festival	[féstəvəl] n.	축제
24	tour guide	[tuər gaid] n.	관광가이드
25	seasickness	[síːsìknis] n.	배멀미
26	carsickness	[kɑ́ːrsìknis] n.	차멀미
27	infirmary	[infə́ːrməri] n.	진료소
28	cable car	[kéibəl kɑːr] n.	케이블카

⋯ **There are lots of tourist attractions in Seoul.**
서울에는 많은 관광명소가 있습니다.

⋯ **I need medicine for carsickness.**
차멀미 약이 필요합니다.

⋯ **We went to an observation platform to look out over downtown.**
우리는 시내를 내려다보기 위해 전망대로 갔습니다.

⋯ **Foreigners enjoy street performances in Insa-dong on the weekends.**
외국인들은 인사동의 주말 거리 공연을 즐겼습니다.

⋯ **A tour guide explains the history of the ancient palaces to the visitors.**
관광 안내원은 방문객들에게 고궁의 역사에 대해 설명합니다.

*	need	필요로 하다
*	negative	부정적인 / 소극적인
*	neighbor	이웃
*	neither	~도 또한 ~아니다
*	nervous	초조한 / 신경성의
*	new	새로운
*	nickname	애칭 / 별칭
*	nod	(머리) 끄덕이다
*	noise	소음
*	normal	보통의
*	notice	주의 / 통지
*	number	숫자

Part 078 Hotel

호텔

A
- luxurious hotel
- city hotel
- international chain hotel
- resort
- inn
- motel

B
- wake-up call service
- facilities
- sauna
- fitness center
- indoor swimming pool
- complimentary shuttle
- in-house phone

C
- single room
- twin room
- double room
- suite room
- room rate
- vacancy
- room change

D
- front desk
- receptionist
- cashier
- bellhop
- check in
- check out
- room service

#				
1	luxurious hotel	[lʌgzúəriəs houtél] n.	호화호텔
2	city hotel	[síti houtél] n.	시내 호텔
3	international chain hotel	[ìntərnǽʃənəl tʃein houtél] n.	국제 체인 호텔
4	resort	[rizɔ́:rt] n.	휴양 리조트
5	inn	[in] n.	여관
6	motel	[moutél] n.	모텔(차고가 방 옆에 달린)
7	wake-up call service	[weikʌp kɔ:l sə́:rvis] n.	모닝콜 서비스
8	facilities	[fəsílətiz] n.	시설물
9	sauna	[sáunə] n.	사우나
10	fitness center	[fítnis séntər] n.	헬스클럽
11	indoor swimming pool	[índɔ:r swímiŋ pu:l] n.	실내 수영장
12	complimentary shuttle	[kàmpləméntəri ʃʌ́tl] n.	무료 셔틀버스
13	in-house phone	[inhaus foun] n.	관내 전화
14	single room	[síŋgl ru:m] n.	싱글 룸
15	twin room	[twin ru:m] n.	트윈 룸
16	double room	[dʌ́bl ru:m] n.	더블 룸(더블 침대가 있는)
17	suite room	[swi:t ru:m] n.	특실
18	room rate	[ru:m reit] n.	숙박 요금
19	vacancy	[véikənsi] n.	빈방
20	room change	[ru:m tʃeindʒ] n.	방 바꾸기
21	front desk	[frʌnt desk] n.	프론트 데스크
22	receptionist	[risépʃənist] n.	접수원
23	cashier	[kǽʃiər] n.	계산원
24	bellhop	[bélhàp] n.	벨보이
25	check in	[tʃekin] n. v.	체크인(하다)
26	check out	[təkaut] n. v.	체크아웃(하다)
27	room service	[ru:m sə́:rvis] n.	룸서비스

- I'm here to check in.
  체크인하려고 합니다.
- Do you have any vacancies?
  빈 방 있습니까?
- I asked for a nonsmoking room.
  금연실을 부탁했습니다만.
- Let's get room service.
  룸서비스를 시킵시다.
- I'd like a 7am wake-up call.
  아침 7시에 모닝콜을 해 주세요.

* **graveyard**	[gréivjà:rd] n.	야간 밤샘 업무
* **occupancy rate**	[ákjəpənsi reit] n.	점유율
* **breakfast coupon**	[brékfəst kjú:pan] n.	아침식사 쿠폰
* **service charge**	[sə́:rvis tʃɑ:rdʒ] n.	봉사료
* **concierge**	[kànsiɛ́ərʒ] n.	콘시어지
* **luggage cart**	[lʌ́gidʒ kɑ:rt] n.	짐 운반용 카트

Part 079 Airport 공항

A
- economy class
- business class
- first class
- one-way
- round-trip
- nonstop flight
- waiting list

B
- flight attendant
- pilot
- check-in counter
- check-in baggage
- carry-on bag
- flight ticket
- boarding pass

C
- window seat
- aisle seat
- delay
- stopover
- in-flight service
- baggage claim
- jet lag

D
- Customs
- clear
- declare
- duty-free shop
- airport limousine
- emergency exit
- security check

#	Term	Pronunciation	Korean
1	**economy class**	[ikánəmi klæs] n.	일반석
2	**business class**	[bíznis klæs] n.	일등석
3	**first class**	[fəːrst klæs] n.	특별석
4	**one-way**	[wʌn wei] n.	편도권
5	**round-trip**	[raund trip] n.	왕복권
6	**nonstop flight**	[nánstáp flait] n.	직항편
7	**waiting list**	[wéitiŋ list] n.	대기자 명단
8	**flight attendant**	[flait əténdənt] n.	승무원
9	**pilot**	[páilət] n.	조종사
10	**check-in counter**	[tʃekin káuntər] n.	탑승 수속 창구
11	**check-in baggage**	[tʃekin bǽgidʒ] n.	탁송 화물
12	**carry-on bag**	[kǽri ɔn bæg] n.	기내 반입 가능한 가방
13	**flight ticket**	[flait tíkit] n.	항공권
14	**boarding pass**	[bɔ́ːrdiŋ pæs] n.	탑승권
15	**window seat**	[wíndou siːt] n.	창가쪽 좌석
16	**aisle seat**	[ail siːt] n.	통로쪽 좌석
17	**delay**	[diléi] n. v.	연착(하다)
18	**stopover**	[stəpòuvər] n.	중간 기착지
19	**in-flight service**	[in flait sə́ːrvis] n.	기내 서비스
20	**baggage claim**	[bǽgidʒ kleim] n.	짐 찾는 곳
21	**jet lag**	[dʒet læg] n.	시차 때문에 느끼는 피로
22	**Customs**	[kʌ́stəmz] n.	세관
23	**clear**	[kliər] v.	통관 절차를 밟다
24	**declare**	[dikléər] v.	(구입 물건등을)신고하다
25	**duty-free shop**	[djúːti friː ʃɑp] n.	면세점
26	**airport limousine**	[ɛərpɔ̀ːrt líməziːn] n.	공항버스
27	**emergency exit**	[imə́ːrdʒənsi éksit] n.	비상구
28	**security check**	[sikjúəriti tʃek] n.	보안 검색

⋯ **Please show your boarding pass.**
    탑승권을 보여주세요.

⋯ **You're in economy class.**
    보통 좌석을 갖고 계시군요.

⋯ **Where is the baggage claim?**
    짐 찾는 곳이 어디죠?

⋯ **Do you have anything to declare?**
    신고하실 물건이 있습니까?

⋯ **Are there any nonstop flights to Miami?**
    마이애미까지 직항편이 있습니까?

* **suitcase**   [súːtkèis] n.   옷가방
* **quarantine**   [kwɔ́ːrəntìːn] n.   검역소
* **departure lounge**   [dipáːrtʃər laundʒ] n.   출발 로비
* **moving sidewalk**   [múːviŋ sáidwɔ̀ːk] n.   움직이는 보도
* **baggage compartment**
    [bǽgidʒ kəmpáːrtmənt] n.   머리 윗쪽의 물품 보관 선반

Part 080 Shopping

쇼핑 1

A
- gift wrapping counter
- gift shop
- souvenir shop
- food court
- lost and found
- shopping mall
- snack bar

B
- department store
- parking lot
- Lady's Wear
- Men's Wear
- elevator
- escalator
- sporting goods counter

C
- pay
- check-out counter
- refund
- exchange
- shop around
- try on

D
- operating hours
- open
- closed
- fitting room
- tight-fitting
- loose

1	gift wrapping counter	[gift ræpiŋ káuntər] n.	선물 포장 코너
2	gift shop	[gift ʃɑp] n.	선물 가게
3	souvenir shop	[sùːvəníər ʃɑp] n.	기념품 가게
4	food court	[fuːd kɔːrt] n.	식당가
5	lost and found	[lɔ(ː)st ən faund] n.	분실물 센타
6	shopping mall	[ʃɑpiŋ mɔːl] n.	쇼핑몰
7	snack bar	[snæk bɑːr] n.	스낵바
8	department store	[dipɑ́ːrtmənt stɔːr] n.	백화점
9	parking lot	[pɑ́ːrkiŋ lɑt] n.	주차장
10	Lady's Wear	[léidiz wɛər] n.	여성복 매장
11	Men's Wear	[menz wɛər] n.	남성복 매장
12	elevator	[éləvèitər] n.	엘리베이터
13	escalator	[éskəlèitər] n.	에스컬레이터
14	sporting goods counter	[spɔ́ːrtiŋ gudz káuntər] n.	스포츠 용품 코너
15	pay	[pei] v.	지불하다
16	check-out counter	[tʃekaut kauntər] n.	계산대
17	refund	[ríːfʌnd] n. v.	환불(하다)
18	exchange	[ikstʃéindʒ] n. v.	교환(하다)
19	shop around	[ʃɑp əráund] v.	(가격을 비교하여) 여러 곳을 돌아다니다
20	try on	[trai ɔn] v.	(한번) 입어보다
21	operating hours	[ɑ́pərèitiŋ áuərz] n.	영업시간
22	open	[óupən] a.	개점(영업중인)
23	closed	[klóuzd] a.	폐점
24	fitting room	[fítiŋ ruːm] n.	옷 입어 보는 곳
25	tight-fitting	[taitfítiŋ] a.	꼭 끼는
26	loose	[luːs] a.	헐거운

⋯▸ **Where can I get a refund?**
어디로 가야 환불을 받을 수 있습니까?

⋯▸ **Lady's Wear is on the fourth floor.**
여성복 매장은 4층입니다.

⋯▸ **Can I try this on?**
이거 한번 입어봐도 될까요?

⋯▸ **Of course, the fitting room is over there.**
물론입니다. 탈의실은 저쪽이예요.

⋯▸ **How late does the store stay open?**
얼마나 늦게까지 가게를 엽니까?

✶	obey	복종하다 / 따르다
✶	obtain	획득하다
✶	occur	일어나다 / 떠오르다
✶	only	단지 / 오직 / 유일한
✶	open	열린 / 개방된
✶	operator	전화 교환수
✶	ordinary	보통의 / 평범한
✶	oriental	동양의
✶	origin	기원
✶	other	다른 / 그밖의
✶	otherwise	그렇지 않으면
✶	ought to	~해야 한다

Part 081 Shopping

쇼핑 2

A
- tourist trap
- overcharge
- clearance sale
- out of stock
- on sale
- on display

B
- cash register
- ring up
- brand-new product
- catalog
- price tag
- fixed price

C
- haggle
- buy in bulk
- pay in cash
- buy outright
- put on a credit card
- pay in installments

D
- come down
- give a discount
- warranty
- price range
- down payment
- customer service department

1	**tourist trap**	[túərist træp] n.	관광객에게 바가지 씌우는 곳
2	**overcharge**	[òuvərtʃá:rdʒ] v.	바가지 씌우다
3	**clearance sale**	[klíərəns seil] n.	정리 세일
4	**out of stock**	[autɔv stɑk] a.	재고가 없는
5	**on sale**	[ɔn seil] a.	세일중인
6	**on display**	[ɔn displéi] a.	진열되어 있는
7	**cash register**	[kæʃ rédʒəstər] n.	금전 등록기
8	**ring up**	[riŋʌp] v.	(금전 등록기로) 계산하다
9	**brand-new product**	[brænnju: prádəkt] n.	신상품
10	**catalog**	[kǽtəlɔ̀:g] n.	카탈로그
11	**price tag**	[prais tæg] n.	가격표
12	**fixed price**	[fikst prais] n.	정가
13	**haggle**	[hǽgl] v.	흥정하다
14	**buy in bulk**	[bai in bʌlk] v.	대량 구입하다
15	**pay in cash**	[pei in kæʃ] v.	현금 구입하다
16	**buy outright**	[bai áutráit] v.	즉석에서 현찰로 구입하다
17	**put on a credit card**	[putɔn ə krédit kɑ:rd] v.	카드로 지불하다
18	**pay in installments**	[pei in instɔ́:lmənts] v.	할부로 계산하다
19	**come down**	[kʌm daun] v.	(가격을) 내리다
20	**give a discount**	[givə dískaunt] v.	할인해주다
21	**warranty**	[wɔ́(:)rənti] n.	제품 보증
22	**price range**	[prais reindʒ] n.	가격대
23	**down payment**	[daun péimənt] n.	계약금, 보증금
24	**customer service department**	[kʌ́stəmər sə́:rvis dipɑ́:rtmənt] n.	고객 서비스 부

⋯ We're going to have a big clearance sale next week.
다음주에 대대적으로 정리세일을 할 예정입니다.

⋯ What is your price range?
생각하시는 가격대가 어느 정도 입니까?

⋯ Can you come down a little more on this?
가격을 좀더 할인해 주실 수 있습니까?

⋯ There is no down payment.
보증금은 없습니다.

⋯ This item is on sale.
그 제품은 세일중입니다.

* out of	~의 밖으로 / 떨어져서
* outdoor	집 밖의 / 야외의
* overall	전반적인
* overcome	이기다 / 극복하다
* overhear	엿듣다
* own	자신의
* ox	황소
* pain	고통
* painful	아픈 / 고통을 주는
* pair	한 쌍
* pal	친구
* palace	궁전

Part 082 Sports

스포츠 1

A
- player
- coach
- referee
- director
- win a game
- end in a tie
- cheering

B
- exercise
- baseball
- soccer
- football
- volleyball
- basketball

C
- table tennis
- bowling
- cycling
- swimming
- billiard/pool
- tennis
- marathon

D
- field and track events
- skateboarding
- badminton
- inlineskating
- hockey
- skydiving
- judo

#	영어	발음	한국어
1	player	[pléiər] n.	선수
2	coach	[koutʃ] n.	코치
3	referee	[rèfərí:] n.	심판
4	director	[diréktər] n.	감독
5	win a game	[winə geim] v.	게임에 이기다
6	end in a tie	[endinə tai] v.	무승부로 끝나다
7	cheering	[tʃíəriŋ] n.	응원
8	exercise	[éksərsàiz] n.	운동
9	baseball	[béisbɔ̀:l] n.	야구
10	soccer	[sákər] n.	축구
11	football	[fútbɔ̀:l] n.	미식 축구
12	volleyball	[válibɔ̀:l] n.	배구
13	basketball	[bǽskitbɔ̀:l] n.	농구
14	table tennis	[téibl ténis] n.	탁구
15	bowling	[bóuliŋ] n.	볼링
16	cycling	[sáikliŋ] n.	사이클링
17	swimming	[swímiŋ] n.	수영
18	billiard/pool	[bíljərd]/[pu:l] n.	당구 / 포켓볼
19	tennis	[ténis] n.	테니스
20	marathon	[mǽrəθàn] n.	마라톤
21	field and track events	[fi:ld ən træk ivénts] n.	육상경기
22	skateboarding	[skeitbɔ́:rdiŋ] n.	스케이트보드타기
23	badminton	[bǽdmintən] n.	배드민턴
24	inlineskating	[ínlàinskéitiŋ] n.	인라인스케이트 타기
25	hockey	[háki] n.	하키
26	skydiving	[skaídàiviŋ]	스카이다이빙
27	judo	[dʒú:dou] n.	유도

⋯⋯ What sports do you like most?
　　스포츠 중에서 무엇을 가장 좋아합니까?
⋯⋯ My sister is good at golf.
　　동생은 골프를 잘합니다.
⋯⋯ He won a gold medal in judo.
　　그는 유도에서 금메달을 땄습니다.
⋯⋯ My dad was selected as an umpire for the Olympic Games.
　　아버지는 올림픽 심판으로 선발되었습니다.
⋯⋯ Ski season is coming soon.
　　이제 곧 스키 시즌입니다.

✽ paper	종이
✽ parade	퍼레이드
✽ part	부분 / 역할
✽ particular	특별한
✽ partner	파트너
✽ path	통로
✽ pattern	패턴
✽ peaceful	평화스러운
✽ peak	산꼭대기
✽ people	사람들
✽ perform	실행하다 / 상연하다
✽ perhaps	아마도

Part 083 Sports

스포츠 2

A
- sit-up
- push-up
- chin-up
- weight lifting
- sitting bike
- golf

B
- stadium
- jog
- run
- swim
- throw
- beat

C
- fencing
- rugby
- shooting
- boxing
- softball
- gymnastics

D
- extended game
- rope-jumping
- martial arts
- horseback riding
- rule
- foul
- penalty

#	Word	Pronunciation	Meaning
1	**sit-up**	[sitʌp] n.	윗몸 일으키기
2	**push-up**	[puʃʌp] n.	팔굽혀펴기
3	**chin-up**	[tʃinʌp] n.	턱걸이
4	**weight lifting**	[weit liftiŋ] n.	역도
5	**sitting bike**	[sitiŋ baik] n.	자전거 타기
6	**golf**	[gɑlf] n.	골프
7	**stadium**	[stéidiəm] n.	경기장
8	**jog**	[dʒɑg] v.	조깅하다
9	**run**	[rʌn] v.	달리다
10	**swim**	[swim] v.	수영하다
11	**throw**	[θruː] v.	던지다
12	**beat**	[biːt] v.	치다 / 이기다
13	**fencing**	[fénsiŋ] n.	펜싱
14	**rugby**	[rʌ́gbi] n.	럭비
15	**shooting**	[ʃúːtiŋ] n.	사격
16	**boxing**	[bɑ́ksiŋ] n.	권투
17	**softball**	[sɔ́ːftbɔ́ːl] n.	소프트 볼
18	**gymnastics**	[dʒimnǽstiks] n.	체조
19	**extended game**	[iksténdid geim] n.	연장전
20	**rope-jumping**	[roup dʒʌ́mpiŋ] n.	줄넘기
21	**martial arts**	[mɑːrʃəl ɑːrtz] n.	무술
22	**horseback riding**	[hɔ́ːrsbǽk ráidiŋ] n.	승마
23	**rule**	[ruːl] n.	규칙
24	**foul**	[faul] n.	반칙
25	**penalty**	[pénəlti] n.	반칙에 대한 벌칙

Part 9 — Hobbies & Leisure

⋯ **My brother does more than 50 push-ups every morning.**
남동생은 매일 아침 팔굽혀펴기를 50회이상 합니다.

⋯ **The doctor advised my mother to learn how to swim.**
의사가 엄마에게 수영을 배울 것을 권했습니다.

⋯ **We went to jamsil Stadium to see a concert.**
우리는 콘서트를 보러 잠실 운동장에 갔습니다.

⋯ **The chance for a penalty kick was given to him.**
페널티의 킥의 기회가 그에게 주어졌습니다.

⋯ **He has been learning martial arts since he was 6 years old.**
그는 6살 이후로 무술을 배우고 있습니다.

* permit	허가하다 / 허락하다
* person	사람
* phrase	구문
* picture	그림 / 사진
* piece	조각
* peach	복숭아
* place	장소
* plate	접시
* plenty	많은
* point	가리키다
* poison	독
* pole	막대기 / 장대 / 기둥

Part 084 Entertainment 놀이

A
- toy
- playground
- square/plaza
- game
- play cards
- gamble
- lottery

B
- theme park
- amusement park
- ride
- roller coaster
- merry-go-round
- cotton candy
- face painting

C
- rest
- admission ticket
- skiing ground
- beach
- picnic
- horse race

D
- golf course
- driving range
- hunt
- playing hide-and-seek
- flying kite
- top spinning
- playing with dolls

#			
1	**toy**	[tɔi] n.	장난감
2	**playground**	[pléigràund]	놀이터
3	**square/plaza**	[skwɛəːr] / [pláːzə] n.	광장
4	**game**	[geim] n.	게임 / 경기
5	**play cards**	[plei kɑːrdz] v.	카드놀이하다
6	**gamble**	[gǽmbl] n.	도박
7	**lottery**	[látəri] n.	복권
8	**theme park**	[θiːm pɑːrk] n.	테마파크
9	**amusement park**	[əmjúːzmənt pɑːrk] n.	놀이공원
10	**ride**	[raid] n.	놀이기구
11	**roller coaster**	[róulər kóustər] n.	롤러코스터
12	**merry-go-round**	[méri gou raund] n.	회전목마
13	**cotton candy**	[kátn kǽndi] n.	솜사탕
14	**face painting**	[feis péintiŋ] n.	얼굴 페인팅
15	**rest**	[rest] n.	휴식
16	**admission ticket**	[ədmíʃən tíkit] n.	입장권
17	**skiing ground**	[skíːiŋ graund] n.	스키장
18	**beach**	[biːtʃ] n.	해변
19	**picnic**	[píːnik] n.	소풍
20	**horse race**	[hɔːrs reis] n.	경마
21	**golf course**	[gɑlf kɔːrs] n.	골프장
22	**driving range**	[dráiviŋ reindʒ] n.	골프연습장
23	**hunt**	[hʌnt] n. v.	사냥(하다)
24	**playing hide-and-seek**	[pleiŋ haid ən siːk] n.	술래잡기
25	**flying kite**	[fláiiŋ kait] n.	연날리기
26	**top spinning**	[tɑp spíniŋ] n.	팽이치기
27	**playing with dolls**	[pleiŋ wið dɑlz] n.	인형놀이

⋯▸ We bought admission tickets and entered the zoo.
　　입장권을 사서 동물원에 들어갔습니다.

⋯▸ I used to play with dolls.
　　인형 놀이를 하면서 놀곤 했습니다.

⋯▸ My father goes to the horse races once a week.
　　아버지는 일주일에 한번 경마를 보러 가십니다.

⋯▸ My friends and I played slot machines in Japan.
　　저는 친구들과 일본에서 파칭코를 했습니다.

⋯▸ I won the lottery.
　　복권에 당첨되었습니다.

✳	politely	예의 바르게
✳	pony	조랑말
✳	popular	대중의 / 인기 있는
✳	port	항구 / 무역항
✳	possess	소유하다
✳	possible	가능한
✳	pound	(무게) 파운드
✳	pour	따르다 / 붓다 / 쏟다
✳	practice	실행 / 연습(하다)
✳	praise	칭찬(하다)
✳	prefer	더 좋아하다 / 선호하다
✳	prepare	준비하다

10 Culture & Art

Part 085 Music 음악

A
- sing
- song
- performance
- popular song
- children's song
- composition

B
- lyrics
- writing songs
- beat/rhythm
- Soprano
- Alto
- solo
- recital

C
- musical instrument
- guitar
- piano
- violin
- drum
- flute
- cello

D
- classic
- jazz
- orchestra
- chorus
- conductor
- melody

#	영단어	발음	뜻
1	sing	[siŋ] v.	노래하다
2	song	[sɔ(:)ŋ] n.	노래
3	performance	[pərfɔ́:rməns] n.	공연
4	popular song	[pápjələr sɔ(:)ŋ] n.	가요
5	children's song	[tʃíldrənz sɔ(:)ŋ] n.	동요
6	composition	[kàmpəzíʃən] n.	작곡
7	lyrics	[líriks] n.	가사
8	writing songs	[ráitiŋ sɔ(:)ŋz] n.	작사
9	beat/rhythm	[bi:t]/[ríðəm] n.	박자
10	Soprano	[səprǽnou] n.	소프라노
11	Alto	[ǽltou] n.	엘토
12	solo	[sóulou] n.	독창
13	recital	[risáitl] n.	독주
14	musical instrument	[mjú:zikəl ínstrəmənt] n.	악기
15	guitar	[gitá:r] n.	기타
16	piano	[piǽnou] n.	피아노
17	violin	[vàiəlín] n.	바이올린
18	drum	[drʌm] n.	북
19	flute	[flu:t] n.	피리
20	cello	[tʃélou] n.	첼로
21	classic	[klǽsik] n.	고전음악
22	jazz	[dʒæz] n.	재즈
23	orchestra	[ɔ́:rkəstrə] n.	오케스트라
24	chorus	[kɔ́:rəs] n.	합창
25	conductor	[kəndʌ́ktər] n.	지휘자
26	melody	[mélədi] n.	멜로디

⋯▶ Can you play the piano?
　　피아노를 칠 수 있습니까?
⋯▶ The sound of the cello is similar to the human voice.
　　첼로의 음은 인간의 목소리와 닮았습니다.
⋯▶ He became a great trumpet player.
　　그는 훌륭한 트럼펫 연주가가 되었습니다.
⋯▶ I've been learning guitar since elementary school.
　　초등학교 때부터 기타를 배우고 있습니다.
⋯▶ She is a music teacher in a high school.
　　그녀는 고등학교 음악교사입니다.

＊ **Korean harp**	[kəríːən hɑːrp] n.	거문고
＊ **harmonica**	[hɑːrmánikə] n.	하모니카
＊ **bugle**	[bjúːgl] n.	나팔
＊ **trumpet**	[trʌ́mpit] n.	트럼펫
＊ **xylophone**	[záiləfòun] n.	실로폰
＊ **harp**	[hɑːrp] n.	하프
＊ **organ**	[ɔ́ːrgən] n.	오르간
＊ **electronic organ**	[ilèktránik ɔ́ːrgən] n.	전자 오르간

Part 086 Literature 문학

A
- novel
- detective novel
- poem
- essay
- story
- fable
- fairy tale

B
- myth
- autobiography
- biography
- diary
- poet
- language
- sentence

C
- explanation
- word
- main character
- character
- author/writer
- expression

D
- manuscript
- publication
- mark
- printing
- edit
- work

#	영어	발음	뜻
1	**novel**	[návəl] n.	소설
2	**detective novel**	[ditéktiv návəl] n.	탐정(추리)소설
3	**poem**	[póuim] n.	시
4	**essay**	[ései] n.	수필
5	**story**	[stɔ́:ri] n.	이야기
6	**fable**	[féibl] n.	우화
7	**fairy tale**	[fɛ́əri teil] n.	동화
8	**myth**	[miθ] n.	신화
9	**autobiography**	[ɔ̀:təbaiágrəfi] n.	자서전
10	**biography**	[baiágrəfi] n.	전기 / 일대기
11	**diary**	[dáiəri] n.	일기
12	**poet**	[póuit] n.	시인
13	**language**	[lǽŋgwidʒ] n.	언어
14	**sentence**	[séntəns] n.	문장
15	**explanation**	[èksplənéiʃən] n.	설명
16	**word**	[wə:rd] n.	단어
17	**main character**	[mein kǽriktər] n.	주인공
18	**character**	[kǽriktər] n.	인물
19	**author/writer**	[ɔ́:θər] / [ráitər] n.	저자
20	**expression**	[ikspréʃən] n.	표현
21	**manuscript**	[mǽnjuskrìpt] n.	원고
22	**publication**	[pʌ̀bləkéiʃən] n.	출판
23	**mark**	[mɑ:rk] n.	표지
24	**printing**	[príntiŋ] n.	인쇄
25	**edit**	[édit] n. vt.	편집(하다)
26	**work**	[wə:rk] n.	작품

···▶ He knows the pleasure of enjoying literature.
그는 문학을 즐기는 기쁨을 알고 있습니다.

···▶ Who is the author of this novel?
이 소설의 저자는 누구입니까?

···▶ She describes Mother Nature in her poem.
그녀는 자작 시에서 대자연을 묘사하고 있습니다.

···▶ Scary stories are very popular among children.
무서운 이야기는 어린이들 사이에 매우 인기가 있습니다.

···▶ I indulge in reading fantasy novels.
저는 판타지 소설을 읽는 것에 빠졌어요.

∗ **compose**	[kəmpóuz] v.	작문하다 / 작곡하다
∗ **describe**	[diskráib] vt.	묘사하다
∗ **create**	[kriéit] v.	창조하다 / 창작하다
∗ **express**	[iksprés] v.	표현하다
∗ **write**	[rait] v.	쓰다

Part 087 Fashion & Cosmetics
패션 및 화장품

A
- fashion
- fashion leader
- makeup
- cosmetics
- skin lotion
- perfume
- lipstick

B
- lotion
- cream
- foundation
- blusher
- eye shadow
- mascara
- massage

C
- soap
- shampoo
- hair conditioner
- treatment
- body shampoo
- lip cream
- cleansing lotion(cream)

D
- skin care
- pedicure
- hair spray
- mousse
- nail polish
- have hair cut
- get a perm

#			
1	fashion	[fǽʃən] n.	유행 / 패션
2	fashion leader	[fǽʃən líːdər] n.	패션 리더(유행 선도자)
3	makeup	[méikʌp] n.	화장
4	cosmetics	[kɑzmétiks] n.	화장품
5	skin lotion	[skin lóuʃən] n.	스킨로션
6	perfume	[pə́ːrfjuːm] n.	향수
7	lipstick	[lípstik] n.	립스틱
8	lotion	[lóuʃən] n.	로션
9	cream	[kriːm] n.	크림
10	foundation	[faundéiʃən] n.	파운데이션
11	blusher	[blʌʃər] n.	볼터치
12	eye shadow	[ai ʃǽdou] n.	아이쉐도우
13	mascara	[mæskǽrə] n.	마스카라
14	massage	[məsάːʒ] n.	마사지
15	soap	[soup] n.	비누
16	shampoo	[ʃæmpúː] n.	샴푸
17	hair conditioner	[hɛər kəndíʃənər] n.	린스
18	treatment	[tríːtmənt] n.	트리트먼트
19	body shampoo	[bάdi ʃæmpúː] n.	바디샴푸
20	lip cream	[lip kriːm] n.	입술 보호제
21	cleansing lotion(cream)	[klénziŋ lóuʃən (kriːm)] n.	세안제
22	skin care	[skin kɛər] n.	피부미용관리
23	pedicure	[pédikjuər] n.	발에 관련된 케어
24	hair spray	[hɛər sprei] n.	스프레이
25	mousse	[muːs] n.	무스
26	nail polish	[neil páliʃ] n.	매니큐어
27	have hair cut	[hæv hɛər kʌt] v.	머리를 커트 하다
28	get a perm	[getə pəːrm] v.	파마하다

- Can you tell me the latest fashion trend?
  최근의 유행에 대해 얘기해 주세요.
- Let's remove makeup completely with cleansing lotion.
  세안제로 깨끗이 화장을 지웁시다.
- She is a fashion leader.
  그녀는 유행을 선도합니다.
- I go to a nail shop at least once a week.
  적어도 일주일에 한번은 손톱 손질하러 갑니다.
- She put on a new lipstick today.
  그녀는 오늘 새로운 립스틱을 발랐습니다.

* **design**	[dizáin] n.	디자인
* **nail shop**	[neil ʃɑp] n.	손톱 손질 해주는 곳
* **pack**	[pæk] n.	팩
* **wax**	[wæks] n.	왁스

11 Culture & Society

Part 088 Social Relations
사교

A
- greet
- greeting
- introduce
- invite
- invitation
- visit
- welcome

B
- relationship
- close friend
- colleague/coworker
- friendship
- advice
- manners
- behavior

C
- activity
- participation
- business card
- meeting
- rumor
- apology
- attitude

D
- guide
- shake hands
- quarrel
- bother
- applaud
- humanity
- congratulatory gift

#	Word	Pronunciation	Meaning
1	greet	[griːt] v.	인사하다
2	greeting	[gríːtiŋ] n.	인사
3	introduce	[ìntrədjúːs] v.	소개하다 / 도입하다
4	invite	[inváit] v.	초대하다 / 초청하다
5	invitation	[ìnvətéiʃən] n.	초대
6	visit	[vízit] n. v.	방문(하다)
7	welcome	[wélkəm] n. v.	환영(하다)
8	relationship	[riléiʃənʃip] n.	관계
9	close friend	[klous frend] n.	친한 친구
10	colleague/co-worker	[káliːg] / [kóuwəːrkər] n.	동료
11	friendship	[fréndʃip] n.	우정
12	advice	[ædváis] n.	충고
13	manners	[mǽnərz] n.	예의
14	behavior	[bihéivjər] n.	행동
15	activity	[æktívəti] n.	활동
16	participation	[pɑːrtìsəpéiʃən] n.	참가
17	business card	[bíznis kɑːrd] n.	명함
18	meeting	[míːtiŋ] n.	모임
19	rumor	[rúːmər] n.	소문
20	apology	[əpálədʒi] n.	사과
21	attitude	[ǽtitjùːd] n.	태도
22	guide	[gaid] n. v.	안내(하다)
23	shake hands	[ʃeik hændz] v.	악수하다
24	quarrel	[kwɔ́ːrəl] n.	말다툼
25	bother	[báðər] v.	폐를 끼치다
26	applaud	[əplɔ́ːd] v.	박수갈채를 보내다
27	humanity	[hjuːmǽnəti] n.	인정
28	congratulatory gift	[kəngrǽtʃələtɔ̀ːri gift] n.	축하선물

⋯→ We exchanged business cards with each other.
우리는 서로 명함을 교환했습니다.

⋯→ This is my best friend, Young.
이쪽은 저의 친한 친구 Young 입니다.

⋯→ Let's get along well with each other from now on.
지금부터 잘 지내도록 합시다.

⋯→ I was invited to the party in her house.
그녀의 집에서 여는 파티에 초대되었습니다.

⋯→ Could you give me some advice about this matter?
이 문제에 관해서 충고 좀 해주시겠습니까?

∗ **appreciate**	[əpríːʃièit] v.	감사하다 / 감상하다
∗ **meet**	[miːt] v.	만나다
∗ **be indebted to**	[bi indétid tu] v.	신세지다

Part 089 Love & Dating
사랑 및 교제

A
- miss
- have a crush on
- propose
- break up with
- dump
- have a love affair
- divorce

B
- engagement
- fiance
- marriage
- wedding ceremony
- bridegroom
- bride
- wedding hall

C
- remarriage
- arranged marriage
- love marriage
- matchmaker
- fate
- favor

D
- scar
- charm
- popularity
- memories
- first love
- lover/boyfriend
- dating

Part 11

Culture & Society

#			
1	**miss**	[mis] v.	그리워하다
2	**have a crush on**	[hævə krʌʃ ɔn] v.	짝사랑하다
3	**propose**	[prəpóuz] n. v.	청혼(하다)
4	**break up with**	[breikʌp wið] v.	-와 헤어지다
5	**dump**	[dʌmp] v.	차버리다
6	**have an affair**	[hævən əféər] v.	바람피우다
7	**divorce**	[divɔ́:rs] n. v.	이혼(하다)
8	**engagement**	[engéidʒmənt] n.	약혼
9	**fiance**	[fi:ɑ:nséi] n.	약혼자(남자)
10	**marriage**	[mǽridʒ] n.	결혼
11	**wedding ceremony**	[wédiŋ sérəmòuni] n.	결혼식
12	**bridegroom**	[bráidgrù(:)m] n.	신랑
13	**bride**	[braid] n.	신부
14	**wedding hall**	[wédiŋ hɔ:l] n.	예식장
15	**remarriage**	[rimǽridʒ] n.	재혼
16	**arranged marriage**	[əréindʒid mǽridʒ] n.	중매결혼
17	**love marriage**	[lʌv mǽridʒ] n.	연애결혼
18	**matchmaker**	[mǽtʃmèikər] n.	중매인
19	**fate**	[feit] n.	운명
20	**favor**	[féivər] n.	호의
21	**scar**	[skɑ:r] n.	상처
22	**charm**	[tʃɑ:rm] n.	매력
23	**popularity**	[pàpjəlǽrəti] n.	인기
24	**memories**	[méməriz] n.	추억
25	**first love**	[fə:rst lʌv] n.	첫사랑
26	**lover/boyfriend**	[lʌ́vər]/[bɔ́ifrènd] n.	애인
27	**dating**	[deitiŋ] n.	교제

⋯▸ Do you love her?
　　그녀를 사랑합니까?

⋯▸ I have been dating out with her for two years.
　　저는 그녀와 2년째 사귀고 있습니다.

⋯▸ I received the wedding invitation from my cousin.
　　저는 사촌의 결혼식 초대장을 받았습니다.

⋯▸ He had a crush on me.
　　그는 나에게 첫눈에 반했었습니다.

⋯▸ He got divorced and remarried right away.
　　그는 이혼하자마자 곧 재혼했습니다.

✳ hug	[hʌg] v.	껴안다
✳ kiss	[kis] n. v.	입맞춤(하다)
✳ marry	[mǽri] v.	~와 결혼하다
✳ like	[laik] v.	좋아하다 / 바라다
✳ attractive	[ətrǽktiv] a.	매력적인
✳ cute	[kjuːt] a.	귀여운
✳ lovely	[lʌ́vli] a.	사랑스러운 / 아름다운
✳ reconciliation	[rèkənsìliéiʃən] n.	화해

Part 090 Religion

신앙 1

A
- God
- evil
- ghost
- devil
- sin
- heaven
- hell

B
- believer
- Bible
- baptism
- Christianity
- Christian
- Catholic
- Protestant

C
- Mass
- service
- minister
- priest
- cathedral
- church
- shrine

D
- temple
- Buddhism
- Buddhist
- Buddha
- monk
- shaman
- shamanism

#	Word	Pronunciation	Meaning
1	God	[gɑd] n.	신/하느님
2	evil	[íːvəl] n.	악
3	ghost	[goust] n.	도깨비, 귀신
4	devil	[dévl] n.	악마(마귀)
5	sin	[sin] n.	죄
6	heaven	[hévən] n.	천국
7	hell	[hel] n.	지옥
8	believer	[bilíːvə] n.	신자
9	Bible	[báibl] n.	성경
10	baptism	[bǽptizəm] n.	세례
11	Christianity	[krìstʃiǽnəti] n.	기독교
12	Christian	[krístʃən] n.	기독교도
13	Catholic	[kǽθəlik] n.	카톨릭 교도
14	Protestant	[prátəstənt] n.	신교도
15	Mass	[mæs] n.	미사
16	service	[sə́ːrvis] n.	예배
17	minister	[mínistər] n.	목사
18	priest	[priːst] n.	신부
19	cathedral	[kəθíːdrəl] n.	성당
20	church	[tʃəːrtʃ] n.	교회
21	shrine	[ʃrain] n.	신사
22	temple	[témpl] n.	절
23	Buddhism	[búədizəm] n.	불교
24	Buddhist	[búːdist] n.	불교도
25	Buddha	[búːdə] n.	부처
26	monk	[mʌŋk] n.	스님
27	shaman	[ʃɑ́ːmən] n.	주술사 / 무당
28	shamanism	[ʃɑ́ːmənìzəm] n.	샤머니즘

⋯▸ Father's funeral was held last week.
  지난주 아버지의 장례식이 치러졌습니다.

⋯▸ I've been to the ancestral grave.
  성묘에 갔다 왔습니다.

⋯▸ Let's pray to God together.
  함께 신에게 기도합시다.

⋯▸ My family goes to church on Sundays.
  우리 가족은 일요일 교회에 갑니다.

⋯▸ She is a Catholic.
  그녀는 카톨릭 신자입니다.

⋯▸ A baby is being baptized.
  아기가 세례를 받고 있습니다.

* present	주다 / 선물
* press	누르다 / 압박하다
* pretend	~인 체하다
* prevent	막다 / 방해하다
* primary	제1의 / 주요한 / 최초의
* private	개인적인 / 사적인
* problem	문제
* progress	전진 / 진행
* promote	홍보하다 / 조장하다
* proper	적당한 / 알맞은
* protect	보호하다
* provide	제공하다

Part 091 Religion 신앙 2

A
- religious
- theology
- cardinal
- bishop
- Confucianism
- Hinduism
- Muslim

B
- Resurrection
- holy
- hymn
- cross
- angel
- paradise

C
- pray
- preach
- oath
- predict
- believe
- bless

D
- funeral
- burial
- tomb stone
- tomb/grave
- cremation
- anniversary of somebody's death
- visit one's ancestral graves

1	**religious**	[rilídʒəs] a.	종교적인
2	**theology**	[θiːálədʒi] n.	신학
3	**cardinal**	[káːrdənl] n.	추기경
4	**bishop**	[bíʃəp] n.	주교
5	**Confucianism**	[kənfjúːʃənizəm] n.	유교
6	**Hinduism**	[híndu:ìzəm] n.	힌두교
7	**Muslim**	[mʌ́zləm] n.	이슬람교도
8	**Resurrection**	[rèzərékʃən] n.	부활
9	**holy**	[hóuli] a.	신성한
10	**hymn**	[him] n.	찬송가 / 성가
11	**cross**	[krɔːs] n.	십자가
12	**angel**	[éindʒəl] n.	천사
13	**paradise**	[pǽrədàis] n.	낙원
14	**pray**	[prei] n. v.	기도(하다)
15	**preach**	[priːtʃ] n. v.	설교(하다)
16	**oath**	[ouθ] n.	맹세
17	**predict**	[pridíkt] v.	예언하다
18	**believe**	[bilíːv] v.	믿다
19	**bless**	[bles] vt.	축복하다
20	**funeral**	[fjúːnərəl] n.	장례식
21	**burial**	[bériəl] n.	매장
22	**tomb stone**	[tuːm stoun] n.	묘비
23	**tomb/grave**	[tuːm] / [greiv] n.	무덤
24	**cremation**	[kriméiʃən] n.	화장
25	**anniversary of somebody's death**	[ænəvə́ːrsəri ɔv sʌ́mbàdiz deθ] n.	기일
26	**visit one's ancestral graves**	[vísit wʌns ænséstrəl greivz] n.	성묘하다

⋯▸ My uncle studied theology at the University.
　　삼촌은 대학에서 신학을 공부했습니다.

⋯▸ Chosun Dynasty was a society ruled by Confucianism.
　　조선왕조는 유교에 의해 통치된 사회였습니다.

⋯▸ He sincerely believes in God.
　　그는 독실한 신자입니다.

⋯▸ Tomorrow is the anniversary of my grandmother's death.
　　내일은 할머니의 기일입니다.

⋯▸ I saw the Cardinal at the special Mass.
　　특별 미사에서 추기경을 보았습니다.

✳ public	공적인
✳ pull	당기다 / 끌다
✳ punish	벌주다
✳ pure	순수한
✳ purpose	목적
✳ push	밀다
✳ put	놓다 / 두다
✳ puzzle	수수께끼 / 당혹하게 만들다
✳ qualify	자격을 주다
✳ quantify	양을 재다
✳ quickly	빨리
✳ quiet	조용한

Part 092 Communication 의사소통

A
- alphabet
- spelling
- word
- accent
- intonation
- pronunciation

B
- standard language
- dialect
- slang
- translation
- interpretation
- proverb
- gender

C
- topic
- birth date
- introduction
- conversation
- gesture
- discussion
- argument

D
- meaning
- foreigner
- opinion
- speech
- joke
- quotation

#	영어	발음	뜻
1	**alphabet**	[ǽlfəbèt] n.	알파벳
2	**spelling**	[spéliŋ] n.	철자법
3	**word**	[wɔːrd] n.	단어 / 말
4	**accent**	[ǽksent] n.	악센트
5	**intonation**	[ìntənéiʃən] n.	억양
6	**pronunciation**	[prənʌ̀nsiéiʃən] n.	발음
7	**standard language**	[stǽndəːrd lǽŋgwidʒ] n.	표준어
8	**dialect**	[dáiəlèkt] n.	방언
9	**slang**	[slæŋ] n.	속어
10	**translation**	[trænsléiʃən] n.	번역
11	**interpretation**	[intə̀rprətéiʃən] n.	통역
12	**proverb**	[právərb] n.	속담
13	**gender**	[dʒéndər] n.	성별
14	**topic**	[tápik] n.	화제 / 주제
15	**birth date**	[bəːrθ deit] n.	생년월일
16	**introduction**	[ìntrədʌ́kʃən] n.	자기소개
17	**conversation**	[kànvərséiʃən] n.	대화
18	**gesture**	[dʒéstʃər] n.	제스처
19	**discussion**	[diskʌ́ʃən] n.	토론
20	**argument**	[áːrgjumənt] n.	언쟁
21	**meaning**	[míːniŋ] n.	의미
22	**foreigner**	[fɔ́(ː)rinər] n.	외국인
23	**opinion**	[əpínjən] n.	의견
24	**speech**	[spiːtʃ] n.	연설
25	**joke**	[dʒouk] n.	농담
26	**quotation**	[kwoutéiʃən] n.	인용

···▸ **The conversation class just started.**
회화수업이 막 시작되었습니다.

···▸ **You have to practice pronunciation more.**
발음 연습을 더 해야 합니다.

···▸ **What is today's topic of the discussion class?**
오늘의 토론수업 주제가 뭐지요?

···▸ **Let me introduce myself.**
자기소개를 하겠습니다.

···▸ **She wants be a great interpreter.**
그녀는 훌륭한 통역사가 되고 싶어 합니다.

∗ **argue**	[ɑ́ːrgjuː] v.	논쟁하다 / 주장하다
∗ **ask**	[æsk] v.	묻다 / 부탁하다
∗ **discuss**	[diskʌ́s] v.	토론하다
∗ **mention**	[ménʃən] v.	언급하다
∗ **tell/say/talk/speak**	[tel]/[sei]/[tɔːk]/[spiːk] v.	말하다
∗ **holiday**	[hɑ́lədèi] n.	휴일
∗ **event**	[ivént] n.	행사 / 사건
∗ **festival**	[féstəvəl] n.	축제 / 잔치
∗ **feast**	[fiːst] n.	축제 / 잔치
∗ **recreation**	[rèkriéiʃən] n.	휴양 / 레크레이션

12 Science & Technology

Part 093 Universe

우주

A
- Galaxy
- Milky Way
- planet
- Sun
- star
- moon
- satellite

B
- space shuttle
- space station
- astronaut
- unidentified flying object (UFO)
- orbit
- zero gravity
- spacewalk

C
- Solar system
- Mercury
- Venus
- Earth
- Mars
- Jupiter
- Saturn

D
- eclipse
- comet
- meteor
- the North Star
- alien
- solar
- lunar

#	Word	Pronunciation	Meaning
1	Galaxy	[gǽləksi] n.	은하계
2	Milky Way	[mílki wei] n.	은하수
3	planet	[plǽnət] n.	행성
4	Sun	[sʌn] n.	태양
5	star	[stɑːr] n.	별
6	moon	[muːn] n.	달
7	satellite	[sǽtəlàit] n.	(인공)위성
8	space shuttle	[speis ʃʌ́tl] n.	우주 왕복선
9	space station	[speis stéiʃən] n.	우주 정거장
10	astronaut	[ǽstrənɔ̀ːt] n.	우주 비행사
11	unidentified flying object(UFO)	[ʌ̀naidéntəfàid fláiiŋ ábdʒikt] n.	미확인 비행 물체
12	orbit	[ɔ́ːrbit] n.	궤도
13	zero gravity	[zíərou grǽvəti] n.	무중력
14	spacewalk	[spéiswɔ̀ːk] n.	우주유영
15	Solar system	[sóulər sístəm] n.	태양계
16	Mercury	[mə́ːrkjuri] n.	수성
17	Venus	[víːnəs] n.	금성
18	Earth	[əːrθ] n.	지구
19	Mars	[mɑːrz] n.	화성
20	Jupiter	[dʒúːpətər] n.	목성
21	Saturn	[sǽtəːrn] n.	토성
22	eclipse	[iklíps] n.	일식
23	comet	[kámit] n.	혜성
24	meteor	[míːtiər] n.	운석
25	the North Star	[nɔːrθ stɑːr] n.	북극성
26	alien	[éiljən] n.	외계인
27	solar	[sóulər] a.	태양의
28	lunar	[lúːnər] a.	달의

Science & Technology

⋯▸ Do you believe in the existence of aliens?
외계인의 존재를 믿습니까?

⋯▸ People found the evidence that there used to be water on Mars.
사람들은 화성에 물이 존재했었다는 증거를 발견하였습니다.

⋯▸ The North Star is sparkling in the sky.
북극성이 하늘에서 반짝이고 있습니다.

⋯▸ There are nine planets in this Solar System including the Earth.
지구를 포함해서 태양계에는 9개의 행성이 있습니다.

⋯▸ UFO stands for unidentified flying object.
UFO는 미확인 비행 물체를 의미합니다.

✽ quit	그만두다
✽ quite	아주 / 꽤
✽ rage	노여움
✽ rail	난간 / 가로대
✽ rainy	비가 오는
✽ raise	올리다 / 기르다 / 모으다
✽ random	임의의 / 되는 대로의
✽ rapidly	빨리
✽ rather	오히려 / 다소
✽ raw	날것의
✽ ready	준비된
✽ realize	깨닫다 / 실현하다

P·a·r·t 094 The Earth
지구 1

A
- mountain
- mountain range
- valley
- hill
- slope
- continent

B
- ocean
- sea
- river
- pond
- lake
- spring
- well

C
- coast
- beach
- wave
- waterfall
- stone
- pebbles
- sand

D
- land
- farm/field
- soil
- mud
- flatland
- rock
- jungle

1	**mountain**	[máuntən] n.	산
2	**mountain range**	[máuntən reindʒ] n.	산맥
3	**valley**	[væli] n.	골짜기(계곡)
4	**hill**	[hil] n.	언덕
5	**slope**	[sloup] n.	비탈 / 경사지
6	**continent**	[kántənənt] n.	대륙
7	**ocean**	[óuʃən] n.	대양
8	**sea**	[siː] n.	바다
9	**river**	[rívər] n.	강
10	**pond**	[pɑnd] n.	연못
11	**lake**	[leik] n.	호수
12	**spring**	[spriŋ] n.	샘
13	**well**	[wel] n.	우물
14	**coast**	[koust] n.	해안 / 연안
15	**beach**	[biːtʃ] n.	해변
16	**wave**	[weiv] n.	파도
17	**waterfall**	[wɔ́ːtərfɔ̀ːl] n.	폭포
18	**stone**	[stoun] n.	돌
19	**pebbles**	[péblz] n.	자갈
20	**sand**	[sænd] n.	모래 / 사막
21	**land**	[lænd] n.	육지 / 땅 / 나라 / 토지
22	**farm/field**	[fɑrm] / [fiːld] n.	밭
23	**soil**	[sɔil] n.	흙 / 땅
24	**mud**	[mʌd] n.	진흙
25	**flatland**	[flǽtlænd] n.	평지
26	**rock**	[rɑk] n.	바위
27	**jungle**	[dʒʌ́ŋgl] n.	정글(밀림지대)

- Mother Nature is vital to human beings.
  대자연은 인간에게 매우 중요한 것이다.
- Farmers are busy with rice planting in their paddy fields.
  농부들은 논에서 모내기를 하느라 바쁩니다.
- We traveled the country from coast to coast.
  우리는 해변을 따라서 그 나라를 여행했습니다.
- My hobby is mountain climbing.
  취미는 등산입니다.
- Today we have big waves.
  오늘은 커다란 파도가 치고 있습니다.

※ **shine** [ʃain] v. 빛나다
※ **surround** [səráund] v. 둘러싸다
※ **alive** [əláiv] a. 살아 있는
※ **natural** [nǽtʃərəl] a. 자연의 / 당연한
※ **vital** [váitl] a. 생명의 / 매우 중요한 / 생생한

Part 095 The Earth
지구 2

A
- village
- island
- sky
- air
- ozone layer
- bush
- forest

B
- life
- creature
- latitude
- longitude
- the North Pole
- the South Pole

C
- equator
- desert
- oasis
- volcano
- glacier
- iceberg
- swamp

D
- the Atlantic
- the Pacific
- peninsula
- sunlight
- ultraviolet ray
- horizon

#	Word	Pronunciation	Meaning
1	village	[vílidʒ] n.	마을
2	island	[áilənd] n.	섬
3	sky	[skai] n.	하늘
4	air	[ɛər] n.	공기
5	ozone layer	[óuzoun léiər] n.	오존층
6	bush	[buʃ] n.	수풀
7	forest	[fɔ́(ː)rist] n.	숲
8	life	[laif] n.	생명
9	creature	[kríːtʃər] n.	생물
10	latitude	[lǽtətjùːd] n.	위도
11	longitude	[lándʒətjùːd] n.	경도
12	the North Pole	[nɔːrθ poul] n.	북극
13	the South Pole	[sauθ poul] n.	남극
14	equator	[ikwéitər] n.	적도
15	desert	[dézərt] n.	사막
16	oasis	[ouéisis] n.	오아시스
17	volcano	[vɑlkéinou] n.	화산
18	glacier	[gléiʃər] n.	빙하
19	iceberg	[áisbəːrg] n.	빙산
20	swamp	[swɔmp] n.	늪
21	the Atlantic	[ði ətlǽntik] n.	대서양
22	the Pacific	[ðə pəsífik] n.	태평양
23	peninsula	[pinínsjulə] n.	반도
24	sunlight	[sʌ́nlàit] n.	햇살
25	ultraviolet ray	[ʌ̀ltrəváiəlit rei] n.	자외선
26	horizon	[həráizən] n.	수평선 / 지평선

⋯› Finally they found an oasis in the desert.
드디어 그들은 사막에서 오아시스를 발견했습니다.

⋯› We have to preserve the environment of the Earth.
지구의 환경을 보존해야 합니다.

⋯› The countries around the equator are always hot throughout the year.
적도 근처의 나라들은 일년 내내 항상 덥습니다.

⋯› Japan is an island.
일본은 섬나라이다.

⋯› This lotion protects your skin from ultraviolet rays.
이 로션은 자외선으로부터 피부를 보호합니다.

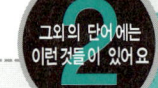

＊ **natural**	[nǽtʃərəl]	a.	천연의
＊ **gravitation**	[græ̀vətéiʃən]	n.	인력
＊ **the Northern Hemisphere**	[nɔ́:rðə:rn hémisfìər]	n.	북반구
＊ **the Southern Hemisphere**	[sʌ́ðə:rn hémisfìər]	n.	남반구

Part 096 Internet 인터넷

A
- personal computer(PC)
- laptop
- mouse
- keyboard
- local area network(LAN)
- program
- Internet shopping mall

B
- home page
- web site
- web designer
- World Wide Web(WWW)
- messenger
- chatting
- email

C
- print
- click
- delete
- copy
- paste
- Identification (ID)
- password

D
- log on
- log off
- online
- offline
- computer virus
- computer vaccine
- computer crime

#			
1	**personal computer(PC)**	[pə́ːrsənəl kəmpjúːtər] n.	개인용 컴퓨터
2	**laptop**	[lǽptɑ̀p] n.	노트북
3	**mouse**	[maus] n.	마우스
4	**keyboard**	[kíːbɔ̀ːrd] n. v.	키보드(를 쳐서 입력하다)
5	**local area network(LAN)**	[lóukəl ɛ́əríə nétwə̀ːrk] n.	근거리 통신망
6	**program**	[próugræm] nʒ	프로그램
7	**Internet shopping mall**	[íntərnèt ʃɑ́piŋ mɔːl] n.	인터넷 쇼핑몰
8	**home page**	[houm peidʒ] n.	홈페이지
9	**web site**	[web sait] n.	웹 사이트
10	**web designer**	[web dizáinər] n.	웹 사이트 디자이너
11	**World Wide Web(WWW)**	[wəːrld waid web] n.	월드 와이드 웹
12	**messenger**	[mésəndʒər] n.	인터넷상의 즉석 대화
13	**chatting**	[tʃǽtiŋ] n.	챗팅
14	**email**	[íːmeil] n. v.	이메일(을 보내다)
15	**print**	[print] n. v.	인쇄(하다)
16	**click**	[klik] n. v.	클릭(하다)
17	**delete**	[dilíːt] v.	삭제(하다)
18	**copy**	[kɑ́pi] n. v.	복사(하다)
19	**paste**	[peist] v.	붙이다
20	**Identification (ID)**	[aidèntəfikéiʃən] n.	아이디
21	**password**	[pǽswə̀ːrd] n.	비밀번호
22	**log on**	[lɔ(ː)gɔn] v.	컴퓨터를 시작하다
23	**log off**	[lɔ(ː)gɔf] v.	프로그램을 끝내다
24	**online**	[ɑ́nlain] a.	컴퓨터에 연결되어 있는
25	**offline**	[ɔ́ːflain] a.	연결되어 있지 않은
26	**computer virus** n.	[kəmpjúːtər váiərəs] n.	컴퓨터 바이러스
27	**computer vaccine** n.	[kəmpjúːtər vǽksi(ː)n] n.	컴퓨터 백신
28	**computer crime** n.	[kəmpjúːtər kraim] n.	컴퓨터 범죄

⋯→ **Please give me your email address.**
　이메일주소를 알려주세요.

⋯→ **Log on the computer.**
　컴퓨터를 켜세요.

⋯→ **He's online chatting for an hour everyday.**
　그는 매일 한 시간씩 컴퓨터 채팅을 합니다.

⋯→ **I ordered books from the internet bookstore.**
　인터넷 서점에서 책을 주문하였습니다.

⋯→ **More information will be available on the web site.**
　더 많은 정보가 웹 사이트에 있습니다.

* really		정말로
* receive		받다
* recommend		추천하다 / 권하다
* record		기록하다
* recover		되찾다 / 회복하다
* refuse		거절하다
* regular		규칙적인 / 정기적인
* relate		관련시키다 / 이야기하다
* remain		남다 / ~인 채로 있다
* remember		기억하다
* remove		제거하다
* repay		보답하다 / 되갚다

P·a·r·t 097 Chemistry

화학

A
- experiment
- laboratory/lab
- microscope
- equipment
- catalyst
- test tube

B
- phenomenon
- principle
- analysis
- status
- material
- substance

C
- hypothesis
- assumption
- classification
- observation
- energy
- reaction
- chain reaction

D
- object
- theory
- reason
- result
- preparation
- react

#	Word	Pronunciation	Meaning
1	experiment	[ikspérəmənt] n.	실험
2	laboratory/lab	[lǽbərətɔ̀ːri]/[læb] n.	실험실
3	microscope	[máikrəskòup] n.	현미경
4	equipment	[ikwípmənt] n.	장비
5	catalyst	[kǽtəlist] n.	촉매제
6	test tube	[test tjuːb] n.	시험관
7	phenomenon	[finámənàn] n.	현상
8	principle	[prínsəpl] n.	원리
9	analysis	[ənǽləsis] n.	분석
10	status	[stéitəs] n.	상태
11	material	[mətíəriəl] n.	물질
12	substance	[sʌ́bstəns] n.	성분
13	hypothesis	[haipáθəsis] n.	가설
14	assumption	[əsʌ́mpʃən] n.	가정
15	classification	[klæ̀səfikéiʃən] n.	분류
16	observation	[àbzərvéiʃən] n.	관찰
17	energy	[énərdʒi] n.	에너지
18	reaction	[riːǽkʃən] n.	반응
19	chain reaction	[tʃein riːǽkʃən] n.	연쇄 반응
20	object	[ábdʒikt] n.	물체
21	theory	[θíːəri] n.	이론
22	reason	[ríːzən] n.	원인
23	result	[rizʌ́lt] n.	결과
24	preparation	[prèpəréiʃən] n.	준비
25	react	[riːǽkt] v.	반응하다 / 반작용하다

⋯→ We set up a hypothesis and performed an experiment to test it.
우리는 가설을 세우고 이에 대한 실험을 했습니다.

⋯→ I observed the hair through a microscope.
현미경으로 머리카락을 관찰했습니다.

⋯→ Can you find out the result of the chemical reaction?
그 화학반응의 결과를 알아봐 주시겠습니까?

⋯→ The Company runs a lab with good facilities.
그 회사는 시설이 잘 된 실험실을 운영합니다.

⋯→ So, let's analyze the substance.
그렇다면 그 성분을 분석합시다.

*	repeat	반복하다
*	reply	대답하다
*	report	보고하다
*	represent	나타내다 / 대표하다
*	require	요구하다 / 필요로 하다
*	reserve	예약하다
*	resident	주민
*	resist	저항하다
*	restrict	제한하다 / 한정하다
*	return	돌아오다
*	reveal	드러나다
*	riddle	수수께끼

13 Miscellaneous

Part 098 Material

물질 1

A
- gold
- silver
- bronze
- iron
- steel
- oil
- coal

B
- electricity
- solid
- gas
- liquid
- gasoline
- existence

C
- atom
- molecule
- hydrogen
- carbon
- oxygen
- synthesis
- liquid crystal

D
- size
- height
- length
- width
- thickness
- weight
- strength

#	Word	Pronunciation	Meaning
1	**gold**	[gould] n.	금
2	**silver**	[sílvər] n.	은
3	**bronze**	[brɑnz] n.	동(청동)
4	**iron**	[áiərn] n.	철
5	**steel**	[sti:l] n.	강철
6	**oil**	[ɔil] n.	석유
7	**coal**	[koul] n.	석탄
8	**electricity**	[ilèktrísəti] n.	전기
9	**solid**	[sálid] n.	고체
10	**gas**	[gæs] n.	기체
11	**liquid**	[líkwid] n.	액체
12	**gasoline**	[gǽsəlí:n] n.	휘발유
13	**existence**	[igzístəns] n.	존재
14	**atom**	[ǽtəm] n.	원자
15	**molecule**	[máləkjù:l] n.	분자
16	**hydrogen**	[háidrədʒən] n.	수소
17	**carbon**	[ká:rbən] n.	탄소
18	**oxygen**	[áksidʒən] n.	산소
19	**synthesis**	[sínθəsis] n.	합성
20	**liquid crystal**	[líkwid krístl] n.	액정
21	**size**	[saiz] n.	크기
22	**height**	[hait] n.	높이 / 신장
23	**length**	[leŋθ] n.	길이
24	**width**	[widθ] n.	넓이, 폭
25	**thickness**	[θíknis] n.	굵기
26	**weight**	[weit] n.	무게
27	**strength**	[streŋθ] n.	세기 / 힘 / 강점

⋯▸ **Water is a liquid, and ice is a solid.**
물은 액체이고, 얼음은 고체입니다.

⋯▸ **Human beings can't live without oxygen.**
산소가 없이는 인간은 살 수 없습니다.

⋯▸ **It is made of bronze and steel.**
이것은 동과 철로 만들어져 있습니다.

⋯▸ **Liquid crystal is a material in a state between solid and liquid.**
액정은 고체와 액체의 중간상태의 물질입니다.

⋯▸ **Strike while the iron is hot.**
쇠가 뜨거운 동안 쳐라. (즉, 기회를 놓치지 말라는 뜻)

⋯▸ **Do you know the height of Mt. Huji?**
후지산의 높이를 아십니까?

∗	ridiculous	우스꽝스러운
∗	right	옳은
∗	ring	반지
∗	rise	오르다 / 일어서다
∗	role	역할
∗	roll	구르다 / 말다
∗	rotate	회전하다
∗	rough	거친 / 대략의
∗	round	둥근 / 왕복의
∗	ruin	파멸 / 몰락
∗	rush	돌진하다

Part 099 Material

물질 2

A
- voice
- sound
- taste
- power
- fire
- light
- heat

B
- smoke
- shade
- metal
- lead
- aluminium
- alloy

C
- temperature
- speed
- rust
- ash
- powder
- charcoal
- acid

D
- steam
- fiber
- cotton
- silk
- hemp
- solar energy

1	**voice**	[vɔis] n.		목소리
2	**sound**	[saund] n.		소리
3	**taste**	[teist] n.		맛
4	**power**	[páuər] n.		힘
5	**fire**	[faiər] n.		불
6	**light**	[lait] n.		빛
7	**heat**	[hiːt] n.		열
8	**smoke**	[smouk] n.		연기
9	**shade**	[ʃeid] n.		그림자
10	**metal**	[métl] n.		금속
11	**lead**	[led] n.		납
12	**aluminium**	[æljúminiəm] n.		알루미늄
13	**alloy**	[ǽlɔi] n.		합금
14	**temperature**	[témpərətʃuəːr] n.		온도
15	**speed**	[spiːd] n.		속도
16	**rust**	[rʌst] n.		녹
17	**ash**	[æʃ] n.		재
18	**powder**	[páudər] n.		가루
19	**charcoal**	[tʃáːrkòul] n.		숯
20	**acid**	[ǽsid] a.		산성의
21	**steam**	[stiːm] n.		증기
22	**fiber**	[fáibər] n.		섬유
23	**cotton**	[kátn] n.		면
24	**silk**	[silk] n.		실크
25	**hemp**	[hemp] n.		마
26	**solar energy**	[sóulə énərdʒi] n.		태양 에너지

Miscellaneous

- Acid rain is caused by pollution in the air.
  대기 오염 때문에 산성비가 내립니다.
- I was worried to notice my baby has a fever.
  아기가 열이 나는 것을 보고 걱정이 되었습니다.
- Fire fighters are working on putting out the wildfire.
  소방수들이 산불을 진압하려고 노력하고 있습니다.
- Solar energy will be an alternative energy source in the future.
  태양 에너지는 미래의 대체 에너지원이 될 겁니다.

*	sacrifice	희생하다
*	sail	항해하다
*	saying	속담
*	scarcely	거의 ~않다
*	scare	두려워하다
*	scene	장면
*	scold	꾸짖다 / 잔소리하다
*	score	득점
*	scream	(비명)지르다
*	search	찾다 / 조사하다
*	seat	자리 / 좌석

Part 100 Abstract Nouns
추상명사 1

A
- liberty/freedom
- equality
- peace
- hope
- pride
- spirit

B
- mercy
- wisdom
- truth
- ignorance
- imagination
- courage
- guess

C
- realization
- preparedness
- suffering
- expectation
- rebellion
- worries

D
- temptation
- harmony
- depression
- regret
- order
- instinct

추상명사 1

#	Word	Pronunciation	Meaning
1	liberty/freedom	[líbərti]/[frí:dəm] n.	자유
2	equality	[i(:)kwáləti] n.	평등
3	peace	[pi:s] n.	평화
4	hope	[houp] n.	희망
5	pride	[praid] n.	자존심
6	spirit	[spírit] n.	정신
7	mercy	[mə́:rsi] n.	자비
8	wisdom	[wízdəm] n.	지혜
9	truth	[tru:θ] n.	진리
10	ignorance	[ígnərəns] n.	무시
11	imagination	[imædʒənéiʃən] n.	상상
12	courage	[kə́:ridʒ] n.	용기
13	guess	[ges] n. v.	추측(하다)
14	realization	[rì:əlaizéiʃən] n.	실감
15	preparedness	[pripέərdnis] n.	각오
16	suffering	[sʌ́fəriŋ] n.	고통
17	expectation	[èkspektéiʃən] n.	기대
18	rebellion	[ribéljən] n.	반항
19	worries	[wə́:riz] n.	고민
20	temptation	[temptéiʃən] n.	유혹
21	harmony	[hɑ́:rməni] n.	조화
22	depression	[dipréʃən] n.	절망
23	regret	[rigrét] n. v.	후회(하다)
24	order	[ɔ́:rdər] n.	질서
25	instinct	[ínstiŋkt] n.	본능

⋯▶ You can enjoy more freedom if you live alone.
　　혼자 살면 좀더 자유를 즐길 수 있습니다.

⋯▶ She is courageous enough to testify in court.
　　그녀는 법정에서 증언할 정도로 용기가 있습니다.

⋯▶ Ignorance is bliss.
　　모르는 게 약.

⋯▶ Everything in the room is in order.
　　방안의 모든 것이 정리가 잘 되어 있습니다.

⋯▶ He is the pride of his parents.
　　그는 부모님의 자랑거리입니다.

＊ associate	[əsóuʃièit] v.	연상하다 / 관련시키다
＊ boast	[boust] v.	자랑하다
＊ bore	[bɔːr] v.	지루하게 하다
＊ consider	[kənsídər] v.	고려하다
＊ forget	[fərgét] v.	잊다
＊ forgive	[fəːrgív] v.	용서하다
＊ ignore	[ignɔ́ːr] v.	무시하다
＊ imagine	[imǽdʒin] v.	상상하다 / 생각하다
＊ misunderstand	[mìsʌndəːrstǽnd] v.	오해하다
＊ persuade	[pəːrswéid] v.	설득하다
＊ comfoːrtable	[kʌ́mfərtəbəl] a.	편안한
＊ eager	[íːgər] a.	열망하는
＊ generous	[dʒénərəs] a.	관대한

Part 101 Abstract Nouns
추상명사 2

A
- perfection
- perfectionist
- safety
- refusal
- memory
- appreciation

B
- honesty
- emphasis
- ideal
- stimulation
- will
- ability

C
- excitement
- tension
- respect
- admiration
- illusion
- prejudice

D
- silence
- intelligence
- contempt
- advice
- confusion
- consideration

Part 13

1	**perfection**	[pərfékʃən] n.	완벽
2	**perfectionist**	[pərfékʃənist] n.	완벽주의자
3	**safety**	[séifti] n.	안전
4	**refusal**	[rifjúːzəl] n.	사양
5	**memory**	[méməri] n.	기억
6	**appreciation**	[əpriːʃiéiʃən] n.	감사
7	**honesty**	[ánisti] n.	정직
8	**emphasis**	[émfəsis] n.	강조
9	**ideal**	[aidíːəl] n.	이상
10	**stimulation**	[stìmjəléiʃən] n.	자극
11	**will**	[wil] n.	의지
12	**ability**	[əbíləti] n.	능력
13	**excitement**	[iksáitmənt] n.	흥분
14	**tension**	[ténʃən] n.	긴장
15	**respect**	[rispékt] n. v.	존경(하다)
16	**admiration**	[æ̀dməréiʃən] n.	감탄
17	**illusion**	[ilúːʒən] n.	착각
18	**prejudice**	[prédʒudis] n.	편견
19	**silence**	[sáiləns] n.	침묵
20	**intelligence**	[intélədʒəns] n.	지성
21	**contempt**	[kəntémpt] n.	경멸
22	**advice**	[ədváis] n.	충고
23	**confusion**	[kənfjúːʒən] n.	혼동
24	**consideration**	[kənsìdəréiʃən] n.	고려

Miscellaneous

단어를 예문으로 만들어 볼까요?

⋯▸ **The kid has a good memory.**
그 아이는 기억력이 좋습니다.

⋯▸ **It's all your fault.**
모두 당신 탓이에요.

⋯▸ **We must respect others without prejudice.**
편견없이 타인들을 존중해야 합니다.

⋯▸ **Honesty is the best policy.**
정직이 최상의 정책.

⋯▸ **My father is a perfectionist.**
제 아버지는 완벽주의자이십니다.

⋯▸ **You need strong will power to achieve your goal.**
목표를 달성하기 위해서는 강한 의지력이 필요합니다.

기초가 되는 단어를 외워두면 좋아요

* seek	구하다
* seem	~처럼 보이다 / ~인 것 같다
* select	선발하다
* send	보내다
* sense	감각
* sentence	문장 / 구형
* separate	떼어놓다
* serve	섬기다 / 봉사하다 / 시중들다
* several	몇몇의
* shadow	그림자
* shake	흔들다 / 흔들리다
* shallow	얕은 / 천박한

Index

A

abacus	86	add	188	aisle seat	255
abalone	137	address	61 / 220	alarm	19
ability	180 / 326	administration	27	alarm clock	73
able	19	admiral	227	album	47
aboard	56	admiration	94 / 326	alcohol	151
above	39	admire	96	alcoholic beverage	152
above zero	24	admission ticket	270	algae	137
abroad	19	admit	19	alien	301
absence	185	adolescent	111	alive	305
absent	186	adopt	111	all-you-can-eat restaurant	155
absorb	19	adoptee	111	all day long	18
absorption	159	adult	111	all year long	21
abstract nouns	322	advance	19	allergy	162
academic	177	advance ticket	55	allied forces	226
academic subject	178	adventure	244	allied nations	226
academy	173	advertisement	229	alligator	130
accent	297	advice	285 / 326	allowance	199
accept	112	affect	19	alloy	320
accessaries	78	afraid	96	almond	115
accident	234	Africa	30	almost	19
according to	19	after school	185	alphabet	297
account	188	aftershock	235	Alto	275
accountant	214	agony	93	aluminium	320
Accounting Dept.	202	agree	19	alumni	176
accuse	233	agricultural chemicals	205	always	22
achieve	112	agriculture	205	amaze	96
acid	320	ahead	19	amazing	22
acquit	238	aim	180	ambulance	168
across	53	air	307	ambush	226
acting	230	air conditioner	70	American	30
active	100	air force	226	amethyst	80
activity	285	airlines	246	amount	188
actor	214	airmail	220	amusement	93
actress	214	airplane	55	amusement park	270
actually	19	airport	246 / 254	analysis	313
		airport limousine	255	ancestor	44

328

anchor	229	apricot	124	astronaut	217 / 301
ancient palace	249	April	21	astronomy	179
angel	294	apron	67	at dawn	18
anger	93	aquarium	249	at midnight	15
angle	188	Arbor Day	36	at night	18
angry	96	archaeology	182	at noon	15
animal	129	architect	217	at sunrise	18
animation	243	area	39	at sunset	18
ankle	102	argue	298	at the beginning of	18
anniversary of		argument	297	at the beginning of the month	
somebody's death	294	arm	102		21
announcement	230	armchair	73	at the end of	18
announcer	214	army	226	at the end of the month	
annoy	96	arranged marriage	288		21
another	22	arrest	232	at the moment	15
answer the phone	58	arrival date	220	athlete's foot	162
answering machine	58	arrive	56	athlete	214
ant	133	arson	232	atom	317
antenna	230	art gallery	249	attach	34
anthropology	179 / 182	arteries	105	attack	226
anxiety	93	article	229	attend a class	185
anxious	96	artist	217	attendance	185
anyway	22	ash	320	attic	64
apartment	61	ashamed	96	attitude	285
apology	285	ashtray	82	attractive	289
appeal	22	Asia	30	auditorium	176
appear	22	ask	298	August	21
appendix	105	asparagus	127	aunt	43
appetite	22	assassination	233	Australia/Australian	30
appetizer	155	assemble	22	author	217 / 278
applaud	285	Assembly	211	autobiography	278
apple	124	assign	22	automatic teller	
apply	22	assist	22	machine(ATM)	223
appoint	22	assistant manager	199	automobile	55
appreciate	286	associate	324	autumn	21
appreciation	326	assumption	313	available	34
approval	238	asthma	162	avocado	124

329

Index

avoid	34	bankrupt	196	bee	133
awful	96	baptism	291	beef	149
awfully	34	bar	88	beetle	133
ax	34	barbecue	144	beg	37
azalea	121	barber	217	behave	37
		barber shop	88	behavior	285
B		bargain	193	behind	37
		barley	115	beige	33
baby-sitter	217	barley tea	152	believe	294
baby	111	baseball	264	believer	291
bachelor's degree	173	basement	61 / 64	bell pepper	127
back	39 / 102	basic	34	bellhop	252
backpacker	246	basket	34	belong	37
backpacking	246	basketball	264	below	39
bacon	155	bat	34	below zero	24
badminton	264	bathroom	64	belt	82
bag	82	bathtub	46	bench	73
baggage	246	battery	46	besides	37
baggage claim	255	battle	226	betray	37
baggage compartment	256	be fined	52	between	39
bake	34	be in charge of	202	beyond	37
bakery	88	be indebted to	286	Bible	291
balance	34	be late for class	185	bicycle/bike	55
balcony	65	beach	270 / 304	big	37
bald	108	beads	79	bill	140
ball-point pen	85	bean	115	billiard	264
ball	34	bean sprout	127	billion	9
balloon	34	bear	112 / 130	billionth	12
bamboo	118	beard	108	bind	37
bamboo shoot	127	beast	37	biography	278
banana	124	beat	267 / 275	Biology	179
bandage	165	beautiful	109	bird	138
bank	222	beauty salon	88	bird watching	243
bank account	223	become	112	birth	37
bank account number	223	bed clothes	73	birth date	297
bank note	223	bed cover	46	birthmark	108
banker	214	bedroom	64	biscuit	155

bishop	294	borrow	50	brief	50
bite	37	botanical garden	249	bright	33
bitter	146	both sides	39	bring	50
black	33	bother	285	Briton	30
black tea	152	bottle opener	47	broad	40
blackboard	85	bottom	39	broadcast	229
blanket	46	Bottoms up!	152	broccoli	127
bleed	50	boulevard	53	bronze	317
bleeding	162	bow	50	brooch	79
blender	67	bowels	105	broom	46
bless	294	bowl	67	broth	149
blind	106	bowling	264	brother	43
block	52	box	85	brown	33
blood	105	boxing	267	brown seaweed	137
blood pressure	159	boy	111	brown sugar	146
blood test	165	boyfriend	288	brownish gold	33
blood type	165	bra	76	bruise	162
blouse	76	bracelet	79	brush	50 / 85
blow	24	brain	102	brush one's teeth	49
blue	33 / 96	branch	118 / 199	bubble	47
blueberries	124	brand-new product	261	bud	121
bluish	33	brandy	152	Buddha	291
blusher	281	brave	99	Buddhism	291
boarding house	61	break	50	Buddhist	291
boarding pass	255	break the law	238	bugle	276
boast	324	break up with	288	build	61
body shampoo	281	breakfast	149	building	62
boil	50	breakfast coupon	253	bulb	121
boiled egg	149	breast	102	bullet train	55
bomb	226	breath	105 / 159	bullying	176
bone	105	breathe	106	bunk bed	73
bonus	199	breeding	205	burdock	128
bookshelf	73	bribery	232	burial	294
bookstore	88	brick	65	burn	162 / 235
boots	76	bride	288	bury	50
border	50	bridegroom	288	bus	55
bore	324	bridge	249	bus stop	52

Index

bush 118 / 121 / 307	camper 56	cash card 223
business 195	can opener 59	cash register 261
business administration 179	Canada/Canadian 30	cashier 252
business card 85 / 285	canal 59	cassette tape 47
business class 255	cancel 247	cast 165
business partner 196	cancer 162	castle 59
businessman 214	candidacy 212	casual 59
busy 50	candidate 211	cat 130
butcher 88	candle 46	catalog 251
butter 155	cannon 226	catalyst 313
butterfly 133	cap 82	caterpillar 133
buttocks 103	capable 59	cathedral 291
buy in bulk 261	capital 193	Catholic 291
buy outright 261	capital city 27	cauliflower 127
	capital punishment 238	cavity 162
C	capitalism 27	CD player 70
	capsule 168	cease-fire 226
	captain 59	cease 59
cabbage 127	car accident 235	ceiling 64
cabinet 27 / 67	caramel 153	celebrate 59
cable 229	carbon 317	celery 127
cable car 249	cardigan 76	cell 105
cactus 121	cardinal 294	cello 275
cafeteria 155	cardinal number 9	cellular phone 58
cage 139	careful 99	Celsius 24
cake 152	carefully 59	cemetery 59
calculate 188	careless 100	censorship 249
calculator 70	carnation 121	center 39
calendar 18	carp 137	centipede 133
calf 103	carpenter 217	Central and South America 31
call 50 / 58	carpet 46	Central Asia 31
call back 58	carrot 127	cereal 59
calligraphy 243	carry-on bag 255	ceremony 71
calm 96	carry 59	certain 71
camel 130	carsickness 249	chain 71
camera 70	cartoon 243	chain reaction 313
camp 247	cash 223	

332

chair	73	chestnut	115	cinema	71
chairman	199	chestnut tree	118	circle	188
chalk	85	chew	149	citizen	27
challenge	71	chewing gum	152	city	61
champagne	152	chick	139	City Hall	88
chance	71	chicken	149	city hotel	252
chandelier	73	chicken pox	162	city sightseeing	249
change	182	child-care facilities	173	civil	28
changes	196	child	111	civil officer	214
channel	230	child birth	111	civilization	182
character	278	childhood	112	claim	208
charcoal	320	Children's Day	36	clam	136
charm	288	children's song	275	clap	71
charming	71	chill	162	class monitor	185
chase	232	chimney	65	class teacher	185
chatting	310	chimpanzee	131	classes	184
cheap	197	chin-up	267	classic	275
check-in baggage	255	chin	108	classification	313
check-in counter	255	China/Chinese	30	classify	71
check-out counter	258	chinese cabbage	127	classmate	176
check	223	chinese character	179	classroom	176
check in	252	chinese date	124	claw	137
check out	252	Chinese food	143	clay	71
cheek	108	chinese ink	85	clean the house	49
cheerfulness	93	chocolate	152	cleansing lotion(cream)	281
cheering	264	choice	71 / 211	clear	25 / 255
Cheers!	152	choose	197	clear a table	49
cheese	155	chop	144	clear strained rice wine	153
chef's special	143	chopstick	67		
chef	214	chorus	275	clearance sale	261
chemist	217	Christian	291	clerk	202
chemistry	179 / 312	Christianity	291	clever	71
cherries	124	Christmas Day	36	click	310
cherry blossom	121	chrysanthemum	121	climate	24
cherry tree	118	church	291	clinic	165
chess	244	cider	152	clip	86
chest	102	cigarette	82	clock	73

333

Index

close friend	285	colony	74	computer crime	310
closed	258	color	32	computer vaccine	310
closet	73	colorful	74	computer virus	310
cloth	74	comb	82	concentrate	186
clothes	75	comb the hair	49	concept	188
cloud	24	combine	74	concern	83
cloudy	74	come	74	concert	243
club	74	come down	261	concierge	253
club activity	185	comedian	214	conclude	83
clue	232	comedy	74	condition	83
coach	264	comet	301	conductor	275
coal	317	comfort	93	confess	233
coal mine	205	comfortable	324	confiscation	208
coast	304	comics	243	conflict	83
coat	76	commercial	229	Confucianism	294
cockroach	133	commercial area	61	confusion	326
cocktail	152	commission	208	congratulate	83
coconut	124	commit	233	congratulatory gift	285
cocoon	133	common	74	Congress	211
coffee break	149	communicate	74	connect	58 / 83
coffee maker	70	communication	296	conservative	211
coffee pot	68	communism	27	consider	324
coffee table	73	communist	27	consideration	326
coin	223	community	74	consist	83
coin collecting	243	commuter	55	constipation	159
coke	152	company	198	Constitution	238
cold	99	company employee	214	Constitution Day	36
cold drink	152	compare	74	construction	61
cold noodle dish	143	compass	85	consumption	193
Cold War	182	compete	193	contact	235
cold wave	235	complain	83	contact lens	82
collapse	182	completely	83	contain	83
colleague/co-worker	285	complexion	109	contempt	326
collect call	58	complimentary shuttle	252	continent	30 / 304
collect data	230	compose	279	continue	83
collection	243	composer	217	control	83
college entrance exam	176	composition	275	convenience store	88

334

convenient	89	courage	323	cucumber	127
conversation	297	course	247	cultural	89
convertible	56	court	238	culture	182
convict	238	cousin	43	cup	116
cook	214	cover the story	230	curious	99
cook dinner	49	cow	130	curl	116
cooked rice	149	coward	99	currency	223
cookie	152	cowboy	89	curry	155
cooking	142	crab	136	curry and rice	143
cool	89	cradle	73	curtain	46 / 116
cooperate	202	cram school	173	curve	116
cooperation	211	crane	139	cushion	46 / 73
copy	310	crash	235	customer	196
coral	79	cream	33 / 281	customer service	
core	40	create	279	department	261
corn	115	creature	307	customs	208 / 255
corner	89	credible	100	cut	116
corporation	196	credit	176 / 223	cute	289
correct	89	credit card	223	cutting board	67
correction fluid	85	cremation	294	cycling	264
correspond	89	cricket	133		
corridor	64	crime	231		
corruption	212	criminal	232		
cosmetics	281	crisis	89	dad	43
cosmos	121	criticize	230	daffodil	121
cost	208	croissant	155	daily activities	48
cost of living	193	crop	205	daily necessities	45
cottage	61	cross	294	damage	116
cotton	320	crosswalk	52	dance	243
cotton candy	270	crow	139	dandelion	121
cotton plant	118	crowded	89	danger	235
couch	73	crown	89	dare	116
cough	159	crown daisy	128	dark	33
cough syrup	168	cruise	249	dash	116
counseling	168 / 238	cry	89	data	116
country	26 / 61	crystal	79	dating	288
coup	226	cube	89	daughter-in-law	43

daughter	43	depend	119	differ	119
day	17	deposit	61	difficulty	119
day off	199	deposit money	223	digestion	159
day trip	246	depressed	100	diligent	99
dead	112	depression	193 / 323	dimple	108
deaf	106	dermatology	169	dining room table	73
deal	193	descendant	44	dinner	149
death	111	describe	279	dinosaur	131
debt	196	desert	307	diplomacy	27
deceive	233	design	282	diplomat	27
December	21	designer	214	direction	39 / 226
decide	247	desk	73	director	199 / 264
declare	255	dessert	151 / 155	directory assistance	58
decorate	80	destroy	119	dirt	47
deep	116	destruction	182	dirt road	52
deep fry	144	detect	119	dirty	119
deer	130	detective	214	disappear	119
defeat	226	detective novel	278	disappoint	96
defend	226	detergent	46	disappointed	97
defendant	238	develop	180	disappointment	93
deficit	196	developed country	27	disapproval	238
defrost	144	developing country	27	disaster	234
degree	25	development	182	discharge from the military service	227
delay	255	deviation	235		
delete	310	devil	291	discoloration	108
delicate	100	devise	180	discount	193
delicious	149	devote	119	discover	119
deliver	116	dew	25	discovery	179
delivery room	168	diabetes	162	discuss	298
demand	193	dial	58	discussion	297
democracy	27	dialect	297	disease	161
democrat	27	diamond	79	disgusting	159
dentist	217	diarrhea	162	dish	67
deny	116	diary	278	dish cloth	67
department	202	dice	86 / 144	dish soap	67
department store	88 / 258	dictionary	180	dishwasher	70
departure lounge	256	die	111	disinfection	165

dislike	119	draft	223	dump	288
dissatisfaction	94	draft beer	152	dumpling	143
distance	119	drag	122	dumpling soup	143
distant	53	dragon fly	133	duodenum	106
distribution	188	drama	229	during	122
distributor	196	draw	244	during the week	16
district	39	drawer	73	dust	49
divide	188	dream	94	duster	46
divorce	288	dreamer	99	dustpan	46
dizziness	159	dresser	73	duty-free shop	255
do good on the exam	185	dressing	146	dye	122
do the laundry	49	drier	70	**E**	
doctor	217	drink	122		
doctorate	173	drive-in restaurant	155	e-mail	310
documentary	229	drive	243	eager	319
dog	130	driver's license	55	eagle	139
doll	119	driver	214	ear-wax	109
dollar	224	driving range	270	ear	108
dolphin	136	driving without a license	52	early	122
domestic animal	205	drizzle	24	earn	202
domestic call	58	drizzling	25	earphone	47
domestic travel	246	drop	122	earrings	79
donkey	130	drop out of school	173	Earth	301 / 303
doorbell	64	dropout	176	earthquake	235
doorplate	65	drought	235	earthworm	133
dormitory	176	drown	235	easily	122
double eyelid	108	drug	165 / 232	east	39
double major	176	drugstore	88	Easter	36
double room	252	drum	275	eastern	40
doubt	122	drunk driving	235	easy	122
down jacket	77	dry	122	eat out	143
down payment	261	dry cleaner's	88	eclipse	301
downpour	24	duck	139	ecology	180
downstairs	65	due	224	economics	179 / 192
downtown	61	dull	122	economy class	255
dozen	122	dumb	106	edit	278

Index

editor	217	emerald	79	eraser	85
editorial	229	emergency exit	255	error	134
education	172 / 179	emergency room	168	escalator	258
eel	136	emotion	93	escape	233
effort	180	emphasis	326	especially	134
egg beater	68	empire	125	essay	278
eggplant	127	employ	202	establish	202
eight	9	employee	196	estimate	208
eighteen	9	employer	196	etc.	134
eighteenth	12	empty	125	Ethics	179
eighth	12	end	15	Europe	30
eightieth	13	end in a tie	264	eve	18
eighty	10	enemy	226	even	134
elbow	102	energy	313	even number	10
elder	125	engagement	288	evening paper	229
elect	211	engineer	217	event	298
election	211	English	179	ever	15
election campaign	211	English literature	180	every	134
electric	125	enjoy	244	every year	16
electric appliances	69	enough	125	evidence	232 / 238
electric bill	65	enter a hospital	165	evil	291
electric blanket	70	enter the school	173	exact	134
electric razor	70	enterprise	193	examine	165
electric rice cooker	67	entertain	244	example	134
electricity	317	entertainer	214	excellent	134
electronic organ	276	entertainment	269	except	134
element	125	entire	125	exchange	258
elementary	125	entrance ceremony	173	exchange money	223
elementary school	173	entree	155	exchange rate	208 / 223
elephant	130	envelope	85 / 220	excite	96
elevator	258	environment	62	excitement	93 / 326
eleven	9	envy	93	executive	199
eleventh	12	equal	125	exercise	264
else	125	equality	323	exhaust fan	67
embarrass	125	equator	307	exhibit	134
embassy	27	equip	125	exhibition	249
embroidery	243	equipment	313	exist	134

existence	317	Fahrenheit	24	fear	93
expect	134	fail	193	feast	298
expectation	94 / 323	fail in an exam	185	February	21
expenditure	193	failure	194	feces	159
expensive	197	fair	147	fee	150
experiment	313	fairy	147	feed	150
explain	147	fairy tale	278	feel	96
explanation	278	fake	79	feel dizzy	159
explode	235	fall	147	feeling	92
exploration	247	fallen leaves	118	female	150
export	208	false	147	fence	64
express	56 / 279	familiar	147	fencing	267
express highway	55	family	42	ferry	55
express mail	220	family court	238	fertilizer	205
expression	278	famous	147	festival	249 / 298
extend	147	fan	82	fetus	111
extended game	267	far	39	fever	159
extension number	58	fare	55 / 208	few	150
extra	147	farewell party	36	fiance	288
extreme	147	farm	205 / 304	fiber	320
eye-drops	168	farm land	205	field	150 / 304
eye-wax	109	farmer	205	field and track events	264
eye	108	fashion	281	fifteen	9
eye shadow	281	fashion leader	281	fifteenth	12
eyebrow	108	fast	56	fifth	12
eyelashes	108	fast food	143	fiftieth	13
eyelid	108	fast food restaurant	155	fifty	10
		fasten	147	fig	124
		fasten the seat belt	52	fight	150
F		fat	150	fighting	182
fable	278	fate	288	file	86
face	107	father-in-law	43	file a suit	238
face painting	270	father	43	file cabinet	86
facilities	252	faucet	46	film	150
facsimile/fax	70	fault	150	final	185
fact	147	favor	150 / 288	finally	150
factory	205	favorite	150	financial	224

339

Index

find	156	float	156	forgive	324
fine	52	flood	235	fork	67
fine art	179	floor	64	form	160
finger	102	floor cloth	46	fortieth	12
fingerprint	232	florist	88	fortunately	160
finish the work	199	floss one's teeth	49	fortune	160
fire	202 / 320 / 235	flour	115	forty	9
fire alarm	64	flow	156	forward	15
firefly	133	flower bed	121	foul	267
fireman	214	flower pot	121	found	160
fireplace	64	flowers	120	foundation	281
first	12 / 15	flute	275	Foundation Day	36 / 176
first class	255	fly	133	fountain pen	85
first love	288	flying kite	270	four	9
fish	135	foe	156	fourteen	9
fisherman	205	fog	24	fourteenth	12
fishing	205 / 243	foggy	25	fourth	12
fishing boat	205	fold	156	fox	130
fist	103	Folk Village	249	fraction	188
fitness center	252	follow	156	fracture	162
fitting room	258	food	141 / 156	fragrance	80
five	9	food court	258	frame	160
fix	70	foolish	156	France/French	30
fixed price	261	foot	102	frankly	160
flag	156	football	264	fraud	232
flamingo	140	footwear shelf	65	freckle	108
flash	156	for the first time	15	free	160
flashlight	46	force	160	freedom	323
flat	156	forehead	108	freeze	24
flatfish	137	foreign country	27	Freeze!	232
flatland	304	foreign languages		freezer	67
flea	133	school	173	freezing	25
flee	233	foreigner	297	freight	208
flesh	105	forest	307	freight train	55
flight	156	forestry	205	French fries	143
flight attendant	255	forever	15	fresh	160
flight ticket	255	forget	324	freshman	176

friction	208	garbage can	46	giant	174
Friday	18	garden	64	gift	174 / 180
fried egg	155	garlic	127	gift shop	258
fried rice	143	gas	317	gift wrapping counter	258
friend	160	gas bill	65	ginger	127
friendship	285	gas range	67	ginkgo tree	118
frog	136	gas station	52	ginseng	127
front	39	gasoline	317	giraffe	130
front desk	252	gastric cancer	163	girl	111
front door	64	gastritis	163	give	174
frost	24	gate	166	give a discount	261
fruit	118 / 123	gather	166	give up your seat to	56
fruit shop	88	gay	166	glacier	307
fry	160	gender	297	glad	96
frying pan	67	general	227	glass	64
full	149	general affairs Dept.	202	glasses	82
fun	160	general goods	81	glory	174
function	166	general manager	202	gloves	79 / 82
fund	166	generally	166	glue stick	85
funeral	111 / 294	generous	100 / 324	go Dutch	143
funny	96	Genetics	179	go into bankruptcy	196
furious	166	genius	180	go on a business trip	199
furnished	62	gentle	99	go straight	52
furniture	72	gentleman	111	go to bed	49
furniture store	88	genuine	79 / 166	go to study	49
future	15	German millet	115	go to the movies	49
		Germany/German	30	go to work	49 / 199
		gesture	297	goal	180
G		get	166	goat	130
		get a job	199	God	291
gain	166	get a perm	281	going to the movies	243
Galaxy	301	get a raise	99	gold	33 / 79 / 317
gall bladder	105	get a ticket	52	golden-bell	121
gamble	270	get along with	43	golden	33
game	270	get the phone	58	golf	267
gap	166	get up	49	golf course	270
garage	64	ghost	291	good	174
garbage	166				

341

Index

goods	193	green onion	127	hamster	183
goose	139	green pea	115	hand	102
gorilla	130	green tea	152	handbag	79
govern	27	greenhouse	183	handcuffs	232
government	27	greet	285	handicap	183
government office	88	greeting	285	handkerchief	82
grace	174	grill	183	handle	183
grade	176	grocery	88	handshake	183
gradual	174	ground	183	handsome	109
graduate	176	group	183	hang	183
graduate from school	173	grow	112	hang up the phone	58
graduate school	173	growth	110	hanger	46
graduation ceremony	173	guerilla	226	Hangul Proclamation Day	
grain	114	guess	323		36
grammar	174	guest	196	happen	235
grand	174	guide	285	happiness	93
granddaughter	43	guilty	233 / 238	happy	96
grandfather	43	guitar	275	harbor	189
grandmother	43	gum	108	hard	189
grandparents	43	gym	176	hardly	189
grandson	43	gymnasitcs	267	hardworking	100
grant	174	gynecology	169	harmful	189
grapefruit	124			harmonica	276
grapes	124	**H**		harmony	323
grass	64			harp	276
grasshopper	133	haggle	261	harsh	189
grate	144	hail	24	harvest	205
grateful	174	hair	102 / 139	hastily	189
grave	294	hair conditioner	281	hat	82
graveyard	253	hair designer	217	hatch	139
gravitation	308	hair spray	281	hate	96
gray	33	half	15 / 188	hatred	93
great	174	half past three	15	have	189
Greece/Greek	30	half year	16	have (catch) a cold	159
greedy	183	Halloween	36	have a baby	111
green	33	hamburger	155	have a bloody nose	159
green layer	137	hammer	46	have a crush on	288

have a flu	159	herb tea	152	hook	200
have a great success in life	197	hero	189	hope	93 / 323
		hiccups	161	horizon	307
have a runny nose	158	hide	200	horizontal	188
have a sore throat	159	high	200	horn	203
have a wrong number	58	high blood pressure	162	horrible	96
have an affair	288	high heels	76	horse	130
have an injection(shot)	159	high price	196	horse meat	149
		high school	173	horse race	270
have breakfast	49	highlighter	85	horseback riding	267
have hair cut	281	hike	200	hospital	164
Hawaii	30	hiking	243	hospital gown	165
hawk	139	hill	304	hostage	232
hay	189	Hinduism	294	hot	203
head	40 / 102	hint	200	hot chocolate	152
headache	162	historic sites	246	hot dog	155
headquarter	199	historical	182	hot spring	246
health	158	history	179 / 181	hotel	246 / 251
health insurance	168	hobbies	242	house	61 / 63
healthy	159	hockey	264	house chores	46
hear	189	hold	200	housewarming party	36
heart	93 / 105	Hold on the line please.	58	housing	60
heart attack	162	hole	200	how	203
heart disease	162	holiday	298	howl	203
heat	320	hollow	200	hug	289
heating pad	165	holy	294	huge	203
heaven	291	home page	310	human	203
heavy	25	homesick	200	human body	101
heel	102	hometown	61	human disaster	235
height	317	homework	185	humanity	285
heir	111	honest	99	humid	24
helicopter	55	honesty	326	humidifier	70
hell	291	honey	200	humor	203
helpful	189	honeymoon	246	humorous	96
hemp	320	honor	200	hump	131
hen	139	hood	200	hundred	9
herb	189			hundred million	10

Index

hundred millionth	13	important	206	infirmary	249
hundredth	12	impossible	206	inform	209
hundredth day after birth	36	impress	96	informal	209
		impression	94	information	209
hungry	149	improve	206	inheritance	182
hunt	270	improvement	182	injection	165
hurrah	203	in-flight service	255	injury	226
hurricane	25	in-house phone	252	ink	85
hurry	203	in-laws	43	inlineskating	264
hurt	203	in the afternoon	18	inn	246 / 252
husband	43	in the evening	18	inner	39
hut	203	in the middle of	18	innocent	233 / 238
hydrogen	317	in the middle of summer	21	insect	132
hyena	130			inside	39
hymn	294	in the middle of winter	21	insist	209
hypothesis	313	in the morning	18	installment savings	223
		include	206	instant cup noodles	143
I		income	193	instant food	143
		income and expenditure	196	instead	209
I'd like to talk to	58			instinct	323
ice	203	increase	206	institute	173
ice cream	152	indeed	206	instruct	209
ice cream sundae	153	independence	226	instructor	173
ice pack	165	Independence Day	36	intelligence	326
ice tray	67	Independence Movement Day	36	intend	209
iceberg	307			interest	223
ideal	326	independent	206	interesting	97
identification (ID)	310	indicate	206	internal medicine	168
idler	99	individual	206	international	31
ignorance	323	indoor	206	international call	58
ignore	324	indoor swimming pool	252	international chain hotel	252
illusion	326	industry	204	internet	309
image	206	infant	111	Internet shopping mall	310
imagination	93 / 323	inferior	209	interpretation	297
imagine	324	inferior goods	208	interpreter	217
immediately	206				
import	208				

344

interrogation	238	jazz	275	keep	215
interrupt	209	jealous	99	kelp	137
intersection	52	jealousy	93	ketchup	146
interview	229	jeans	76	kettle	67
intonation	297	jeep	55	key	215
introduce	285	jet lag	255	key ring	79
introduction	208 / 297	jewel	79	keyboard	310
invade	209	jewelry	215	kick	215
invent	209	jog	267	kidnap	232
invention	179	jogging suit	77	kidney	105
investigate	180	join	215	kidney bean	115
investment	196	join a club	173	kill	233
invitation	285	join the army	227	kind	215
invite	285	joke	297	kindergarten	173
involve	209	journalism	229	kindness	93
iron	70 / 317	journalist	217	king	28
iron pot	68	journey	215	kingdom	28
irritate	96	judge	238	kiss	289
island	307	judicature	27	kitchen	66
Italy/Italian	30	judo	264	kitchen knife	67
itchy	163	juice	152	kite	215
item	215	July	21	kiwi fruit	124
itinerary	246	jump	215	knee	102
ivory	79	jumper	77	knitting	243
ivy	118	June	21	knock	218
		jungle	304	know	218
		junior	176	knowledge	180
		junior level	202	koala	130
J		junk mail	220	Korea/Korean	30
jacket	76	Jupiter	301	Korean	179
jail	232	juror	238	Korean food	143
jail break	232	just	215	Korean harp	276
January	21			Korean literature	180
Japan/Japanese	30	**K**		Korean style barbecue	143
Japanese apricot tree	118	kangaroo	131	Korean Thanksgiving Day	36
Japanese cedar	118	karaoke room	88		
jar	215				

345

Index

korean traditional candy		lawyer	214	light	320	
	152	lay	218	light blue	33	
		lay off	202	light green	33	
L		lazy	99	lighter	47	
		lead	320	lighting	61	
		leaf	118	lightning	24	
labor	193	leaf mustard	128	lights	46	
labor union	199	leap year	21	like	289	
laboratory/lab	313	leave	218	lily	121	
ladder	46	leave a message	58	lime	124	
ladle	67	leave earlier	185	line	188	
Lady's Wear	258	leave one's mark	182	linens	73	
lady	111	leave the hospital	165	lines	230	
ladybug	133	leave the office	199	Lines are crossed.	58	
lake	304	lecture	185	lion	130	
lamb	130 / 149	leek	127	lip	108	
lamp	46	leg	102	lip cream	281	
land	56 / 304	legislation	27	lipstick	281	
landowner	61	leisure	244	liquid	317	
landslide	235	lemon	124	liquid crystal	317	
language	278	lemon tea	153	liquid medicine	168	
laptop	310	length	317	listen	109	
large	218	leopard	131	listen to music	49	
large intestines	105	lesson	218	listen to the radio	49	
last	218	let	218	listening to music	243	
last night	18	letter	220	literature	179 / 277	
last year	16	letter paper	220	little	218	
late	15	lettuce	127	live coverage	229	
late riser	100	liar	99	liver	105	
lately	15	liberal	211	livestock	205	
later	15	liberty	323	livestock farming	205	
latitude	307	library	176	living room	64	
laugh	96	lick	109	lizard	130	
laundry	46	life	111 / 307	loan	223	
law	237	life imprisonment	238	lobster	136	
lawmaker	212	lifelong	218	local	218	
lawn	218	lifelong education	173	local area network(LAN)		

346

		310	lyrics	275	margarine	155
local call		58			mark	278
location		38	**M**		marriage	288
lock		221			marry	289
lodge		61	mackerel	136	Mars	301
log		205	mad	221	martial arts	267
log off		310	magazine	229	mascara	281
log on		310	maggot	133	mask	221
loneliness		94	magnolia	118	Mass	291
lonely		96	magpie	139	Mass Media	228
long-distance call		58	mah-jong	244	massage	281
long-sleeved shirt		77	mailbox	220	master's degree	173
long skirt		77	mailman	220	master	236
longitude		307	main character	278	match	47
look like		43	maintenance	182	matchmaker	288
loose		76 / 258	major	221	material	313 / 316
lose		221	major in	176	Mathematics	179 / 187
lost and found		258	make a crank call	58	matter	236
lotion		281	make the bed	49	mattress	73
lottery		270	makeup	281	May	21
lotus root		127	male	221	maybe	236
loud		221	mammal	221	mayonnaise	146
love		93 / 287	man	111	mayor	27
love marriage		288	manage	202	meal	148
lovely		289	manager	199	mean	236
lover		288	managing director	202	meaning	297
low		221	mane	131	measles	162
lucky		221	mango	124	meat	149
luggage cart		253	mankind	221	median	55
lunar		301	manners	285	medical chart	168
lunar calendar		21	mansion	61	medical check-up	165
Lunar New Year's Day			manuscript	278	medical examination	165
		36	map	246	medical insurance	168
lunch		149	maple tree	118	Medical Science	179
lung		105	marathon	264	medicine	165
lung cancer		162	marble	221	medium	155
luxurious hotel		252	March	21	meet	286

347

Index

meet friends	49	mini skirt	77	moss	118
meeting	199 / 285	mining	205	mostly	239
melody	275	minister	291	motel	252
melon	124	minor	82 / 111 / 236	moth	133
melt	236	minor in	176	mother-in-law	43
member	236	misjudgment	238	mother country	27
memorial	249	miss	288	mother/mom	43
Memorial Day	36	missile	227	motion	239
memories	288	mist	25	motorcycle	55
memory	326	mistake	236	mountain	304
Men's Wear	258	misunderstand	324	mountain climbing	243
mental calculation	188	misunderstanding	93	mountain range	304
mention	298	mix	236	mouse	130 / 310
menu	143	model	214	mousse	281
merchant	197	model building	243	mouth	108
Mercury	301	modern	236	move	61
mercy	199	modest	99	movement	53
merry-go-round	270	moist	239	movie theater	243
merry	100	molecule	317	moving sidewalk	256
messenger	310	Monday	18	mud	304
metal	320	money	223	muffler	82
meteor	301	money order	220	mug	239
method	180	money rates	223	mugwort	128
Mexico/Mexican	30	Mongol	31	mulberry tree	118
Microscope	313	Mongolia	31	multi-grain bread	115
microwave oven	67	monk	291	multiply	188
mid-term	185	monkey	130	mung bean	115
middle	39	monopoly	196	murder	232
middle school	173	monsoon season	24	muscle	105
mild	146 / 236	month	20	museum	249
military	226	monthly magazine	230	mushroom	127
milk	152	mood	93	music	179 / 274
Milky Way	301	moody	99	musical	243
million	9	moon	301	musical instrument	275
millionth	12	morning paper	229	musician	217
mince	144	morning sickness	162	Muslim	294
mind	236	mosquito	133	mussel	136

348

mustache	108	neighbor	250	non-smoking area	246
mutton	149	neither	250	nonstop flight	255
mystery	239	nephew	43	normal	250
myth	278	nervous	250	north	39
		nervousness	93	North Korea	30
		nest	139	Northeast	40
N		Netherlands/Dutch	30	Northern	40
nail	102	neurology	169	northwest	40
nail clipper	46	neuron	105	nose	108
nail polish	281	new	250	nose dripping	105
nail shop	282	New Year's Day	36	nose wax	109
name	239	New Year's Eve	36	nostril	108
napkin	239	New Zealand/New		notebook	85
narcotism	165	Zealander	30	notice	250
narrow	239	news	229	novel	278
nasal spray	165	newspaper	229	novelist	217
national highway	53	newspaper office	229	November	21
nationlity	29	next	15	nowadays	15
native	239	next year	16	number	250
natural	305 / 308	nice	109	nurse	217
natural disaster	235	nickname	250	nutrition	159
naughty boy	99	niece	43		
navel	102	nightgown	77	**O**	
navy	226	nightingale	140		
navy blue	33	nightstand	73	oak tree	118
near	39	nine-to-five job	202	oasis	307
nearly	239	nine	9	oat	115
neat	239	nineteen	9	oath	294
necessary	239	nineteenth	12	obesity	162
neck	102	ninetieth	13	obey	259
necklace	79	ninety	10	object	313
necktie	82	ninth	12	obligation	211
necktie pin	82	nipple	103	observation	313
need	250	nod	250	observation platform	249
needle	86	noise	250	observe	180
needy	194	non-alcoholic beverage		obtain	259
negative	250		152	occupancy rate	253

Index

occupation	213	opposite	39	overhear	262
occur	259	opposition party	211	overnight mail	220
ocean	304	orange	33 / 124	overseas travel	246
October	21	orbit	301	overtime	199
octopus	136	orchard	205	overwork	162
odd number	10	orchestra	275	owe	224
off-campus	176	orchid	121	owl	139
offend	96	order	208 / 323	own	262
offer	208	ordinal number	12	ox	262
offline	310	ordinary	259	oxygen	317
oil	146 / 317	organ	76	oyster	136
ointment	165	organization	196	ozone layer	307
old	112	organizer	85		
older brother	44	orient	259		
older sister	44	oriental medicine	168		
on-campus	176	oriental medicine doctor		pack	282
on display	261		168 / 217	package tour	246
on sale	197 / 261	origin	259	pad	86
on weekends	16	original	249	pain	262
once	15	orthopedics	169	painful	262
once upon a time	15	ostrich	139	painkiller	168
one-way	255	other	259	paint	62
one	9	otherwise	259	painter	217
one third	188	ought to	259	painting	243 / 249
one way street	52	out of	262	pair	262
onion	127	out of stock	261	pajama	76
online	305	outdoor	262	pal	262
only	259	outer	39	palace	262
only child	43	outgoing	99	pale	108
open-minded	99	outlet	70	palm	102
open	258 / 259	outside	39	palm tree	118
opera	244	oval	188	pan fry	144
operating hours	258	oven	70	pancreas	105
operation	165	overall	262	pants	76
operator	259	overalls	76	pantyhose	76
ophthalmology	169	overcharge	261	papaya	124
opinion	297	overcome	262	paper	265

paper clip	85	payment	193	personnel	202
parade	265	pea	115	persuade	324
paradise	294	peace	323	pesent	292
parasol	82	peaceful	265	pet	130
parcel	220	peach	33 / 124 / 268	petal	121
Parents'Day	36	peacock	139	pharmacist	168 / 217
parents	43	peak	265	pharmacy	88 / 168
parfait	153	peanut	115	pheasant	139
parking lot	52 / 258	pear	124	phenomenon	313
Parliament	211	pearl	79	Philippines/Filipino	30
parlor	64	pebbles	304	Philosophy	179
parrot	139	pedestrian	52	phone	58
parsley	127	pediatrics	168	phone bill	65
part	265	pedicure	281	phone booth	58
participation	285	peel off	144	photo studio	88
particular	265	pelican	140	photocopier	70
partner	265	pen	85	photography	243
party	35	penalty	267	phrase	268
pass a bill	211	pencil	85	physical	103
pass away	111	pencil case	85	Physical education	179
pass gas	159	peninsula	307	physical therapy	165
pass the test	185	penquin	140	physician	217
passenger	55 / 247	pension	202	physicist	217
password	310	people	265	Physics	179
past	15	pepper	146	Physiology	180
paste	310	perfection	326	piano	275
path	265	perfectionist	326	pick	124
patient	99 / 165	perform	265	pick up the phone	58
patriotism	27	performance	275	pickpocket	232
patrol car	55 / 232	perfume	79 / 281	picnic	270
pattern	265	perhaps	265	picture	268
pay	58	period	182	piece	268
pay in cash	261	permit	268	pig	130
pay in installments	261	persimmon	124	pigeon	139
pay phone	58	person	268	pill	168
pay the bill	143	personal computer(PC)	310	pillar	64
payday	199	personality	98	pillow	46

Index

pilot	214 / 255	policeman	214	potluck party	36
pimple	108	policy	211	pottery	243
PIN number	223	polite	99	pound	271
pine tree	118	politely	271	pour	271
pineapple	124	political	212	powder	168 / 320
pink	33	political party	27 / 211	power	211 / 320
pistol	232	political power	208	practice	271
pizza	155	politician	211	praise	271
place	268	politics	210	pray	294
plaintiff	238	pollack	137	praying mantis	133
planet	301	pollen	121	pre-recorded	229
plant	117	pollution	62	pre-school	173
plastic surgery	168	pomegranate	124	preach	294
platanus	118	pond	249 / 304	precious	79
plate	268	pony	271	predict	294
platform	53	pool	264	prefer	271
platina	80	poor	194	pregnancy	111
play	243 / 244	poplar	118	prejudice	326
play cards	270	popular	271	preparation	313
player	264	popular song	275	prepare	271
playground	176 / 270	popularity	288	preparedness	323
playing hide-and-seek	270	population	61	prescription	168
playing with dolls	270	pork	149	present	15
plaza	270	pork cutlet	155	preservation	182
please	96	porridge	149	President	27 / 199
pleasure	93	port	271	press	292
plenty	268	possess	271	pretend	292
plum	124	possible	271	pretty	109
plum wine	152	Post-It note pad	85	prevent	292
pneumonia	163	post office	219	prevention	235
pocket	77	postal worker	220	preview	185
poem	278	postbox	64	previous	15
poet	278	postcard	220	price	208
point	268	postmark	220	price range	261
poison	268	pot	67	price tag	261
polar bear	131	potato	127	pride	323
pole	268	potato powder	146	priest	291

352

primary	292	public	295	quiet	295
Prime Minister	27	public bathroom	88	quit	302
prince	28	public holiday	35	quite	302
princess	28	public phone	58	quiz	185
principle	313	public transportation	51	quotation	297
print	310	publication	278		
printing	278	publish	229	**R**	
prison	232	pudding	152		
private	292	puffer	137	rabbit	130
problem	292	pull	295	raccoon	131
process	205	pulse	159	radio	70
produce	193	pumpkin	127	radio station	229
producer	229	punish	295	radish	127
product	196	puppet show	244	rage	302
production	193 / 214	purchase	197	rail	302
profile	109	pure	295	railroad	55
profit	193	purple	33	railroad crossing	52
program	310	purpose	295	rain	24
progress	292	purse	79	rainbow	24
prohibition	53	push-up	267	raincoat	77
promote	292	push	295	rainy	302
promotion	202	put	295	raise	302
pronunciation	297	put on a credit card	261	ranch	205
proof	238	put through	58	random	302
proper	292	puzzle	295	range	39
propose	288			ransom	232
prosecutor	233 / 238	**Q**		rape	232
prosperity	182 / 193			rapid	53
protect	292	quail	140	rapidly	302
Protestant	291	qualify	295	rare	155
prove	233	quality	193	rash	163
proverb	297	quantify	295	rat	130
provide	292	quarantine	256	rather	302
province	62	quarrel	285	ratio	188
Psychology	179	quarter	15 / 188	rattlesnake	137
pub	88	queen	28	raw	302
puberty	111	quickly	295	re-run	229

353

Index

react	313	refrigerator	67	reservation	246
reaction	313	refuge	235	reserve	314
reading	244	refund	258	residence	61
ready	302	refusal	326	resident	314
real	79	refuse	311	resident bird	139
real estate agency	88	registered letter	220	residential area	61
realization	323	regret	96 / 323	resignation	202
realize	302	regular	311	resist	314
really	311	regular price	196	resort	252
reason	313	relate	311	respect	326
rebellion	323	relationship	285	responsibility	211
receipt	196	relatives	43	responsible	99
receive	311	relax	244	rest	270
recently	15	relief	93	restaurant	88 / 154
reception desk	202	religion	290	restrict	314
receptionist	252	religious	294	result	313
recipe	143	remain	311	Resurrection	294
recital	275	remains	182	retail sale	193
recommend	311	remarriage	288	retire	199
reconciliation	289	remember	311	retirement	202
record	311	remittance	224	return	314
recover	311	remote control	70	return address	220
recreation	298	remove	311	reveal	314
recreation room	88	rent	61	review	185
rectangle	188	repair	70	reward	61
recycle	47	repay	311	rhythm	275
red	33	repeat	314	rib	02
red bean	115	reply	314	rib meat	143
red pepper paste	143 / 146	report	314	ribbon	82
red pepper powder	146	report card	185	rice	115
red snapper	137	reporter	217 / 229	rice and soup	143
red wine	153	represent	314	rice farming	205
redial	58	representative	212	rice plant	115
reed	121	require	314	rice planting	205
referee	264	required subject	186	rice scoop	67
reference book	185	research	179	rich	194
refined rice wine	153	resemble	43	riddle	314

354

ride	270	rumor	285	saury	136
ridiculous	318	run	267	sausage	155
right	211 / 318	run away from home	235	save money	223
ring	79 / 318	rush	318	say	298
ring up	261	Russia/Russian	30	saying	321
rise	318	rust	320	scale	85 / 220
river	304	rye	115	scallion	127
roast	144			scar	162 / 288
robber	232	**S**		scarcely	321
rock	304			scare	321
role	318	sacrifice	321	scarf	79 / 82
roll	318	sad	96	scene	321
roller coaster	270	sadness	93	scholar	179
rooftop	64	safety	326	scholarship	185
room change	252	sail	321	scholarship recipient	186
room rate	252	salad bar	155		
room service	252	salary	202	school	175
root	118	sales	208	school cafeteria	176
rope-jumping	267	saliva	105	school excursion	246
rose	121	salmon	136	school reunion	176
rotate	318	salt	146	Science	179
rough	318	salt farm	205	scientific	180
round-trip	255	salty	146	scissors	85
round	318	sample	208	scold	321
row	56	sand	304	score	321
royal	28	sandals	76	score points	188
rub	47	sandwich	155	scorpion	133
rubber band	85	sanitation	159	scream	321
rubber plant	118	sapphire	80	screw	47
ruby	79	sardine	136	scrubber	68
rude	99	satellite	229 / 301	sculpting	243
rug	73	satisfaction	94	sculptor	217
rugby	267	satisfy	96	sea	304
ruin	318	Saturday	18	sea animal	135
rule	27 / 226 / 267	Saturn	301	sea horse	136
ruler	85	sauce	146	sea mail	220
ruling party	211	sauna	252	sea slug	136

Index

sea urchin	136	separate	327	shine	305
seagull	140	September	21	shipment	205
search	321	sequela	163	shipping	208
seasickness	249	serious	100	shipping date	220
season	21	serve	327	shoe store	88
seasonal bird	139	service	291	shoe string	77
seasonings	145	service charge	253	shoes	76
seat	321	sesame	115	shooting	267
seat belt	55	sesame oil	146	shop around	258
seats for the elderly	55	sesame salt	146	shopping	257
seaweed	136	set a table	49	shopping mall	258
second	12	seven	9	short-sleeved shirt	77
secret	227	seventeen	9	shortcut	52
secretary	199	seventeenth	12	shorts	76
section	202	seventh	12	shot	165
security	223	seventieth	13	shoulder	102
security check	255	seventy	10	shower	24 / 47
security guard	223	several	327	shred	144
seed	118 / 205	sewing	243	shredded pepper	146
seedling	118	sewing machine	70	shrimp	136
seek	327	shade	320	shrine	291
seem	327	shadow	327	shy	99
select	327	shake	327	siblings	43
self-service	143	shake hands	285	side	39
selfish	99	shallow	327	side dishes	149
sell	197	shaman	291	side street	52
semester	176	shamanism	291	sideburns	108
Senator	211	shame	93	sidewalk	52
send	327	shampoo	281	sightseeing	246 / 248
send email	220	shark	136	sign acontract	208
send money	223	sharp pencil	86	sign up for a class	176
senior	176	shave	49	silence	326
senior citizen	111	shawl	79	silk	320
seniority system	199	sheep	130	silkworm	133
sense	327	shelf	73	silver	33 / 79 / 317
sentence	238 / 278 / 327	shell	137	simulcast	229
sentiment	94	shelter	235	sin	291

sincere	100	small intestines	105	sometimes	15
sing	275	smoke	320	son-in-law	43
singer	214	smoke detector	65	son	43
single bed	73	smoking area	246	song	275
single eyelid	108	smuggling	208	sophomore	176
single room	252	snack bar	258	Soprano	275
sink	47 / 67	snacks between meals		sound	320
sister	43		152	soup	149
sit-up	267	snail	133	sour	146
sitting bike	267	snake	136	south	39
situation	182	sneakers	76	southeast	40
six	9	sneeze	105	Southeast Asian	
sixteen	9	snot	109	southern	40
sixteenth	12	snow	24	southwest	40
sixth	12	snowstorm	24	souvenir	246
sixtieth	13	soap	281	souvenir shop	258
sixty	10	soccer	264	soy bean	115
size	317	social relations	284	soy bean paste	146
skateboarding	264	socialism	27	soy sauce	146
skiing ground	270	Sociology	179	space	39
skin	105 / 118	socks	82	space shuttle	301
skin care	281	sofa	73	space station	301
skin lotion	281	soft drink	152	spacewalk	301
skip a class	185	softball	267	spaghetti	155
skirt	76	soil	304	Spain/Spaniard	30
sky	307	Soju tent	88	sparrow	139
skydiving	264	solar	301	speak	298
skylark	139	solar calendar	21	Speaking.	58
slang	297	solar energy	320	speech	297
sleeping pill	168	Solar system	301	speed	320
slice	144	sold-out	196	speeding ticket	52
sling	165	soldier	226	spelling	297
slippers	77	solid	317	spend	194
slope	304	solitude	94	spices	146
slow train	56	solo	275	spicy	146
slowly	53	solve	188	spider	133
slug	133	someday	15	spinach	127

357

Index

spine	105	stimulation	326	suburb	61
spirit	323	stir fry	144	subway	55
sponsor	229	stock	199	succeed	193
spoon	67	stockholder	199	success	194
sporting goods counter	258	stockings	76	successful	194
		stomach	102	suffering	323
sports	263	stomach ulcer	163	sugar	146
spouse	111	stone	304	sugar cube	146
spring	21 / 304	stop	53	suicide	232
spring vacation	177	stopover	255	suit	76
spy	226	stores	87	suitcase	82 / 256
square	188 / 270	storm	25 / 235	suite room	252
squid	136	storm waves	235	summer	21
stadium	267	story	278	summer vacation	177
stairs	64	stove	70	Sun	301
stamp	85 / 220	strain	144	sunburn	163
stamp collecting	243	strawberries	124	Sunday	18
stamp pad	86	street light	52	sunflower	121
stand	70	strength	317	sunglasses	82
standard language	297	stress	162	sunlight	307
stapler	85	stressed	96	supervisor	202
star	301	stripes	131	supper	149
starfish	136	stroke	162	supplier	196
starve	149	structure	196	supply	193
stationery	84 / 88	struggle	227	support	211
statistics	188	stubborn	99	suppuration	163
statue	249	student	173	Supreme Court	238
status	313	studio	61	surface	39
stay up all night	18	study	64	surface mail	220
steak	155	study abroad	173	surgeon	217
steal	233	stuffed	149	surgery	168
steam	320	stupid	99	surplus	196
steel	317	subcontract	193	surprise party	36
steering wheel	53	submission	186	surrender	226
stem	118	subordinate	202	surround	305
stereo	70	substance	313	suspect	232
stewardess	214	subtract	188	swallow	139

swamp	307	tax affairs	202	testimony	238
swan	139	taxi	55	text message	58
sweat	105 / 159	taxi stand	52	textbook	185
sweater	76	teach	186	Thailand/Thai	30
sweet and sour pork	143	Teacher's Day	36	the 60th birthday	36
sweet potato	127	teacher	173	the ancient times	182
swim	267	teachers' room	186	the Atlantic	307
swimming	264	teaching method	173	the day after tomorrow	18
swimsuit	76	team spirit training	227	the day before yesterday	18
switch	65	teapot	68		
Switzerland/Swiss	30	tear	105 / 159		
swollen	163	teasing	177	the end of the month	16
syllabus	186	technology	193	the end of the year	16
sympathy	93	teenager	111	the first birthday	36
symptom	162	telegram	220	the first World War	182
synthesis	317	telephone	57	the handicapped	163
system	196	television	70	the last	15
		television station	229	The line is busy.	58
T		tell	298	the Middle Ages	182
		temperature	24 / 320	the modern times	182
T-shirt	76	temple	108 / 291	the nape of the nec	103
table tennis	264	temptation	323	the North Pole	307
tablecloth	67	ten	9	the North Star	301
tablet	168	ten million	10	the Northern Hemisphere	308
tadpole	136	ten millionth	13		
tail	139	ten thousand	9	the Pacific	307
take a bath	49	ten thousandth	12	the place of origin	208
take a nap	49	tenant	61	the present times	182
take a shower	49	tendon	105	the rose of Sharon	121
taking a walk	243	tennis	264	the South Pole	307
talent	180	tension	326	the Southern Hemisphere	308
talk	298	tenth	12		
talkative	99	term	76	the summer solstice	21
tangerine	124	termite	133	the time for payment	208
taro	128	terrible	97	The United Kingdom	30
taste	320	terrorist	226	The United States	30
tax	208	test tube	313	the winter solstice	21

359

Index

the year after next	16	tile	62	translation	297
the year before last	16	time	14	translator	217
theft	232	toast	155	transportation	53
theme park	270	toaster	67 / 70	transportation card case	82
theology	294	today	18	travel	245
theory	313	toe	102	travel agency	246
thermometer	25	toiletries	46	traveler's check	223
these days	15	tomato	127	traveler	246
thesis	185	tomb	294	tray	67
thickness	317	tomb stone	294	treasure	79
thief	232	tomorrow	18	treatment	165 / 281
thigh	102	tone	106	tree	117
third	12	tonight	18	trial	238
thirsty	149	tooth	108	triangle	188
thirteen	9	toothpaste	46	trillion	10
thirteenth	12	top	39	trousers	76
thirtieth	12	top spinning	270	trout	136
thirty	9	topic	297	truck	55
this year	16	tornado	25	trumpet	276
thousand	9	tortoise	136	trunk	131
thousandth	12	tour guide	249	truth	323
thread	82	tourist	246	try on	258
three-hole punch	86	tourist attractions	246	tuberculosis	163
three	9	tourist trap	261	Tuesday	18
thrilled	97	towel	46	tuitions and fees	185
throat	102	toy	270	tulip	121
throw	267	toy shop	88	tuna	136
throw up	163	trade	207	turkey	149
thumb	102	traditional market	88	Turkey/Turkish	30
thumbtack	86	traditional tea shop	249	turn on(off)	70
thunder	24	traffic law	52	turn right(left)	52
Thursday	18	traffic light	52	turnip	128
ticket window	55	train	55	turnstile	55
tie clip	79	train station	52	turtle	136
tiger	130	transaction	196	turtleneck	76
tight-fitting	258	transfer	56 / 58	tusk	131
tight	76	transfer to a school	185		

tuxedo	77	**V**		vital	305	
twelfth	12			vitamins	165	
twelve	9	vacancy	252	voice	320	
twentieth	12	vacation	246	volcano	307	
twenty	9	vacuum	49	volleyball	264	
twin room	252	vacuum cleaner	70	vomit	163	
twins	44	Valentine's Day	36	vomiting	162	
two-year college	173	valley	304	vote	211	
two	9	value	196	voter	211	
two thirds	188	vase	73	voting right	211	
typhoon	24	vegetable	126	voyage	247	
typical	100	vehicle	54			
		vein	105	**W**		
U		vein of ore	205			
		vending machine	56	wage	202	
ultraviolet ray	307	Venus	301	waist	102	
umbrella	82	verdict	238	wait in line	55	
uncle	43	vertical	188	waiter	214	
underdeveloped country	27	vest	76	waiting list	255	
		vice president	202	waitress	214	
underneath	40	Vice Prime Minister	27	wake-up call service	252	
underpass	52	victory	226	wake up	49	
understand	180	video	70	wall	64	
underwear	76	video rental shop	88	wallet	82	
unemployment	202	view	61	wallpaper	64	
unfurnished	62	village	307	walnut	115	
unidentified flying object (UFO)	301	vine	121	war	225	
		vinegar	146	ward	168	
uniform	76	violate traffic law	52	wardrobe	73	
universe	300	violence	232	warm	24	
university	173	violet	121	warranty	261	
university days	112	violin	275	warship	226	
unripe bean	115	visit	285	warthog	131	
unsatisfactory	97	visit a sick person	165	wash one's face	49	
upstairs	65	visit one's ancestral graves	294	wash the dishes	49	
urine	159			washer	70	
utilities	64	visitor	249	wasp	133	

361

Index

waste	193	white	33	wrinkle	108
watch TV	49	white wine	153	wrist	102
water bill	65	Who's calling?	58	wrist watch	79
water parks	249	whole wheat	115	write	279
waterfall	304	wholesale	193	write an essay	185
watermelon	124	wicked	100	writer	217 / 278
wave	304	width	317	writing songs	275
wax	282	wife	43	World Wide Web(WWW)	310
way of cooking	143	wild goose	139		
weak	159	wildfire	235	**X**	
wealthy	194	will	326		
weapon	226	win a game	264	X-rays	165
weather	23	win an election	211	xylophone	276
weather forecast	24	wind	24		
web	133	window	64 / 220	**Y**	
web designer	310	window seat	255		
web site	310	wine glass	153	yam	128
wedding anniversary	36	wing	139	yard	64
wedding ceremony	288	winter	21	yawn	106
wedding hall	288	winter vacation	177	year-end party	36
Wednesday	18	wisdom	323	yearning	105
weekly magazine	230	wise	99	yellow	33
weight	317	withdraw money	223	yen	224
weight lifting	267	woman	111	yesterday	18
welcome	285	womb	103	yogurt	152
welcome party	36	won	224	young	112
well-done	155	woodpecker	140	young days	112
well	304	woolong tea	153	young man	111
west	39	word	278 / 297	youth	112
western	40	work	196 / 278		
western food	154	work full-time	214	**Z**	
wet	24	work part-time	214		
whale	136	work place	199	zebra	130
wheat	115	workaholic	202	zero	10
wheelchair	168	worker	214	zero gravity	301
whiskers	131	works of art	249	zip code	220
whiskey	153	worries	93 / 323	zoo	249

회화를 제대로 살리는 주제별 영단어

1판 1쇄 발행 | 2004년 9월 20일
2판 9쇄 발행 | 2010년 4월 10일

지은이 | 정희영 · 봉영아 공저
펴낸이 | 윤다시
펴낸곳 | 도서출판 예가

주소 | 서울시 영등포구 당산동 1가 191-10
전화 | 02)2633-5462
팩스 | 02)2633-5463
E-mail | yegabook@hanmail.net
등록번호 | 제 8-216호

ISBN 978-89-7567-450-1 13730

※ 잘못된 책은 바꿔드립니다.
※ 가격은 표지 뒷면에 있습니다.
※ 인지는 저자와의 합의하에 생략합니다.